The Bible and Literature

SCM CORE TEXT

The Bible and Literature

Alison M. Jack

scm press

© Alison M. Jack 2012

Published in 2012 by SCM Press
Editorial office
3rd Floor, Invicta House,
108–114 Golden Lane,
London EC1Y 0TG, UK

SCM Press is an imprint of Hymns Ancient & Modern Ltd
(a registered charity)
13A Hellesdon Park Road
Norwich NR6 5DR, UK

www.scmpress.co.uk

British Library Cataloguing in Publication data

A catalogue record for this book is available
from the British Library

978-0-334-04166-5
Kindle 978-0-334-04474-1

Originated by The Manila Typesetting Company
Printed and bound by
CPI Group (UK), Croydon

Contents

Introduction

This book offers an introduction to the massive field that is covered by the phrase 'the Bible and Literature'. In the process, it juggles literary and biblical texts, literary critical approaches to texts, and the notion of the location of meaning. Many texts and authors, theories and their key proponents are introduced. Questions are asked and a variety of answers offered about the relationship between the Bible and literature. While it is not possible to cover every conceivable aspect of that relationship, or to consider any of the texts and theories in detail, the aim of the book is to at least give its readers an understanding of the issues involved, and to encourage further study in those areas that spark most interest.

Because of its wide subject matter, by its nature interdisciplinary, readers may find some aspects of the book overly simplified. I assume little knowledge of the Bible, and little knowledge of the literary texts covered: but there will be few readers, I imagine, who come to this book with little knowledge of either field. I hope, however, that enough is said of interest in each chapter to both groups that the reading of it all will be deemed worthwhile – and that my necessary condensing of scholarship will not cause too much offence. Throughout, I aim to bring texts and readers into conversation with each other, and to enable each to have enough understanding of the other for that conversation to be meaningful from the beginning. But there will always be more to be said!

My background is in the study of the New Testament and in Scottish fiction from the nineteenth century. I have tried to move beyond these comfort zones in the writing of this book, but readers will quickly become aware that there is a little more about the New Testament than the Old Testament here; and that the literary texts discussed are predominantly although by no means exclusively from the Victorian period. I have included texts from a variety of English-speaking literary cultures, which I hope have given the book a wide appeal, although astute readers will probably be able to tell in which literary areas I feel most at home. While the readings of specific texts are important, and readers will gain most from the book if they have carefully read the texts under discussion, it is hoped that the methods used will be applicable to other texts also. The questions given at the end of each chapter often direct readers to consider other texts they are familiar with, both biblical and literary, from the perspective offered.

All of the literary texts used here should be widely available. Indeed, in a university setting, the novels and poems discussed are likely to be held in multiple copies in a university library, as they have been chosen, on the whole, because they are likely to be mainstream texts in undergraduate English studies. The poems, in particular, may often be found online: although readers should be careful to ensure they have consulted the whole of a particular poem under discussion. Recently several of my students attended my class on the first of T. S. Eliot's *Four Quartets*, having assumed that the one stanza they had found online was the poem in its entirety, and were perplexed when the rest of us started to discuss stanzas two to five. The next week, I was in the same position with regard to a poem by Christina Rossetti, which I had consulted in haste from an internet site! The books and articles that are considered in detail as key contributions to the various debates may be slightly less generally accessible. With regard to these texts, I have attempted to give a full exposition of the argument made, with a generous use of quotations.

The first two chapters consider what it means to talk about the Bible *in* literature and the Bible *as* literature. In the first, the story of the Bible and the story the Bible tells are introduced; something of the background to the King James or Authorized Version of the Bible is given, and three short examples of the Bible in specific poems are offered. In the second, the rise of the idea of the Bible as literature is discussed, and some of the challenges to this idea, from a variety of perspectives, are outlined. In Chapters 3 and 9, the recurring biblical themes of creation and apocalypse respectively are traced within the Bible itself, and in later literature. Three of the remaining chapters take an approach to a text from the world of literary criticism (theories of intertextuality, narrative criticism and reader-response criticism), and seek to demonstrate what a reading of both a literary and a biblical text from this approach might look like. In Chapter 7, feminist readings of the biblical texts of Ruth and the parable of the foolish virgins are offered; and Margaret Atwood's novel *The Handmaid's Tale* is read as a feminist critique of biblical themes. Chapter 8 takes the ancient reading strategy of the rabbis, midrash, and asks if it is a useful way to think about the re-reading of biblical texts in later literature, as some literary critics have recently argued. Finally, in Chapter 10, something of the future of the field is suggested, in light of the development of literary studies away from the rigid application of theory, which has been so attractive up until now to those in biblical studies with an interest in literary matters. The context of the reader, with its disputed role in the understanding of the location of meaning in any text, will be in view throughout. A good exercise for any reader of this text will be, self-consciously, to monitor their own reaction to the readings offered, and to ask why one reading makes more sense than another, or even provokes the strongest positive or negative reaction.

Over several years I have taught a Bible and Literature Honours class at New College, the School of Divinity of the University of Edinburgh. When the course began, it was co-taught with Professor Ian Campbell, then Professor of Scottish and Victorian Literature in the Department of English at Edinburgh. Once he retired, he continued to participate in the class on a voluntary basis, and was often named in student evaluation forms in response to the question, 'What was the best thing about this course?' With these students, I have learned a huge amount from Ian's knowledge of literature and, although he plays this down, his knowledge of the Bible too. I have also benefited from the enthusiasm and insights of the many students who have taken the course – and this is a much better book as a result of their interaction with the ideas contained here. I should also add that we all found John B. Gabel et al, *The Bible as Literature: An Introduction* (Oxford: Oxford University Press, 2006) to be a very useful textbook, and I have been inspired by the approach taken there, particularly with regard to Apocalyptic Literature.

I would also like to thank my editors at SCM Press for their patience. I can only hope the result is worth their long wait and their willingness to believe in me. And I thank the many friends who have shared in discussions that my thinking and reading for this book have provoked, especially Abigail Clark and Mark Elliott.

1

The Bible in Literature

The idea of reading literary texts for their allusions and references to the Bible is a familiar and safe one. That the Bible has had an influence on literature throughout the ages is hardly surprising, textually foundational as it is to many cultures. And so we begin our discussion of 'the Bible and literature' by considering 'the Bible *in* literature'. However, the question of what is 'literature' and what is 'the Bible' still needs to be defined in order to make sure the ground we aim to cover is shared terrain.

The focus of this chapter, indeed this book, is literature in English, mainly of the recent past (the last couple of centuries or so), focusing on the genres of poetry, short story and novel. The selection that has been made reflects my academic background and areas of interest, but it also, I hope, offers a suitable and stimulating variety of examples from a range of texts that are easily available and within the generally accepted canon of literature in English. The texts are accessible in the fullest sense of that word.

The Bible in question is generally the translation known as the King James Version (KJV) or as the Authorized Version. While other translations have long been available, and indeed modern translations are now much more readily heard in acts of worship, it is the KJV that has had an undisputed influence on English, Scottish and American literature. A book covering the influence of the Revised Standard Version of the Bible or the Good News Bible on contemporary literature in English would be a slim volume indeed. By asserting that an English translation of the Bible, and one from the seventeenth century at that, is generally the Bible under discussion, this book is removing itself from the accepted genre of Bible criticism. The focus throughout is on readings and readings of readings, not on a search for the interpretation that is the earliest or the closest to the original reading. The most significant Bible in literary terms, both as a literary text itself and as a source of influence in literary texts, is the KJV.

In this chapter, a brief history of the genesis of the KJV, and of its influence in English Literature, will be given. The story the Bible tells, and the story of the Bible itself, will then be introduced, in order that the field that is the study of the Bible in literature may be explored meaningfully by those unfamiliar with the content and history of the biblical text.

A later chapter will seek to understand and discuss the specific ways in which the Bible reappears in literature through various modern theories of intertextuality. Here we will focus on the history of the Bible in literature, and consider ways in which the influence of the one on the other may be read as a barometer of literary and/or theological trends.

The King James Version of the Bible

Alister McGrath's statement, in his book, *In the Beginning: The Story of the King James Bible and How it Changed a Nation, a Language, and a Culture*, that '[t]he two greatest influences on the shaping of the English language are the works of William Shakespeare and the English translation of the Bible that appeared in 1611',[1] is surely no overstatement of the case. The convoluted chain of events that led to the translation of the Bible into English initiated by James VI (known as James I in England) in 1603 cannot be covered in any more than a cursory way here, although it is a fascinating story. It should be remembered, however, that the King James Version was not the first English translation, and that it struggled at first to gain acceptance in churches and in homes. During the Elizabethan and much of the Jacobite era, it was the Geneva Bible that was the most widely read Bible in the English-speaking world. Produced in the Geneva of John Calvin and John Knox in 1560 by English exiles from the reign of Mary Tudor, it offered a thoroughly Protestant interpretation of the text it was translating. Produced cheaply yet attractively, it offered prefaces to each book, in defence of Protestant claims; marginal notes anticipating difficulties and clarifying the obscure; illustrations and maps, all with the aim of making engagement with the biblical text as straightforward as possible for each reader. By 1600 it was the Bible of choice for English-speaking Protestants, and it should be noted that it is the Geneva Bible to which Shakespeare alludes and refers. In 1559, Elizabeth I had demanded that there should be an English Bible in every church in England, but even when it became available, the Geneva Bible was not considered suitable for this purpose. Its rampant Protestant emphasis threatened to disturb the uneasy peace between the religious factions of the time, which Elizabeth sought to maintain. Older versions were given official sanction, such as the Great Bible of 1539, and a new one was commissioned from Archbishop Matthew Parker, known as the Bishops' Bible. When James VI of Scotland and I of England came to the throne, no ally of Scottish Presbyterianism, he too refused to endorse the Geneva Bible. At the Hampton Court Conference of 1603 convened to deal with the claims of Anglicans and Puritans, he agreed to authorize

---

1 Alister McGrath, 2001, *In the Beginning: The Story of the King James Bible and How it Changed a Nation, a Language, and a Culture*, New York: Anchor Books, p. 1.

a new translation in order to appease the Puritans who rejected the Bishops' Bible, and to mollify the Anglicans who were deeply opposed to the Geneva Bible, and who hoped they might have the greater influence over the composition of the panel of translators.

The basis of the translation was drawn up, and it appeared that the Anglican faction did indeed have the upper hand. There were to be no marginal notes. Contentious issues were resolved in the Anglicans' favour: 'ekklesia' was to be translated as 'church', not the more individual 'congregation', thus emphasizing the Church as an institution; and whereas 'kings' were sometimes referred to as 'tyrants' in the notes of the Geneva Bible, such anti-monarchy leanings were to be avoided. Psalm 105.15 could indeed stand as a justification of the divine right of kings, which the Geneva Bible had rejected. Thus the political nature of the genesis of the KJV should not be underestimated or ignored. As McGrath comments, summing up the aspirations of those involved in its production:

> The new Bible would be a rallying point for a Protestant English nation. The production, at the king's initiative, of a new English translation of the Bible would reinforce the image of the king as the political and spiritual leader of his people, and might even stimulate the rebirth of that elusive sense of national identity and pride that had blossomed under Elizabeth.[2]

Written in the period in which English was going through an unprecedented process of being shaped and standardized, influenced by the rise of printing, the KJV did not include literary elegance or merit as one of its aims of translation. Rather, the act of translation was seen as an act of service to the people of God, of offering direct access to the Bible, the author of which was God himself. Accuracy was the chief aim: the translation was to be as literal as possible, following the word order of the original; each word was to be given an English equivalent; and where words were added, this was to be indicated. Thus many Hebrew idioms were brought into English use, such as the now familiar 'to set one's face against' (Leviticus 20.3), 'far be it from me' (1 Samuel 20.9) and 'den of thieves' (Mark 11.17).[3] The translators were ordered to use the Bishops' Bible of 1568 wherever possible, which traced its ancestry right back to Tyndale's translation of the New Testament from 1526 (revised in 1534) via Coverdale's complete English Bible of 1535. This accounts for many words and phrases that Tyndale had coined, such as 'the salt of the earth' (Matthew 5.13) and 'a law unto themselves' (Romans 2.14), and

---

2 McGrath, *In the Beginning*, p. 171.

3 See David Norton, 1993, *A History of the Bible as Literature*, Volume 2: *From 1700 to the Present Day*, Cambridge: Cambridge University Press, pp. 340–8 for more examples.

'Jehovah', 'Passover' and 'atonement'. It also explains the predominance of forms that were already considered archaic at the time the KJV was produced, such as 'thee' and 'thy' and the verbal forms ending in –eth. The overall effect was to give the impression that religious language was by necessity from generations before. While the KJV seemed strange at first to some, especially those in regions far away from the south east, where the majority of translators came from, and while it was not whole-heartedly accepted until the reinstatement of the monarchy in 1660, by the mid 1700s it had become not just a symbol of national unity but was considered a great work of religious literature. 'Biblical English', with all its Hebraisms, archaisms and painstaking constructions, came to be seen to possess unassailable literary and cultural as well as religious authority.

Meanwhile, in America, the KJV also attained a powerful status. The first Bible in America was in fact the Geneva Bible, reflecting the Puritan roots of the first English colonists. However, it was the KJV that united American Christians: 'Cut off from their linguistic homeland, the colonists found that the text of the Bible was an important means of sustaining both their religious faith and their English prose. Both their faith and their language was nourished and governed by the King James translation.'[4] Legal restraints and lack of resources meant that Bibles were not printed in America until near the end of the American Revolution. Even after this, cheap imports from Britain and Europe were easily obtained, and it was the KJV that flooded the market.

The widespread authority and dominance of the KJV in Britain and America over the centuries since its inception at a particularly opportune moment in the history of the English language and of the dissemination of printed texts, has given it a powerful literary, cultural and religious status. For many, the KJV has been synonymous with the Bible. For some, it has been evidence of God's providential plan, produced with divine inspiration behind it at the high point of the development of the English language. However, the relationship between the Bible and literature has not stayed constant and static over time. The religious views of individual writers and the broader sweep of theological understanding at any given period may change, and may be in tension. For biblical and literary scholars of our era, I suggest that an assessment of why and how this hugely significant text relates to other, later texts should not avoid the theological contexts in which these later texts were produced. While some modern literary theories may attempt to remove texts from their contexts, and some of these will be considered in this book, it will be argued here that a fruitful way to read literary texts is to understand their interaction with the Bible from the perspective of their theological suppositions.

We have begun our exploration of the topic 'the Bible and Literature' by considering which Bible we generally mean when we want to consider

---

4 McGrath, *In the Beginning*, p. 294.

'the Bible in Literature': the King James Version. Before going further, however, a brief summary of what 'the Bible' is might prove useful for those for whom 'literature' is a well-known concept, but the Bible is something of a closed book.

The Bible's story

One way to do this is to consider two stories that overlap but that do not coincide completely. The first is the story the Bible tells; the second is the story of the Bible.[5]

The story the Bible tells begins with two accounts of the creation of the world. The creative power of God is asserted, and the beginnings of the human race and their fractured relationship with this God are explained. The story of the flood, in response to humanity's refusal to follow God's way, marks a new beginning, but time and again biblical characters such as Noah are revealed to disappoint the responsibilities placed upon them. The story continues with the narrative of the Patriarchs. First comes Abraham, from whom God promises a great nation will descend, and who will live in a land flowing with milk and honey. Abraham's commitment to this God is tested by God's command to sacrifice his only son, Isaac. But the boy is saved at the last moment, and his sons, Jacob and Esau, continue the story. From Jacob's many sons come the 12 tribes of Israel, the name given to Jacob after his defining wrestle with a divine stranger. Joseph, the youngest, gains power in Egypt. Over time, the Israelites descend into slavery in Egypt; but one of their number, Moses, triumphantly leads them out of bondage, through the Red Sea and the 40 years of wilderness wandering, and into the promised land. On the way, Moses is given the Ten Commandments, and a special relationship, or covenant, is established between the people and God. The story of the Exodus, as this narrative is known, is one of the foundational and recurring stories of the Bible. The overarching narrative continues with the people settling as a nation in Canaan, under the rule of the great kings David and then Solomon. In this period, the temple is built in Jerusalem. However, peace does not last and the Israelites are defeated by the Babylonians and many are taken into exile. Eventually, a small number are allowed to return and to begin to rebuild the temple. Exile and return is a second recurring theme in this story. Many more sub-stories are told in the Hebrew Bible,[6] many focused on the struggle to live according to

---

5 For an accessible introduction to the Bible, and particularly to its individual books, see Stephen Harris, 2006, *Understanding the Bible*, 7th edn, Boston: McGraw-Hill.

6 The 'Hebrew Bible' is a more neutral term for those books of the Bible that Christians usually call the 'Old Testament', which implies these texts needed the insights of the 'New Testament' to be complete.

the covenant, and what happens when people individually or collectively fall short of this ideal, or deliberately turn away from it. There is recounting of battles won and lost, and prophets who warn in a variety of ways what the consequences will be if God's way is not taken. However, at its core, the Hebrew Bible tells the story of God's care for the world and for his chosen people in particular.

In the Bible used by the Christian Church, the story does not end with the Old Testament. The events of the birth, life and death of Jesus are told as a continuation of the story of God's interaction with the world, which extends to the founding and spread of the Church in his name. The ongoing presence of Jesus, who is given attributes that link him to Adam, Moses and other Old Testament figures, is asserted and presumed. The Bible closes with a visionary description of the end of the world, and the promise of a new creation in heaven.

If we take the story the Bible tells on its own terms, using its own internal dating, the period covered is around 4000 years, from the time of the creation (famously estimated by some to be the year 4004 BCE) through the lives of the Patriarchs (the beginning of the second millennium BCE) to the end of Paul's career (around 60 CE).[7] While one overarching story may be discerned, involving the central character of the one God, creator and sustainer of the earth, and his relationship with those who accept a relationship with him, and those who do not, there are many different voices behind the books of the Bible. A multitude of literary genres are found here, from long and short narratives to poetry and song, genealogies and historical accounts, biography, letters and apocalyptic writing. These voices tell different versions of the story, from a variety of perspectives, and the relationship between each text, and within texts themselves, is the subject of scholarly debate. This brings us to the second story of interest here, and that is the story of the Bible itself.

As was realized in the nineteenth century with the discovery and translation of a variety of inscriptions from the ancient Near East, there are in the Bible a number of versions of stories that come from a much earlier time. The creation of the world from the watery deep (Genesis 1.2) is considered by many to be a reworking of an earlier story from Babylon, often called 'Enuma Elish'.[8] A Sumerian myth, found in written form from the late third millennium BCE, speaks of a flood sent by the gods, from which only the pious man Ziusudra is destined to survive by building

---

7 To arrive at this figure, the various genealogies in Luke 3 and the adding together of the ages of the Patriarchs from Genesis 5 have all to be taken into account. It was with the discovery of fossilized remains and the ideas put forward by Charles Darwin in the nineteenth century that this figure began to be questioned, and the historical veracity of the whole of the Old Testament scrutinized.

8 This is considered in more detail in Chapter 3.

a large boat. After seven years the sun god appears and Ziusudra is saved and granted eternal life. Over a millennium later, the story was incorporated into an Akkadian epic, which added family members to those who are saved. This story soon became part of an even longer narrative, the 'Gilgamesh epic', forms of which spread widely across the Near East. A comparison of this story with the narrative of Noah and his ark, from Genesis 8.6–12, reveals close parallels, including the sending of birds to test for land.[9] The precise relationship between these earlier texts and the Hebrew Bible stories is hard to establish, beyond pointing to a sharing of traditions within the geographical area, developing no doubt from oral as well as written forms of the narrative. While, at first, many of the nineteenth-century pioneers of archaeology and philology hoped the discovery of these parallel traditions pointed to a shared historical event, it became evident to most that these texts did not point to a single happening, but belonged to a world of myth and story. Each example used local gods and heroes as the main characters, with their own points of view and motivations. Very little of the archaeological material offered historical confirmation of Bible narratives and figures, but some at least brought a new dimension to our understanding of the story of the Bible. It came to be accepted by many that certain of the biblical narratives are held in common with the culture of its time and owe their existence to a period many hundreds of years before the Bible came to be written down.

It is to be expected that many of the texts of the Bible, in both Old and New Testaments, existed within an oral tradition before being committed to writing. Low literacy rates and the high cost of writing materials meant that a strong and widespread oral culture may well have been responsible for much of the development and maintenance of the texts that make up the Bible. While much of this process, by its very nature, is now difficult to reconstruct, we have some understanding of the way in which the texts as they were finally written down may have come to be gathered together and considered canonical.

In the scriptures of Judaism, the books are divided into three categories or sections, each of which was brought into canonical shape at different periods. The Torah ('Law') or Pentateuch ('five scrolls') is made up of the books of Genesis, Exodus, Leviticus, Numbers and Deuteronomy. All of these books claimed to have been written by Moses, and the early scholarly consensus was that they were brought into this canonical shape in the fifth century BCE, in response to the trauma of the exile. Many later scholars refute any suggestion that one person was responsible for all of these books, far less Moses himself, and argue instead that they were written at the beginning of the first millennium BCE by a variety of hands. On this view, the aim of these books was to encourage Jews who

---

9 The story may be read in full in James Pritchard, 1955, *Ancient Near Eastern Texts Relating to the Old Testament*, Princeton: Princeton University Press, pp. 94–5.

had returned from exile by reminding them of the stories that highlighted their beginnings as a people. From such a promising start, their future too promised to be bright.

The next set of books to be brought together and considered scriptural was the Prophets, which includes Joshua, Judges, the books of Samuel and Kings (each one book rather than two in Jewish scripture), Isaiah, Jeremiah and Ezekiel and the minor prophets. These were probably formed into a literary unit by around 200 BCE, and together show that faithfulness to God brings reward, while turning away from him brings catastrophe. The final set, named the Writings, included the Psalms, Proverbs, Job, Daniel and Chronicles. These generally related to the period between the time of David and the return from exile, but many were written much later than this. While the names of figures from the past have been associated with these texts, such as David with the Psalms, and Solomon with Proverbs, this was part of a common literary tradition which accepted the ongoing inspiration lying behind such texts. The book of Daniel, for example, purports to have been written at the time of the exile (Daniel is a hero of the sixth century BCE) but probably comes from the Jerusalem of the second century BCE, when the Jews were facing desperate persecution at the hands of the Greeks and their successors. Reasserting stories from the glorious past of the Jews brought hope in dire circumstances.

The final, combined shape of these texts emerged towards the end of the first century CE, when those who had survived the fall of Jerusalem regrouped and sought to redefine Judaism away from the temple and all that it symbolized.[10] Finally, some texts, which had been included in the earlier Greek translation of the Hebrew Bible known as the Septuagint, were excluded from this final closing of the canon. Mostly written between 200 BCE and 150 CE, these books included Ecclesiasticus (also known as Sirach), Wisdom and the Books of Maccabees. While the scriptures of the early Christian Church (based on the Septuagint) included these texts, the Reformers of the sixteenth century reverted to the canon agreed after the fall of Jerusalem. And thus, the Roman Catholic and Orthodox traditions retain these texts, termed collectively the Apocrypha or the Deuterocanonical books, while Bibles from the Reformed tradition tend to exclude them.

The story of the relationship of the books of the New Testament to the events they refer to, and their establishment as canonical, is similarly complex. The oldest of these texts are the letters of Paul, which probably date to the period 50–60 CE. Not all of the letters attributed to Paul are accepted as having been written by him: but that he wrote letters

---

10 Traditionally this regrouping took place at Jamnia, a village on the coast, far west of Jerusalem, where a collection of Pharisees sought to work out the next steps for their religion and way of life. Whether or not there was a conscious consideration of canonical issues here is uncertain.

for particular situations and to specific communities is accepted by all. That these letters also included general advice for the faithful meant that they were copied and distributed among a wider range of churches. By the middle of the second century CE, a collection of 13 letters by Paul (including 1 and 2 Corinthians, Romans, Philippians and 1 and 2 Timothy), plus the disputed Letter to the Hebrews, was circulating, according to the evidence offered in 2 Peter 3.15–16. As this was over a generation after Paul's death, we can only assume many of his letters had been lost in the interim. However, the collection proved popular and useful, and seven other letters, bearing the names of other apostolic writers, were added, including James, 1 and 2 Peter, and the three letters of John.

The letters of Paul, and possibly James and Jude, were written before any of the Gospels took the final form in which we read them today. In the first century CE, the oral traditions about Jesus merged into written traditions, with several writers/collectors of these traditions presumably working for specific audiences. It is generally agreed that Mark's Gospel was the earliest of the four canonical texts, from around 65–75 CE, and that this Gospel was used by the writers of Matthew and Luke (80–90 CE), who also had a collection of shared sayings and their own unique material at their disposal. John's Gospel is very different from the first three, and is usually considered the latest to be written of the four, perhaps arising between 90–100 CE.

Irenaeus, a forceful figure in the early Church, wrote in around 180 CE that the four Gospels, which had by now been brought into a collection, were to be considered both sufficient and necessary.[11] Gradually, the pressure to exclude views that were deemed heretical, and to promote theological thinking that was deemed orthodox, meant that some texts were added to the nascent canon of the Pauline letters and the four Gospels, while others were considered unsuitable. The Book of Acts, the sequel to the Gospel of Luke, was generally accepted in the second half of the second century, while Hebrews and the Book of Revelation split the Church, with some accepting these books and others rejecting them. Others accepted texts, such as the Letter of Barnabas and the Shepherd of Hermas, which did not receive universal approval. It was not until around 400 CE, when Jerome's Latin translation of the Bible became so influential, that a 27-book canon of the New Testament was fixed and widely agreed. Direct apostolic succession was a key principle in making canonical decisions, interpreted rather more strictly than the prophetic inspiration that generally guided the canonical debates behind the Hebrew Bible. A connection with Jesus himself was deemed important, perhaps increasingly so as the original disciples died. However, inevitably,

---

11 'The Gospels could not possibly be either more or less in number than they are.' (*Adversus Haereses* 3.11). Irenaeus went on to substantiate this claim from the example of the four-fold nature of other religious and natural phenomenon.

with the passing of time and the existence of various texts actually in use in Christian communities, this principle may have been applied after the fact. What is notable for us is that all of the books of the New Testament were written many years after Jesus lived, and, it is argued, with the specific needs of their readers in view. For both the Old and New Testaments, the interplay between historical, literary and rhetorical concerns is not straightforward.

The study of the Bible in literature

The above discussion of both the story the Bible tells and the story of the Bible itself has been brief, and aspects of it will be told in more detail in the chapters to come, where the voices of those who would debate my telling of those stories will be heard also. Here we turn to focus more closely on what the study of the Bible in literature means and has meant. For many, maintaining a distinction between the Bible *as* literature and the Bible *in* literature is not as straightforward as I have perhaps suggested thus far. It is held by literary and biblical critics such as Stephen Prickett, David Norton and David Jasper[12] that the rise of a commonly held understanding of the Bible *as* literature, allied to its loss of status as a sacred text, led directly to its growing influence *within* literature itself. Prickett (2006) has persuasively argued that the loss of the Bible's credence as an inspired text, and its coming to be read instead as a collection of narratives, occurred in conjunction with the rise of the novel. The two movements were related to each other, and this relationship included the integration of biblical themes and allusions into literary texts. The close and complex intertwining of the novel, particularly in the Victorian era, the Bible and the culture of the time, stemmed from a loss of trust in the Bible as the infallible Word of God. Such claims will be considered in more detail in the next chapter, and it should be noted here that they do not go uncontested, as we will also see in the next chapter. Certainly the Bible had been a source of inspiration for literary texts long before the novel form became widespread. Milton's epic poem *Paradise Lost* (published in 1667) and Bunyan's *Pilgrim's Progress* (1678) are two examples that will probably spring to most minds. Few would dispute that the Bible, and in particular the King James Version, has influenced English literature. The levels of that influence will now be considered.

Biblical and literary scholars alike have sought to categorize the various levels of influence between one text and another. The study of intertextuality, considered in Chapter 4, takes this as its aim and focus. In this introductory chapter, we might begin by teasing out the differences between, and significance of, biblical quotations and allusions in literature,

---

12 See the 'Further reading' section of this chapter for details of the work of these scholars.

and leave the more speculative level, which some have called 'echo', to that later chapter.

The Bible in literature: three poetic examples

There are many ways to approach the study of the influence of the Bible in literature. In a recent monograph, *Pen of Iron*, Robert Alter, who has been a pioneer in this field, considers the role of the King James Version in shaping the style of American novels of the nineteenth and twentieth centuries. He explores the recurrence of biblical stylistic features such as parallelism, the invocation of grand themes of flesh and blood, land and curse, and a simplicity of expression without recourse to expansive causal connections, in novels such as Herman Melville's *Moby Dick*, William Faulkner's *Absalom, Absalom!* and Saul Bellow's *Seize the Day*. The aim of this section will be less ambitious and more readily accessible. Here we will consider three well-known, short and easily obtained poems, and compare the ways in which the Bible plays a role in their uses of language, themes and creation of meaning.

The first is T. S. Eliot's 'The Journey of the Magi', published in 1930 in his collection *Ariel Poems*.[13] Its subject is clearly biblical, and relates to the story of the visit of the wise men, or 'magi', from the East to the stable where Jesus was born, related in Matthew 2. However, although the poem relates to a biblical story, there are no direct links to the original story on the level of words or images. The form is that of a dramatic monologue, offering the reader a perspective on events from one of the participants, from a much later period. While the Matthean version offers little in the way of access to motive or reaction, apart from noting that they 'rejoiced with exceeding great joy' (2.10) when they saw the star, and worshipped the child with his mother, the poem focuses on the hardships endured and the new, 'hard' understanding that the experience brought. While the speaker asserts that the place they found 'was (you may say) satisfactory', and he 'would do it again', the experience of 'this Birth' was 'like Death, our death'. In the 'old dispensation' they have returned to, he is 'no longer at ease', and he concludes he would be 'glad of another death'. There is a marked shift in tone and outcome, and the fractured link between the biblical character and story is emphasized by the lack of verbal correspondences. Indeed, the first five lines of the poem are taken from Lancelot Andrewes's 'Nativity Sermon' of 1622: this is a tradition that has been cut loose from its biblical bearings, and given a literary life of its own. The relationship to the first mention of the magi

---

13 T. S. Eliot, 1969, *The Complete Poems of T. S. Eliot*, London: Faber & Faber, p. 103.

in Matthew is oblique and the poem is as informed by later retellings of the story as by the biblical text.

However, there are significant biblical allusions made in the poem, although they tend to relate to the end of the life of Jesus, rather than his birth. In a quasi-symbolic way, Eliot introduces significant, biblical images into the landscape of his poem. Into the central section, with its modern-sounding reflections on a 'temperate valley ... below the snow line' and on the 'water-mill beating the darkness', comes the short, emphatic line 'And three trees on the low sky'. The three trees of course recall the three crosses on the hill of Jesus' crucifixion, while the lowered sky may allude to the image of the heavens opened at the end of time, and the New Jerusalem, part of a new creation to replace the old, being lowered into place (see Revelation 21). Both events, presumably, remain in the future of the speaker, but the experience of his visit to 'the place' brings past and future into a new relationship. The 'old white horse' that runs past suggests the fleeting appearance of the triumphant Messiah of the Book of Revelation (6.2), sent to conquer the earth. In place of the blood of the lamb of Passover (Exodus 12.7) smeared on the doorpost of the houses of the Israelites, there are 'vine-leaves' on the 'lintel' of the 'tavern' where the magi seek information, without success. Blood, wine and sacrifice, and the image from John 15 of Jesus as the vine, and his followers as the branches, are all alluded to here. The 'empty wine-skins' which the gamblers kick points to a perception of a lack of fruitfulness as a result of Christ's coming, and also recalls Jesus' teaching about new wine to be poured into new rather than old wine-skins, from Luke 5.33–9: the speaker's sadness and disillusionment is expressed in significant biblical images. Perhaps the clearest allusion in this central section of the poem is found in the reference to the hands of three people 'dicing for pieces of silver' at 'an open door'. The pieces of silver recall the money Judas was given to betray Jesus, which, in Matthew's Gospel, he throws back into the temple, before hanging himself (27.3–10). The reference to gambling suggests the soldiers throwing dice for Jesus' garment at the scene of the crucifixion (Matthew 27.35). The 'open door' is reminiscent of various assertions in Revelation about doors, from the 'open door' of Revelation 3.8, set before believers by Jesus which no man can shut, to the open door in heaven of Revelation 4.1, through which the Seer ascends to receive his vision, to the door at which Jesus famously stands and knocks and waits to be allowed through (Revelation 3.20). The 'open door' of the poem, however, is a sign of emptiness and corruption rather than invitation and the possibility of new inspiration and salvation.

'The Journey of the Magi' takes the biblical story and sets it in a new time and perspective. It assumes knowledge of the basic story; and a reader who is familiar with the wider sweep of biblical narrative, from the Exodus to the Book of Revelation, will be rewarded with a deeper understanding of the poem's significance. With its interwoven references to these texts from the past and the future of the narrative moment being described, the timelessness of the experience is stressed. Its potential to affect those who have undergone the moment of revelation is expressed in its final stanza, in the interplay between birth and death. The Wise Man has known both birth and death in the moment: 'hard and bitter agony' (like the Garden of Gethsemane experience of Jesus in Luke 22.44), and leading to a complete dislocation from all that was familiar in the past, 'the old dispensation' among people who are now 'alien'. References to the contrasts so popular in the writings of Paul are hard to avoid: 'For me to live is Christ, and to die is gain' (Philippians 1.21); 'I am crucified with Christ: nevertheless I live; yet not I, but Christ liveth in me: and the life which I now live in the flesh I live by the faith of the Son of God, who loved me, and gave himself for me' (Galatians 2.20). This is no easy, comfortable conversion, but profoundly disturbing. An awareness of the biblical allusions alive in the poem, none of them overtly signalled but all with significance, enriches the experience of reading the text.

The second poem to be considered is W. B. Yeats's 'The Lake Isle of In-nisfree', published in 1893 in the collection *The Rose*.[14] Here, the phrase with which the poem opens, and which recurs at the beginning of the third and final stanza, is a direct quotation from the parable of the Prod-igal Son (Luke 15.18). In the parable, the younger son asks his father for his half of his inheritance, which he takes to a far country and wastes in excessive living. The country is in the grip of a famine, and the son ends up looking after a herd of pigs, and coveting their feed. He finally 'comes to himself', and mentally prepares to return to his father's household and ask to be accepted there as a servant: 'I will arise and go to my father . . .', he decides. As is well-known, his father has been watching for his return, runs to greet him, re-establishes him as a member of the family and throws a party for him; for, as he explains to the truculent older son, 'this my son was dead, and is alive again; he was lost, and is found' (15.24).

Yeats's poem begins with this reference, but its setting proves to be very different in some ways at least: 'I will arise and go now, and go to Innisfree' (l.1). The poem continues to imagine the scene that awaits the speaker there, of 'peace', and harmony with nature, and beauty for all the senses. It is only at the end of the poem, in the final two lines, that the current, contrasting experience of the speaker is described, standing 'on the pavements grey'. The use of the opening phrase, however, might lead a reader to expect such a stark contrast, following the pattern of the parable that also highlights the contrast between the comforts of home and the denigrated state of the younger son. While the parable describes an actual return to the place of welcome and restoration, the concluding line of the poem offers a different interpretation. A physical return is

---

14 W. B. Yeats, 1981, *The Collected Poems of W. B. Yeats*, 2nd edn, London: Macmillan, p. 44.

not envisaged, because the experience is of a different order, and comes from 'the deep heart's core'. As in T. S. Eliot's poem, the introduction of the biblical reference in this way emphasizes the timeless and universal quality of the central theme of the poem. The repetition of the phrase from the parable gives the imagined scene of life on the island deeper resonance: it speaks of restoration of the soul as well as the body; of homecoming after a profound and unnatural breaking away; and of the possibility of spiritual reintegration. If this use of a biblical phrase in the poem is not recognized, the text is still effective. If it is, a new depth of meaning is discovered.

The third poem similarly opens with a biblical reference, which is later repeated, although even more emphatically. In Dylan Thomas's 'And Death Shall Have no Dominion', published in 1936 in the collection *Twenty-five Poems*,[15] the three stanzas open and close with a statement based on Paul's Letter to the Romans 6.9: 'Knowing that Christ being raised from the dead dieth no more; death hath no more dominion over him'. The tone is similar to that of Paul, too, assertive and rhythmic, and playing with the ideas of death, life, the mortal and immortal body. But here the similarity ends, and the conception of life beyond death is very different in the poem from the Christocentric expectation of Paul. There is a hope, even an expectation, of resurrection ('Though they sink through the sea they shall rise again'), but this is not 'in the likeness of his [Christ's] resurrection' (Romans 6.5). Rather, the images stacked up are natural and supernatural, mythic and astrological:

Dead men naked they shall be one
With the man in the wind and the west moon;
When their bones are picked clean and the clean bones gone,
They shall have stars at elbow and foot.

(ll.2–5)

The world of the poem is one of 'daisies' and 'gulls', and 'unicorn evils', 'racks' and 'wheels' of torture, but also 'love' that 'shall not' be lost. It is not 'sin' that is the enemy, but unnamed and threatening forces, including the natural process of decay. However, just as for Paul, in the poem, death cannot be avoided (to be 'dead as nails' remains the fate), but for both, there is still the hope that death will not prevail: 'heads of the characters hammer through daisies' (l.25)/ 'that like as Christ was raised up from the dead by the glory of the Father, even so we also should walk in newness of life' (6.4). The vocabulary and the imagery are poles apart, but the outcome is the same. Just as Romans is a difficult text theologically and in terms of its cohesive sense, so Thomas's poem is difficult to

---

15 Dylan Thomas, 1971, *Dylan Thomas: The Poems*, Daniel Jones (ed.), London: Dent & Sons, p. 49.

fathom and to find a thread of sense that runs through it, but in both cases, from different perceived experiences, the expectation of the ultimate powerlessness of death is held to with unshakeable conviction.

While the repetition of the biblical phrase gives this poem an unmistakeably biblical weight and cadence, in fact it is the least biblically based of the three poems we have considered. 'The Journey of the Magi' is based on a biblical story, and uses language from the Bible symbolically throughout. 'The Lake Isle of Innisfree', although it uses only one biblical phrase, depends on an allusion to an underlying biblical story. Thomas's poem uses a similar technique of repeating a familiar, biblical phrase, and asserts a hope for the future that is shared in the writings of Paul, but it expresses that hope in a completely different way, pulling the biblical language and ideas away from their original anchor into a new realm. All depend on the King James Version of the Bible, as this chapter described in its opening paragraph. Knowing something of the KJV, and of the story of the text that lies behind it, leads to an enriched reading experience of later texts such as the ones discussed briefly here. There is much more to say about the Bible in literature, but I hope we have established that studying the Bible in literature is a worthwhile endeavour. As Robert Alter argues, in his exploration of the role of the King James Version in the shaping of the style of American novels:

> The resonant language and the arresting vision of the canonical text, however oldentime they may be, continue to ring in cultural memory. We may break them apart or turn them around, but they are tools we still use on occasion to construct the world around us.[16]

Questions

1. Why, in your opinion, did the King James Version of the Bible become so popular and so dominant in the English-speaking world?
2. Discuss examples of poems, novels or plays you know in which the influence of the Bible may be detected. Is the influence at the level of quotation or allusion, and what effect does recognizing this have on your understanding of the text?

Further reading

Robert Alter, 2010, *Pen of Iron: American Prose and the King James Bible*, Princeton: Princeton University Press.

---

16 Robert Alter, 2010, *Pen of Iron: American Prose and the King James Bible*, Princeton: Princeton University Press, pp. 182–3.

Gordon Campbell, 2010, *Bible: The Story of the King James Version 1611–2011*, Oxford: Oxford University Press.

T. S. Eliot, 1969, *The Complete Poems of T. S. Eliot*, London: Faber & Faber.

Stephen Harris, 2006, *Understanding the Bible*, 7th edn, Boston: McGraw-Hill.

David Jasper, 2009, 'Biblical Hermeneutics and Literary Theory', in R. Lemon, E. Mason, J. Roberts and C. Rowland (eds), *The Blackwell Companion to the Bible in English Literature*, Chichester: Wiley-Blackwell, pp. 22–37.

Alister McGrath, 2001, *In the Beginning: The Story of the King James Bible and How it Changed a Nation, a Language, and a Culture*, New York: Anchor Books.

David Norton, 1993, *A History of the Bible as Literature*, Volume 2: *From 1700 to the Present Day*, Cambridge: Cambridge University Press.

David Norton, 2000, *A History of the English Bible as Literature*, Cambridge: Cambridge University Press.

Stephen Prickett, 2005, *Origins of Narrative: The Romantic Appropriation of the Bible*, Cambridge: Cambridge University Press.

Stephen Prickett, 2006, 'From Novel to Bible: The Aestheticizing of Scripture', in M. Knight and T. Woodman (eds), *Biblical Religion and the Novel, 1700–2000*, Aldershot: Ashgate, pp. 13–24.

Dylan Thomas, 1971, *Dylan Thomas: The Poems*, Daniel Jones (ed.), London: Dent & Sons.

W. B. Yeats, 1981, *The Collected Poems of W. B. Yeats*, 2nd edn, London: Macmillan.

2

Reading the Bible as Literature

While in the previous chapter we focused on the Bible *in* literature, here we consider in more detail the history and implications of reading the Bible *as* literature, a rather different exercise. We will assess what it means to say the Bible is literature, rather than any other sort of text; and we will demonstrate what such an assertion looks like when it is applied to an actual section of the Bible.

First, however, it will be useful to trace the phrase, and its implications, to its genesis. Probably the first person to use the term 'the Bible as literature' was Matthew Arnold, the nineteenth-century Oxford Professor of Poetry and commentator on literary, social and educational issues. In his Introduction to T. H. Ward's *English Poets*, published in 1880, Arnold wrote:

> Our religion has materialized itself in the fact, in the supposed fact; it has attached its emotion to the fact, and now the fact is failing it. But for poetry the idea is everything; the rest is a world of illusion, of divine illusion. Poetry attaches its emotion to the idea; the idea *is* the fact. The strongest part of our religion today is its unconscious poetry.[1]

For Arnold, as for many of his contemporaries, the Bible could no longer be considered 'history' in the sense that term was commonly used. The internal inconsistencies in the Bible accounts, of both the history of Israel in the Old Testament and the portrayal of Jesus in the New, were being considered critically. Archaeological discoveries and evolutionary speculation, supported by new geological understandings of the development of the world, cast doubt on the veracity of either of the two accounts of creation in Genesis. And questions were asked of the two accounts themselves: could they possibly be referring to the same historical event? In the New Testament, could the Jesus depicted in John's Gospel, philosophical and assuming the existence of the Church that would come after him, really be the same person as the terse, enigmatic leader of a band of inadequate followers whom Mark described? Form and source criticism

---

1 Quoted in David Daiches, 1984, *God and the Poets*, Oxford: Oxford University Press, p. 118.

of the Gospels, new ways of understanding and interpreting the texts, pointed to a long process of development of the stories that made up the Gospels, and to the influence of the communities in which the stories were told on the content and shape of each individual Gospel. How far could any one Gospel be read as offering historical information about Jesus the man?

While some struggled to reconcile the notion of the Bible as history, some in the Church clung to the idea of the inerrant inspiration of Scripture: either constructing elaborate explanations for the apparent inconsistencies; or consigning them to the inadequacy of human understanding in comparison to the overarching wisdom of God. The rise of biblical fundamentalism or literalism traces its origins to this unsettling period, and continues to offer a strong voice, at times critical of those who attempt to read the Bible on any other terms, and in particular as literature. While such attempts need not be in opposition to a historical approach, the backstory to the development of the literary study of the Bible sometimes breeds suspicion on both sides. Meanwhile, in the mid nineteenth century, for those who found the Bible an unreliable witness to historical events, such as Matthew Arnold, reading the Bible as literature offered a way to maintain the status and importance of the text, without troublesome historical considerations.

The battle lines were drawn in the nineteenth century, as a result of new critical pressure on the historicity of the Bible: in Arnold's words, 'the fact [as presented in the Bible] is failing it [religion]'. While for some, critical questions might be avoided or subsumed into the language of faith, for the admittedly small percentage of others who cared about the Bible, the answer lay in severing any necessary link between the biblical text and historical reliability. Instead, the discourse of poetry was invoked, which stood for a different understanding of the way language was used. Poetic discourse, on this view, speaks of a truth that is not scientific or true in a historical way; rather, the idea behind the words is the important truth offered by poetry. The Bible offers such religious truths through the medium of its unconscious poetic discourse. As David Daiches has commented, very much standing in this tradition, 'if there is a truth of the imagination, a truth of feeling, a religious truth – and these terms were increasingly being associated – then the Bible can be saved as poetry'.[2] As such, it might induce emotions that elevate feeling and lead to benefits to society and to individuals, and be worth treasuring, without having any connection with literal truth.

If religion, and in particular the expression of religious belief expressed in the Bible, may be saved by its recategorization as poetry rather than historical account, then poetry too is given a new status in society. And not just poetry in the formal sense, but all literary works. A clear and concise discussion, tracing the symbiotic relationship between shifting ways of

---

2 Daiches, *God and the Poets*, p. 118.

reading the Bible and the rise of the novel, is offered by Stephen Prickett in his article, 'From Novel to Bible: The Aestheticizing of Scripture'.[3] According to this view, as the form of the novel developed and grew in popularity in the eighteenth and nineteenth centuries, so the Bible's form, in terms of plot, character, author and story, came to be read in a similar way. At the same time, typological and allegorical readings of particular biblical stories, which had been long-established approaches to the sacred text, fell out of favour. Such allegorical or typological readings took the New Testament as re-interpreting the message of the Old, so Jesus might be read as the new Adam, or Moses, or Abraham, according to the scheme of the individual writer in conjunction with an individual reader. Individual elements of the parables might be understood to represent all manner of different aspects of past or current religious life. Instead, a single meaning was now expected, as one would expect from a novel, and in general this meaning was taken to be historical. When the reliability of this one meaning was put under stress from outside developments in science and biblical criticism, the sceptical reader was vindicated. At the same time, if God was to be viewed as the author of these univocal texts, then his creations were now also open to literary analysis. And so, again, the novel form was elevated, the historicity of the Bible was questioned, and the Bible's literary worth was stressed. At least in some academic and literary spheres, it was the subjective and aesthetic analysis of the literary genres and themes of the Bible that became popular, rather than a didactic or expository reading of the biblical text. Matthew Arnold and S. J. Coleridge were at the forefront of this movement. As Prickett concludes:

> In the space of a little under a hundred years, the Bible had lost its status as a divinely inspired text, been reappraised by hostile critics as a collection of documents of doubtful veracity and even less authority, and finally been appropriated as source of cultural renewal, aesthetic value and literary inspiration . . . Even more significantly, the Bible had, in the process, become the representative literary form, and the paradigm by which other works were to be understood and judged.[4]

It should be stressed, however, that this approach was far from universally accepted, the historical criticism of the Bible continued in academic and ecclesiastical circles unabated, and for many the reading of the Bible and of literature remained distinct operations. But there is no doubt that a movement was begun, in parallel with the rise of the novel, which would

---

3 Stephen Prickett, 2006, 'From Novel to Bible: The Aestheticizing of Scripture', in M. Knight and T. Woodman (eds), *Biblical Religion and the Novel, 1700–2000*, Aldershot: Ashgate, pp. 13–24.

4 Prickett, 'From Novel to Bible', p. 21.

have long-term repercussions for the way the Bible would be viewed over time.

Despite this new appreciation of the Bible as literature, and its corresponding raising of the status of other literary works, the sense of loss in much Victorian literature is palpable. Matthew Arnold's own 'Dover Beach', from 1867,[5] is a famous example, with its retreat of 'The Sea of Faith' to the 'breath/Of the night-wind, down the vast edges drear/ And naked shingles of the world'. The 'eternal note of sadness' marks the realization that there is no higher authority that gives meaning to existence, and the imagery of the sea, dragging pebbles up and down the beach, speaks of creation unformed and unplanned. Even more desolate, James Thomson's 'The City of Dreadful Night', written between 1870 and 1874, imagines London from the perspective of an atheist prophet:

> And now at last authentic word I bring,
> Witnessed by every dead and living thing;
> Good tidings of great joy for you, for all:
> There is no God; no Fiend with names divine
> Made us and tortures us; if we must pine,
> It is to satiate no Being's gall.[6]

If we were considering the Bible *in* literature, as we were in the last chapter, we would note the use of the angel chorus's words to the shepherds from the nativity story of Luke (2.10) in the third line of this quotation: not bringing news of the birth of a Saviour, but the assurance there is no God. The reference in the final line, to 'no Being's gall', echoes the reference in Jeremiah 9.15 to the people who are given the water of gall to drink, because they had sinned against the Lord, itself reused in the crucifixion story in Matthew 27.34, where Jesus is given wine mixed with gall. Gall in all of these references metonymically refers to the restitution demanded by God for sins against him, which, on one view of the atonement, or work of Jesus on the cross, is paid by Jesus himself. To have a full understanding of the meaning of this line of the poem, the reader has to recognize the image's biblical roots. Implicitly here, the Bible's status is established on a literary level at the very moment that its historical and theological veracity is rejected.

Even in the work of avowedly Christian poets, there is often a resigned stoicism in the face of increasing opposition and scepticism. Few writers were more committed to Christianity and a high view of the Bible than Christina Rossetti, yet even for her, the answer to her question, 'Does

---

5 Matthew Arnold, 1979, *The Complete Poems*, 2nd edn, Miriam Allott (ed.), London: Longman, pp. 253–7.

6 James Thomson, 1880, *The City of Dreadful Night*, 1993 edn, Edinburgh: Canongate, p. 56.

the road wind uphill all the way?'[7] is the decidedly resigned 'Yes, to the very end'. The destination of the journey envisaged will be 'beds for all who come', but the 'comfort' offered will be, the dialogue-partner of the narrator asserts, 'Of labour you shall find the sum'. This is no confident, joyful expression of faith-filled, Bible-inspired living, but hard work.

Lifting the Bible out of the realm of faith and into the world of literature, then, seemed a natural step for some at least, particularly those who found the effort of retaining a belief in the Bible's historical veracity beyond them. Of course, reverence for the literary qualities of the Bible, and in particular for the King James Version, had been expressed even before the rise of the novel and the pressure of nineteenth-century Higher Criticism and evolutionary thinking. The intention of the translators of the King James Version was not to produce a text of great literary merit; rather, as the Preface stated, they understood translation as that which 'openeth the window, to let in the light; that breaketh the shell, that we may eat the kernel'. The aim was to give people direct access to the Bible so they might grow spiritually. However, relatively quickly, its literary qualities were recognized and extolled. For many, it was inevitable that the Bible in any translation or form would display literary greatness. In his Seventy-Fifth Sermon, the poet and priest John Donne (1572–1631) praised the Holy Ghost himself as 'an eloquent author, a vehement and an abundant author, but yet not luxuriant'.[8] But much more literary praise was to come for the King James Version in particular. David Norton has charted these expressions of literary interest, and offers an extensive catalogue of examples and analysis, some of which we detail here.

In 1731, while he had expressed some negativity towards the King James Version, John Husbands had exclaimed:

> how beautiful do the holy writings appear . . .? So beautiful that, with a charming and elegant simplicity, they ravish and transport the learned reader, so intelligible that the most unlearned are capable of understanding the greater part of them.[9]

Others in the eighteenth century, while they worried about the accuracy of the translation, and in particular its transposition of verse into prose in the Old Testament, recognized the literary status of the King James Version:

---

7 Christina Rossetti, 1979, *The Complete Poems of Christina Rossetti*, vol. 1, R. W. Crump (ed.), Baton Rouge: Louisiana State University Press, p. 65.

8 Quoted in Alister McGrath, 2001, *In the Beginning: The Story of the King James Bible and How It Changed a Nation, a Language, and a Culture*, New York: Anchor Books, p. 218.

9 John Husbands, 1731, *A Miscellany of Poems by Several Hands*, Oxford: Lichfield, p. 30, quoted in David Norton, 1993, *A History of the Bible as Literature*, Volume 2: *From 1700 to the Present Day*, Cambridge: Cambridge University Press, p. 1.

The translators of our Bible, though ... they may not have perfectly understood the original, did certainly understand their language very well; and accordingly I hold the English Bible to be the best standard of the English language we have at this day.[10]

For the Hebrew lexicographer John Taylor, the King James Version was simply the 'most excellent book in our language'.[11]

Throughout the eighteenth and nineteenth centuries there were voices raised in favour of a new translation of the Bible, on the grounds of accuracy in light of new manuscript discoveries, and in particular in response to the work of Robert Lowth, who championed the recovery of the poetic form of much of the Hebrew scriptures. This blending of historical and aesthetic interests worked as a further and important impetus towards acceptance and understanding of the Bible as literature. However, there was much resistance to change, and for some at least it seems as if the Bible and the King James Version were in fact synonymous, with the literary beauty of the text sometimes invoked as a central proof of the divine inspiration behind it. As Thomas Rennell, Dean of Winchester, asserted:

> the grandeur, dignity and simplicity of [the KJV] is confessed even by those who wish eagerly to promote a revision, and by the most eminent critics, and masters of style[. I]t is allowed to exhibit a more perfect specimen of the *integrity* of the English language, than any other writing which that language can boast.[12]

The Dean of Westminster, Richard Chenevix Trench, called the King James Version 'the first English classic' to be read 'with pleasure' and without alteration.[13] For some, such as George Gilfillan, the 'infinite beauty' of the Bible might be linked with its 'eternal truth': if the beauty is explored further through literary analysis, those who believe might be led to a wider appreciation of the Bible, and those who do not might be

---

10 James Burnett, 1774, *Of the Origin and Progress of Language*, 6 vols. Edinburgh, 1773–92, II, p. 141, quoted in Norton, *A History of the Bible as Literature*, p. 98.

11 John Taylor, 1762, *A Scheme of Scripture-Divinity ... With a vindication of the Sacred Writings*, London, in Richard Watson, 1785, *A Collection of Theological Tracts*, 6 vols, Cambridge, I, pp. 4–219, p. 188, quoted in Norton, *A History of the Bible as Literature*, p. 99.

12 Thomas Rennell, 1801, *Discourses on Various Subjects*, London, p. 240, quoted in Norton, *A History of the Bible as Literature*, p. 177.

13 Richard Chenevix Trench, 1858, *On the Authorised Version of the New Testament*, London, p. 24, quoted in Norton, *A History of the Bible as Literature*, p. 184.

led from the beauty to the truth it expresses.[14] Reading the Bible as literature, then, on this view, might well have religious benefits.

Both religious and pedagogical motives led to a rise in a movement to have the Bible read in schools in America and in the United Kingdom in the nineteenth century. Norton describes America's 'especially intense biblical heritage',[15] which, in the early nineteenth century and through the work of the Bible Society, aimed to make sure everyone had a Bible and the Bible was read in public schools. However, after the Civil War, and with the arrival of a large number of Roman Catholics, the dominant Protestant heritage, which asserted the importance of Bible reading for evangelical purposes, was debated. The question was asked if it was unconstitutional to read the Bible in school, given the firm separation of religion and the state. However, if the Bible could be presented as a classic of literature, rather than a religious manifesto, its place in schools at least could be justified.

Matthew Arnold in the United Kingdom was making a similar case for the Bible in school and wider education, although from a less religiously motivated perspective. His belief in the important effect of 'poetry, philosophy, eloquence' as 'beneficent wonder-working power[s] in education' found a home in the Bible as a great literary rather than religious work.[16] As an ardent schools inspector, Arnold sought to offer the Bible as a coherent set of literary works suitable, even vital, in the education of children, quite separate from its religious worth. He argued passionately that 'the Bible's application and edification belong to the Church, its literary and historical substance to the school'.[17] This drive to separate the reading of the Bible as a religious text from its literary importance, combined with the sceptical critique of its claims to historical accuracy, are important milestones in the history of the idea of the Bible as literature.

While the history of the idea or theory of the Bible as literature has been traced through the nineteenth and early twentieth century, we might ask in what ways this theory was worked out in practice, before attempting our own reading from this perspective. Arnold offered the final 27 chapters of Isaiah for reading in schools, not because they were part of the Bible and had religious significance (although, if pushed, he might agree they were), but because in the King James Version they were English literature of great merit. He would explain in his introduction to these chapters, as arranged for the general reading public:

14 George Gilfillan, 1851, *The Bards of the Bible*, 4th edn, Edinburgh, 1856, p. 11, quoted in Norton, *A History of the Bible as Literature*, p. 211.

15 Norton, *A History of the Bible as Literature*, p. 267.

16 Matthew Arnold, *The Complete Prose Works of Matthew Arnold*, ed. R. H. Super, 11 vols. 1960 onwards, Ann Arbor: University of Michigan Press, VII, pp. 500, 503, quoted in Norton, *A History of the Bible as Literature*, p. 273.

17 Matthew Arnold, *The Complete Prose Works of Matthew Arnold*, VII, p. 510, quoted in Norton, *A History of the Bible as Literature*, pp. 274–5.

By virtue of the original it is a monument of the Hebrew genius at its best, and by virtue of the translation it is a monument of the English language at its best.[18]

Arnold felt the need to offer some changes to the King James Version, and very much had in mind the new Revised Version, which was underway at the time: he attempted to explain some of the incoherences in the text, while admitting some of these come from the original Hebrew version, and he also isolated it from the rest of the Book of Isaiah, and rearranged it on the page in verse form. But he strove to maintain what he argued was the literary value and beauty of the King James Version, and urged other translators to do the same. This perceived need to reposition the text on the page, perhaps removing chapter and verse numbering, and certainly recovering the poetic layout of those sections that were not considered simple narratives, is a common feature of other works that presented the Bible in a literary way.[19] Also common is the confession that a selection of texts has had to be made, and that not all of the Bible is amenable to this approach. Some sections, or even whole books, are considered by implication not to be suitable to be read as literature, while others, such as the Psalms, and Song of Songs, are self-evidently so.

Whether or not the Bible could and should be read 'like any other book' was a point of dispute among these critics, the more religious usually asserting the negative, while the less religious the positive; in practice literary enjoyment of the selected biblical texts was taken for granted. However, it remained comparatively unusual for much of the Bible to find its way into purely literary anthologies of English literature or poetry. It would probably be true to say that even today, interest in the Bible as literature remains more common in the field of biblical studies than in Departments of English Literature, although there are of course exceptions. W. E. Henley was one such exception from the turn of the last century, who offered extensive examples from the Old Testament in his *English Lyrics: Chaucer to Poe, 1340–1809*.[20] The King James Version of texts such as chapters from Job, Song of Songs and Habakkuk were here laid out as free verse. Norton comments that 'the effect is to remove the biblical appearance of the text and to allow the poetry of the KJB to stand as the most substantial achievement of English lyric'.[21] Other

---

18 Matthew Arnold, *The Complete Prose Works of Matthew Arnold*, VII, p. 58, quoted in Norton, *A History of the Bible as Literature*, p. 275.

19 See, for example, James George Frazer, 1895, *Passages of the Bible Chosen for their Literary Beauty and Interest*, 2nd edn, London: Macmillan, 1909; and William Ralph Inge, 1934, *Every Man's Bible: An Anthology Arranged with an Introduction*, London: Longmans.

20 W. E. Henley, 1897, *English Lyrics: Chaucer to Poe, 1340–1809*, 2nd edition, London, 1905.

21 Norton, *A History of the Bible as Literature*, p. 290.

anthologists offered smaller selections, and some felt justified in cutting passages and sections judged to be of poor literary quality. Generally, through the nineteenth and into the twentieth centuries, when the meaning of the phrase 'the Bible as literature' was being formed and explored, it was understood that 'the Bible' was more than literature, and much of it did not sit easily within that categorization. The implications of making that claim for any of it are still being worked out today.

The Bible as literature: objections

Two influential writers of the mid-twentieth century reacted publicly and vociferously against such an approach to the Bible, and for completeness their arguments should be mentioned here. In 1935, T. S. Eliot, the well-respected poet and convert to Christianity, had questioned the basis for the excitement over the idea of the Bible as literature, or as the 'noblest monument of English prose'.[22] For him, the undoubted literary influence of the King James Version, or indeed the Bible in any translation, stemmed from its acceptance as the Word of God. The Bible's religious status has been, he argued, much more important than its literary merits, even when its literary reach is under consideration. The fact that it was now being discussed as literature rather than as scripture, for Eliot signalled that its literary influence was inevitably on the wane. More than 70 years after this assessment, we might wish to challenge Eliot's gloomy prediction about the loss of influence of the Bible in literature, in parallel with its loss of status as a sacred text. Certainly knowledge of the contents of the Bible may be argued to have decreased: but many writers continue to find inspiration and are influenced by the great narratives of the Bible, as we shall see when we trace the themes of creation and apocalypse in literature in later chapters of this book.

C. S. Lewis, in an article from 1950, was similarly suspicious, both of what he understood as the influence of the King James Version on English literature, and of reading the Bible itself as literature. While he agreed that the Bible, and the King James Version of it in particular, has been an important 'source', giving writers themes and ideas to write about, its influence, which he described as that which 'prompts us to write in a certain way', is less significant.[23] More importantly, he argued, with Eliot, that the religious character of the Bible precludes it from being considered a purely literary text:

22 T. S Eliot, 1935, 'Religion and Literature', in *Selected Prose*, 1953, ed. John Hayward, Harmondsworth: Penguin, pp. 31–42, here p. 32.

23 C. S. Lewis, 1950, 'The Literary Influence of the Authorised Version', in *They Asked for a Paper*, 1962, London: Bles, pp. 26–50, here p. 36.

It is . . . not merely a sacred book but a book so remorselessly and con-tinuously sacred that it does not invite, it excludes or repels, the merely aesthetic approach . . . It demands incessantly to be taken on its own terms: it will not continue to give literary delight very long except to those who go to it for something quite different.[24]

For Lewis, the Bible was important and treasured because it was familiar. And it was familiar because it was used and perceived as a sacred text. Attempts to read the Bible as something other than a text with religious significance are forced; and there is something in the text itself that makes such approaches doomed to fail. I have hinted earlier that practitioners of literary studies have been slow to read the Bible, or even parts of it, on the same terms as the literary texts that they routinely handle. When biblical critics try to read the Bible as literature, they struggle to use a translation such as the King James Version without recourse to the origi-nal, or to avoid redaction – critical or theological issues that would rarely be raised when a poem or novel was under consideration. However, in the next section of this chapter, we will consider the work of some mod-ern literary and biblical scholars who have attempted to read the Bible as literature, and thus assess the validity of Lewis's critique.

Reading the Bible as literature: some examples

Although far from the first study of the Bible from a literary perspec-tive (Norton offers examples from a century before), Robert Alter's and Frank Kermode's *The Literary Guide to the Bible* was an influential pub-lication in a growing field. It is often referred to in much later texts on a similar theme, although most often with the aim of showing how far the later writers have come in literary sophistication. The aim of the edited volume was to promote for the general reader 'a new view of the Bible as a work of great literary force and authority, a work of which it is en-tirely credible that it should have shaped the minds and lives of intelligent men and women for two millennia and more'.[25] Alter and Kermode, in their General Introduction, offer to help readers read the text of the Bible *well*, which involves reading it as one would any other text, but does not for them preclude historical, philological or theological insights. They have high hopes for their endeavour, seeing the Bible 'reoccup[ying] the literary culture'[26] and newly of interest to literary critics as well as to biblical scholars who are sensitive to the literary qualities of the text. The commentators they have gathered together, while not offering one

---

24 Lewis, 1950, 'The Literary Influence of the Authorised Version', pp. 48–9.

25 Robert Alter and Frank Kermode (eds), 1987, *The Literary Guide to the Bible*, London: Fontana Press, p. 2.

26 Alter and Kermode, *Literary Guide to the Bible*, p. 3.

view of what a literary reading should look like, all subscribe to the view that a critic's role is to 'help make possible fuller readings of the text, with a particular emphasis on the complex integration of diverse means of communication encountered in most works of literature'.[27] This sort of 'constructive' critic will consider issues such as genre, allusion, style, points of view, voice, the 'operation' of the language. Specifically, critical approaches, such as deconstruction, social scientific or feminist readings, are excluded on the grounds that they do not provide 'illumination' in the way more traditional literary readings do, and of the sort that is needed at a time when the Bible's general popularity is waning.[28] It is for this decision to exclude such readings that *The Literary Guide to the Bible* has been most heavily criticized.

The biblical text we shall use to describe and assess the approach of *The Literary Guide to the Bible* is the Gospel of John. In later chapters, we will consider specific texts from this Gospel in much more detail, such as the opening verses, which will be discussed in Chapter 3. Here I offer the reading of John's Gospel by Frank Kermode in Alter's and Kermode's text, in comparison with other literary readings, hoping to illuminate what it has meant and might mean to read a book of the Bible as literature.

Kermode reminds his readers that for centuries, readers of John have been urged and expected to approach John's Gospel as a literary unit, using the capacities and reading skills at their disposal, including their sensitivity to poetry. The modern attempt to break up the narrative in order to discern its origin in terms of its literary or historical source is to ignore the Gospel's first interest, which is in the stories it tells. In arguing for the Gospel to be read in this way now, for its language and internal relationships to be considered for what they mean to readers today, as the text stands and with the reading capacities we bring to it, Kermode offers close readings of the Prologue (John 1.1–18), the wedding at Cana (2.1–11), the cleansing of the temple (2.13–22), the visit of Nicodemus to Jesus (3.1–10), the conversation between the Samaritan at the well and Jesus (4.1–30) and the healing of the nobleman's son (4.46–54). Interspersing his comments with quotations from literary figures such as W. B. Yeats and John Milton, Kermode seeks out the connections within the whole narrative based on the repetition of significant and resonant words and themes.

Kermode notes that the 'liminal antitheses' of the Prologue, the way in which 'being' and 'becoming' are played with and the eternal and the earthbound are contrasted, extend into the narratives that follow. The notion of 'thresholds' being crossed in the person of Jesus is explored in the miracles and interactions of the central section of the Gospel. For

---

27 Alter and Kermode, *Literary Guide to the Bible*, p. 5.
28 Alter and Kermode, *Literary Guide to the Bible*, p. 6.

example, Kermode suggests that the turning of water into wine at the wedding of Cana (John 2.1–11) signals 'the first act of the Word in the world, and [is] a type of the greater transformation that is to come . . . It foreshadows . . . the final transformation of becoming into being, the last victory that restores the Word to God'. Noting an exact quotation from the opening poem (1.14) in the story regarding the 'glory' of Christ (2.11), he asserts that 'the parabolic narrative is telling us to remember the Prologue, as well as foreshadowing the end' (p. 449).[29] The everyday and the historically plausible are given latent meanings here, which the reader is nudged to acknowledge by the interweaving of repeated words and concepts.

For Kermode, the narrative skill of John is undoubted. His control of his material has an ultimate aim of representing the eternal in the world of the transient, so the accounts in the Synoptic Gospels of miraculous feedings are in John 6 infused with symbolic importance: the bread that is multiplied is both the manna of the Old Testament and the new Eucharistic bread symbolizing the on-going presence of Christ, all set within a framework of Passover. Kermode goes on to claim John as a 'novelist' who introduces themes into his narrative with the skill of a literary storyteller. Themes such as betrayal, glory, sin, are woven into stories that have come from the tradition in a way 'more delicate and more powerful' than the Synoptic writers.

Finally, Kermode considers the passion narratives in John. Arguing that each of the Gospel writers treats the same scenario according to their own creative powers, he offers an explanation for some of the differences between them. One such example, famously, is that John does not describe the Last Supper as a Passover meal, as the others do – so, for Kermode, the connection is made in John between the killing of the Passover lambs before the feast and the death of Jesus. The different portrayals of Judas are also considered, and the key moment described in John by the terse 'And it was night' (13.30) for Kermode signals the acceptance by Judas of his role in the drama, the leaving of the light for the darkness and his becoming the person designated in ancient drama as the one who will bring about the catastrophe. The prediction of Peter's betrayal follows immediately, and works in the same way as betrayal brought about by the earlier action of a specific character. In John's 'And it was night' is an example, for Kermode, of the 'gnomic reticence' of John,[30] who despite a tendency towards expansiveness in the long monologues he puts in the mouth of Jesus, also knows, with a firm grasp of the power of narrative terseness, when to leave something for his readers to work out. The interrogation scene between Jesus and Pilate is another example, as is the character of the Beloved Disciple, who appears, mysteriously, only in this

---

29 Alter and Kermode, *Literary Guide to the Bible*, p. 455.
30 Alter and Kermode, *Literary Guide to the Bible*, p. 463.

Gospel, 'a movable narrative focus . . . at once the instrument of explanation and of reticence'.[31] As Kermode concludes, the Gospel of John, like the rest of the Bible, uses narrative to reveal sense as well as to obscure it. For him, John is a skilled storyteller, whose work is best understood by those who take the power of story seriously and read it as it was intended to be read: with literary sensitivity.

Kermode writes poetically and persuasively of the literary skill of John, from the perspective of a sensitive reader of fiction. What marks his reading of the Gospel as a reading of the text as literature rather than anything else has to be defined, however. There is certainly no reference to the community for which or out of which John wrote, such as might be found in a standard commentary: the emphasis is on those features of the text that a modern, novel-reading reader might notice and appreciate. The insights of poets and novelists are offered as having relevance because of their shared literary interests, and there is no extensive recourse to the work of biblical scholarship, although there is some reference to the history of interpretation of the Gospel. The most obvious features of this reading of the Gospel as literature are the tracing of images, words and concepts through the narrative; and the assumption of narrative unity on which the given significance of these tracings is based. It is John's prowess as storyteller, rather than as historian or as theologian, or the Gospel as the endpoint of a long process of identifiable exegetical moves, which is of interest to Kermode. The role of the reader is acknowledged – it is the reading of a modern literary critic that is offered – but the fixed qualities of the text itself are assumed and are guaranteed by the intention of the skilful author.

Such a reading of the Gospel would be acceptable today to most 'professional' readers of the Bible, whether biblical scholars or those with a confessional interest in and commitment to the text, as one of several possible approaches. Although Kermode does not assert this explicitly, there is an assumption in his writing that other readings are possible: his is not the final word on the Gospel, although it claims to take seriously, in a way that has not happened sufficiently in the past, the literary intention behind the text. Sitting well within the stated parameters of *The Literary Guide to the Bible*, Kermode's contribution exists happily as an approach that does not threaten the status of the Gospel either as historical treasure trove or theological guidebook. Other readings of this text as literature have made rather more revolutionary claims, and while Kermode's work remains a rich and illuminating resource, later commentators have pushed harder on the notion of the Bible as literature, with more controversial results.

Kermode, of course, was not the first commentator to find literary design in the Gospel of John, or any other Gospel, for that matter. We

---

31 Alter and Kermode, *Literary Guide to the Bible*, p. 464.

will consider David Rhoads and Donald Michie's seminal work, *Mark as Story*, from 1982, more in Chapters 5 and 6 on the role of the reader. Perhaps, with regard to the Gospel of John, the most influential in the 1980s and later was R. Alan Culpepper's *Anatomy of the Fourth Gospel: A Study in Literary Design*. In the Preface to Culpepper's book, Kermode writes admiringly of his application of secular narrative analysis to the sacred text, in such a way that the truth of the Gospel is rediscovered through the achievement of 'a proper understanding of the Gospel as story, and of the relation of story to truth'.[32] Although Kermode's contribution to *The Literary Guide to the Bible* does not make use of the language of the narrator, implied reader and characterization that Culpepper was so influential in introducing to biblical studies, both he and Culpepper share the assumption of narrative design in the Gospel. Narrative criticism as an approach to the biblical text is considered in detail in Chapters 5 and 6 of this book. Here, I offer a critique of readings of John's Gospel from this general perspective as offered nearly 30 years after the publication of Culpepper's important book.

In 2008, Tom Thatcher and Stephen D. Moore edited a collection of essays, *Anatomies of Narrative Criticism*, assessing, in the words of its subtitle, *The Past, Present, and Futures of the Fourth Gospel as Literature*.[33] In its introductory chapter, 'Anatomies of the Fourth Gospel: Past, Present and Future Probes', Tom Thatcher reflects on the impact and significance of Culpepper's work, published as it was at a time when the world outside the text was considered to be of highest importance. Culpepper's insistence that the Gospel should be considered as a unified and coherent text in its own right and on its own terms was in conflict with those who saw its usefulness as a window onto the world of Jesus and the early Church. His claim, echoed in Kermode's essay in the *Literary Guide*, that John's Gospel was a sophisticated literary masterpiece of inherent worth and interest to readers *as* readers was to lead both to intense criticism and opposition and to a multitude of new approaches to the text. In particular, it has encouraged scholars to consider where meaning resides, and has led some to move away from the idea that meaning resides in the text itself, towards an interest in the role of the reader in the construction of meaning. This has included a focus on the pervasive influence of the reader's ideology, stated or unstated, on the reading offered. Thatcher's article offers a glimpse of what came after Culpepper's and Kermode's approach, building on their work to give the biblical text status and credibility as a work of literary merit.

---

32 R. Alan Culpepper, 1983, *Anatomy of the Fourth Gospel: A Study in Literary Design*, Philadelphia: Fortress Press, p. v.

33 Tom Thatcher and Stephen D. Moore (eds), 2008, *Anatomies of Narrative Criticism: The Past, Present, and Futures of the Fourth Gospel as Literature*, Atlanta: Society of Biblical Literature.

One of the most significant writers who has pushed such literary read-ings of John's Gospel in the direction of the recovery of the role of the reader as meaning-maker is Robert Kysar, whose work is discussed by Adele Reinhartz in Thatcher and Moore.[34] For Kysar, readings that at-tempt to extrapolate religious or social communities 'behind' the text are inevitably reflections of the readers' own interests or prejudices. This may be traced by comparing readings of John's Gospel over the centuries. Reinhartz quotes Kysar's assertion that texts arise out of the assumptions readers brings to their readings of them, which are irrevocably shaped by their position within complex social structures: 'it is sheer pretence to suppose that any of us can examine the evidence for the past and come up with an objective, unbiased, and true picture of what took place.'[35]

This, of course, is in direct conflict with those scholars who have taken, and continue to take, a historical-critical approach to the text. For Kysar, much more significant than a biased attempt to reconstruct the original world of the text is what the text actually does to the reader who approaches it carefully, as a literary creation with rhetorical power. This includes, for him, incidentally, the text's theological power, and its place in the Church's preaching and witness. While Kysar's deeply sceptical approach has not been widely accepted, it highlights for some the inher-ent dangers of literary readings of the Bible, although for others it has led to a greater openness about their presuppositions, and a new humility regarding what may be known about the world in which the text was written, and with what certainty.

Kysar's critique is not the end of the story, however, and other articles in Thatcher and Moore offer readings that integrate literary sensitivity towards the text with stated ideological purposes and with an interest in its original historical context. The contrast need not be as stark as Kysar, or some of his and Culpepper's opponents, might assume. In the same collection, Colleen M. Conway asks what might be the manifestation of ancient gender ideologies in a text such as John's Gospel. History, on such a reading of the text, is as much redefined in this interdisciplinary approach as the role of the reader and the literary merits and meaning of the Gospel. As Conway explains, 'Although I still read the Gospels as narratives, this work [her most recent book on Greco-Roman mas-culinity as it relates to New Testament presentations of Jesus] has been

---

34 Adele Reinhartz, 2008, 'Building Skyscrapers on Toothpicks: The Literary-Critical Challenge to Historical Criticism', in Thatcher and Moore (eds), *Anatomies of Narrative Criticism*, pp. 55–76.

35 Robert Kysar, 2005, 'The Whence and Whither of the Johannine Community', in John Donahue (ed.), *Life in Abundance: Studies of John's Gospel in Tribute to Raymond E. Brown*, Collegeville, MI: Liturgical Press, pp. 65–81, p. 73, quoted in Reinhartz, p. 67.

influenced by gender theory, postcolonial theory, and new historicism.'[36] Here, the Gospel is situated in its context, in the widest sense of the word, which includes the cultural and rhetorical influence of its setting. An understanding and interpretation of the Roman Empire, and the texts it produced, is an important part of this study, as informed by literary theory and gender studies in particular. Culpepper's initial move towards literary theory as it applied to the Gospel of John involved stepping away from the traditional historical-critical method, and this made possible approaches which took other theoretical perspectives. For many this had significance mainly for the current concerns of readers. But it need not be that literary critical approaches have nothing to say about the historical context of texts such as John's Gospel, even for those who embrace such critical approaches wholeheartedly. In my view, the gulf between historical and literary readings is overstated and hard to sustain with credibility. This book will not aim to cover every critical approach to the text currently in evidence in the discipline, but the reader will notice those which hold some connection to the historical context of the biblical text will be given more space than those which do not. This seems to me to represent the current interdisciplinary nature of the field that is biblical studies.

We have moved a long way from the concerns of C. S. Lewis, that the biblical text actively resists a reading that is based purely on a consideration of the text's aesthetic qualities; and that only those who approach it as other than a sacred book will find much in it to delight in from a literary perspective. All texts are now potentially considered differently since Lewis was writing. The set of contrasting approaches with which he worked, which included the aesthetic, historical and religious or theological, has been expanded hugely to include those which address the cultural and ideological concerns of the reader and of the context in which particular texts were written. The strict boundaries between approaches have been made more permeable. The Bible remains of interest, even perhaps 'delight', to those who view it as sacred in some sense and to those who do not. It was an appreciation and new understanding of particular texts' literary qualities, and specifically their literary design and coherence, which led indirectly to the possibility of reading them in new and still developing ways that Lewis could not have imagined.

I have noted already that there remains some resistance to reading more than selected biblical texts as if they were literature, although the publication by Canongate Press of individual books of the Bible, with

---

36 Colleen M. Conway, 2008, 'There and Back Again: Johannine History on the Other Side of Literary Criticism', in Thatcher and Moore (eds), *Anatomies of Narrative Criticism*, pp. 77–91, here p. 90.

introductions by literary figures, seeks to redress this.[37] But perhaps this is less important than the move to read the Bible as any other text, with shifting literary, historical, ideological and cultural importance for readers themselves. Reading the Bible as literature on these terms puts it in meaningful dialogue with other texts, such as novels and poetry, which are our concern here. This may have implications for literary or historical study, or for education or for theology. It is hoped that the fruits of such an endeavour, as demonstrated in the chapters to come, will convince readers that the exercise is indeed worthwhile.

Questions

1. What has led to modern attempts to read the Bible 'as literature'? Is this a valid move in your view?
2. In what ways does a literary reading of a biblical text differ from that which might be found in a historical-critical commentary?

Further reading

Robert Alter and Frank Kermode (eds), 1987, *The Literary Guide to the Bible*, London: Fontana Press, and in particular, Frank Kermode's article on 'John', pp. 440–66.

Matthew Arnold, 1979, *The Complete Poems*, 2nd edn, Miriam Allott (ed.), London: Longman.

Colleen M. Conway, 2008, 'There and Back Again: Johannine History on the Other Side of Literary Criticism', in Tom Thatcher and Stephen D. Moore (eds), *Anatomies of Narrative Criticism: The Past, Present, and Futures of the Fourth Gospel as Literature*, Atlanta: Society of Biblical Literature, pp. 77–91.

R. Alan Culpepper, 1983, *Anatomy of the Fourth Gospel: A Study in Literary Design*, Philadelphia: Fortress Press.

David Daiches, 1984, *God and the Poets*, Oxford: Oxford University Press.

T. S Eliot, 1935, 'Religion and Literature', in *Selected Prose*, 1953, ed. John Hayward, Harmondsworth: Penguin, pp. 31–42.

C. S. Lewis, 1950, 'The Literary Influence of the Authorised Version', in *They Asked for a Paper*, 1962, London: Bles, pp. 26–50.

Alister McGrath, 2001, *In the Beginning: The Story of the King James Bible and How It Changed a Nation, a Language, and a Culture*, New York: Anchor Books.

David Norton, 1993, *A History of the Bible as Literature*, Volume 2: *From 1700 to the Present Day*, Cambridge: Cambridge University Press.

---

37 See Canongate's Pocket Bible Series, which currently includes the Book of Job introduced by Louis de Bernières, and the Gospel of Mark introduced by Nick Cave (both 1998, Edinburgh: Canongate Press).

David Norton, 2000, *A History of the English Bible as Literature*, Cambridge: Cambridge University Press.

Stephen Prickett, 2006, 'From Novel to Bible: The Aestheticizing of Scripture', in M. Knight and T. Woodman (eds), *Biblical Religion and the Novel, 1700–2000*, Aldershot: Ashgate, pp. 13–24.

Adele Reinhartz, 2008, 'Building Skyscrapers on Toothpicks: The Literary-Critical Challenge to Historical Criticism', in Tom Thatcher and Stephen D. Moore (eds), *Anatomies of Narrative Criticism: The Past, Present, and Futures of the Fourth Gospel as Literature*, Atlanta: Society of Biblical Literature, pp. 55–76.

Christina Rossetti, 1979, *The Complete Poems of Christina Rossetti*, vol. 1, R. W. Crump (ed.), Baton Rouge: Louisiana State University Press.

Tom Thatcher, 2008, 'Anatomies of the Fourth Gospel: Past, Present and Future Probes', in Tom Thatcher and Stephen D. Moore (eds), *Anatomies of Narrative Criticism: The Past, Present, and Futures of the Fourth Gospel as Literature*, Atlanta: Society of Biblical Literature, pp. 1–38.

James Thomson, 1880, *The City of Dreadful Night*, 1993 edn, Edinburgh: Canongate.

3

Recurring Themes: Creation

So far we have considered some of the wider issues involved in defining the relationship between the Bible and literature. Here, and in Chapter 9, we consider that relationship as it plays out through specific biblical themes and literary texts. In Chapter 9, the theme will be apocalypse; here, it is creation.

There can be little argument that creation is a biblical theme that has spread its intertextual influence into literary texts throughout the ages. The poetic cadences of the first version of the creation story, found in Genesis 1, offer a structure, order and divine assurance that is frequently recalled either to be confirmed or subverted in later literature. The narrative of the creation and fall of humanity in Genesis 2 and 3 give human faces in response to age-old dilemmas: where do we come from; where is God in the midst of pain; why is life such a struggle? In this chapter, we will consider the creation stories in Genesis, and their echo in the Prologue to John's Gospel, from a literary perspective, and we will compare two poems that have a direct intertextual relationship with these stories – W. B. Yeats's 'Adam's Curse'[1] and Edwin Muir's 'Adam's Dream'.[2] Here, the contexts of all of these texts, as well as what they say and how they say it, will be of interest, following the model of intertextual Bible reading offered by the literary critic, Steven Marx.

In his *Shakespeare and the Bible*, Marx argues that Shakespeare's use of the Bible in his plays may be read as being based on principles of typology and midrash. Understanding the way the Bible was read in Shakespeare's time offers an insight into biblical themes and echoes in Shakespeare's work, which might be considered as having exegetical concerns. Where the plays wrestle with biblical ideas, a reader may be drawn to read the biblical original in a new way, having experienced the narrative force of the later text. Marx thus highlights the two-way flow of intertextuality, potentially affecting readings of the original text as well as of those which come later. At this stage, it will be useful to consider Marx's approach in

---

1 W. B. Yeats, 1981, *The Collected Poems of W. B. Yeats*, 2nd edn, London: Macmillan, p. 88.
2 Edwin Muir, 1984, *Collected Poems*, London: Faber & Faber, p. 210.

more detail, as it will inform our readings of the creation stories in the poems by Yeats and Muir.

Marx states boldly that 'any imagination being formed in sixteenth- and seventeenth-century England would have been saturated with what was the most powerful cultural influence of its time'.[3] The Bible was used as political propaganda to bolster the position of the monarch: as we have seen in Chapter 1, James I and VI commissioned the translation of what became known as the Authorized or King James Version of the Bible at least in part to quell the more anti-monarch bias of the Geneva Bible. It was also, throughout the period of the Renaissance, a text to be studied and enjoyed as any other, as the work of Valla and Erasmus demonstrate. Its literary value as the work of the Divine Author was praised, and it was taken as the inspiration for many works of art and literature. In addition to its obvious religious significance in powerful ecclesiastical settings, the Bible had a strong influence on the aesthetic and political landscape of Shakespeare's time and place.

The value of Marx's work lies in his skill at bringing together with integrity and plausibility the wider historical context in which the Bible was understood and the role of the Bible in Shakespeare's writing. Marx admits that Shakespeare's own attitude towards the Bible is difficult to ascertain, a fact that is understandable given the shifting religious landscape through which he lived and the potentially dangerous consequences that might follow the obvious taking of a particular religious or non-religious view. Scholars have long disagreed about the level of reverence or irreverence implied by the biblical references in his plays. Marx points out that evidence for both sides of the debate can be found in the texts, and that in places the same biblical reference is used in contrasting ways. He concludes:

> the ambiguity of such allusions and the credibility of both orthodox and sceptical critics leads to the hypothesis that Shakespeare read the Bible with a very wide range of interpretative responses to its vast plenitude of meanings. A corollary premise is that Shakespeare imitated scriptural models with the kind of variety found in later biblically inspired writers such as Milton, . . . Blake, . . . Kafka, . . . and Beckett.[4]

As a playwright of extraordinary skill, Shakespeare might be expected to appreciate and be drawn to explore the metaphorical and narrative complexity of many biblical texts. The prevalence of biblical stories depicted in church interiors and dramatized in the popular liturgical plays makes his familiarity with them unsurprising. Without going into all of the detailed

---

3 Stephen Marx, 2000, *Shakespeare and the Bible*, Oxford: Oxford University Press, p. 3.

4 Marx, *Shakespeare and the Bible*, p. 9.

examples Marx offers, we can appreciate his argument that Shakespeare alludes to biblical texts in shifting, flexible and significant ways, often under the influence of contemporary events and concerns. These new texts in turn may offer later readers new and surprising ways to read the original biblical stories and themes, in the light of Shakespeare's re-working of them. Marx's handling of both aspects of the intertextuality of Shakespeare's plays and the Bible is particularly well-executed and nuanced, and, I suggest, is a helpful model for other readings of the Bible in literary texts.

In specific terms, Marx labels the Bible's influence on Shakespeare as 'typology', a well-established way of identifying correspondences and similarities between the Bible and later ideas, so that one aspect of the text is deemed to represent or stand for another. The reading of the Hebrew Bible as anticipating the New Testament, so that the story of the sacrifice of Isaac by his father Abraham in Genesis 22 makes sense of and is completed by the story of the sacrifice of Jesus by God the father, is a typological reading. Many readings of the parables are in fact typological: identifying each character in the story with another, more representative one, so that figures of authority tend to be identified with God and those who get it wrong in the story are understood to be the Jewish people. The example Marx offers of a typological relationship between the Bible and Shakespeare is the story in Exodus of the Israelites' victory over the mighty Egyptians at the Red Sea and, from *Henry V*, the victory of the English over the more powerful French at Agincourt. Such a typological relationship grants status to the English cause, and highlights the miraculous, God-inspired nature of their triumph. Here, it is the similarity between the two stories that prompts the reading of the relationship.

Marx goes on to offer 'midrash' as the interpretative name for Shakespeare's commentary on or re-writing of the Bible. Classical midrash comes from the third century CE, and refers to the body of writings made by rabbis as they struggled to understand the Hebrew Bible after the destruction of the Temple in Jerusalem. More recently, midrash has been reinvented as a literary method, its playfulness and apparent fluidity chiming well with the more free and indeterminate readings of postmodernism and in particular deconstruction. Midrash as a literary critical approach will be considered in greater detail in Chapter 8. For Marx, midrash 'makes word-play, storytelling, and interpretation come together to liberate pleasure, creativity and knowledge'.[5] He suggests that *King Lear* is a 'midrashic elaboration' of the book of Job: by imitating the biblical tragedy in its characterization, plot and theme, the play re-interprets the theme of the relationship between humanity and God, which Job had wrestled with, for contemporary readers. Here it is in the dissimilarity between the two texts that the new meaning is to be found. For rather

---

5 Marx, *Shakespeare and the Bible*, p. 16.

than being rewarded for his suffering as is the biblical Job, Shakespeare's Job-figure, Lear, dies after cradling his dying daughter in his arms. In this play, and in the theology of sections of the society out of which it arose, God is both less capricious and less all-powerful than the God of the Book of Job, and certainly much less involved in his creation. While there may be hints of the possibility of renewal in Albany's arrival, the overwhelming mood and message is one of despair in the face of suffering. While Job was read in Shakespeare's time as an attempt to justify the ways of God to humanity, the play may be read as either a bitter parody of the theology of Job, or an attempt to show humanity teaching God a lesson about the reality of life. Marx concludes that both texts offer the possibility of different meanings, and encourage the reader to think deeply about the issues both texts raise.

Reading the texts this way, then, invites us to consider both the mapping of biblical characters and stories onto later literature, following the typological model, and a looser relationship between the Bible and literature, which reads biblical themes as they play through the text, developing and changing as they weave a new story out of the old. Finding these correspondences is facilitated, although not constrained, by an understanding of the way the Bible was read at the time the literary text was written. Context, whether of the Prologue of John's Gospel and its use of the Hebrew Bible, or of W. B. Yeats and Edwin Muir and their use of the Bible theme of creation, offers a perspective on the texts that is illuminating and valuable.

Creation themes: Genesis

We turn to read our four texts and the intertextual relationship between them, mindful of the literary and religious context out of which each arose, as far as that is possible to determine, and alert to the typological and midrashic echoes each may bounce off the other.

A multiplicity of commentaries and monographs have been written about the Genesis creation stories. Although the placing of the book of Genesis at the beginning of both the Hebrew and Christian Bibles makes narrative sense, detailing as it does the divine *fiat* out of which the known world came, the majority of scholars do not believe it was among the first books of the Bible to be written. Traditionally, of course, Moses is credited with the authorship of the Pentateuch, the first five books of the Bible, and that view remains a sincerely held one to this day by some. However, in biblical studies, it is the 'documentary hypothesis' that is the prevailing view, and this argues that there are many sources behind the Pentateuch, none from Moses directly as far as that may be determined. Instead, over a period of centuries, writers and editors worked on earlier sources, some from cultures before that of the Jews, re-writing, editing, bringing together and deleting that which seemed appropriate to them. Books such as Genesis, on this view, are themselves products of a long period of intertextual interplay, some of which may be recoverable.

The history of the attempts by scholars in the eighteenth and nineteenth centuries to tease apart the various layers of editorial interventions in the Pentateuch need not detain us here. More information is offered in the 'Further reading' section of this chapter. The opening chapters of Genesis offer us in microcosm enough material for us to understand something of the thrust of the theory, which in turn will inform our reading of the creation stories and their echoes. Obvious to any reader of the first three chapters of Genesis will be the fact that creation is described in two different – many would say – contradictory, ways. This in itself points to an editorial bringing together of sources, rather than one hand at work behind the text.

In Genesis 1–2.4a we have the poetic, formal and balanced story of the creation of the world, its cosmic setting and humanity over a period of seven days. When it refers to God, this story uses the title 'Elohim', which is the plural of *el*, the ancient Semitic word for a god. Many scholars have noted a similarity between this story and the Babylonian creation story 'Enuma Elish'. Both stories describe a victory over a watery expanse, in Hebrew a watery chaos translated as 'the deep' (1.2), the Hebrew word for which, *tehom*, is from the same root as the Akkadian *Tiamat*, the formal name given to the sea that is conquered by the god Marduk. Marduk creates heaven and earth by splitting Tiamat into two parts, and demanding he is acknowledged as the supreme being over all. The sharing of the idea of the creator's victory over a powerful adversary, which allows material creation to take place, is somewhat hidden by the later, more sophisticated nuance of the Genesis editors, perhaps writing in the sixth or fifth century BCE, who downplay the idea of any serious threat to the all powerful creator God: the shadowy Deep is all that remains. It is suggested that the earlier story came to the Hebrew writers via Canaanite literature, and echoes of it can be found elsewhere in the Hebrew Bible in the lingering marine presence of the monstrous Leviathan in passages such as Job 7.12 and Psalm 77.16. Further evidence for what we might call a midrashic relationship between the two stories comes from the similarity in order of elements created, starting with light and culminating in human beings, with joyful rest at the end of it all.

In the second story, God is always referred to as 'Yahweh' or 'Yahweh Elohim', never simply as 'Elohim': 'Yahweh' is taken as the personal name of the god of Israel, said to have been revealed to Moses on Mount Sinai as he received the call to lead the people out of Egypt (Exodus 3.13–18). It is argued that a distinction in terms of style and content may be made between the material in Genesis in which this name is used, and that in which 'Elohim' is used. The distinction points to two different sources within the one text. In terms of their content and structure the two creation stories certainly demand considerable interpretative work if they are to be harmonized. In the second story the scope of creation is limited to the earth, no time frame is mentioned and there is a difference in the ordering of events: humans are created before rather than after the animals, whose purpose is to keep humanity company. Whereas in the first story men and women are created simultaneously, in the second, woman is created from man. In the second story, the two representative humans are put in charge of Eden rather than the world, and the assumption is they are designed to stay there, while the first gives humanity a much broader role. Only in the second story is there any mention of a tree that is hedged around with prohibitions. Both stories demonstrate considerable literary skill, but of a different order, with the first a complete and ordered narrative in itself, and the second seeming to demand more in terms of an expectation of the unfolding history of the first humans and their descendants. Scholars have found this difference in approach to be carried on throughout Genesis. In some places, genealogical order and careful design seem important, with a remote but powerful God behind everything. In others, God plays a part in the narrative, with the telling of intriguing stories such as the Tower of Babel, Isaac and Rebecca and, perhaps most famously of all, Jacob wrestling with an apparently divine force in the dark of the night.

The two stories of creation in Genesis, then, point to a much larger process of intertextuality in the world out of which the text as we have it was finally transmitted. I argue here that that process has continued, both in the New Testament, and in later literature. In this chapter, we will consider the echo of creation in the Prologue to John's Gospel. In a later chapter, we will discover that echo is to be found in the final book of the Christian Bible too, in the Book of Revelation. In the previous chapter, we briefly discussed Frank Kermode's 'literary' reading of John's Gospel. Here, however, we go back a step and offer an introduction to the Gospel for those who may be unfamiliar with it, before considering the relationship between its opening chapter and the creation stories.

Creation themes in the Prologue to the Gospel of John

Just as the composition of the Book of Genesis is the source of much scholarly debate, so the context out of which John's Gospel came into being is hotly disputed. For some, the apostle John, son of Zebedee, follower of Jesus, is the author; for others, the Gospel arose out of a distinct community based on this John's teaching. Others find the link to that John unconvincing, or at least unprovable. The Gospel does in places refer to having an eyewitness account as its basis. See for example John 21.24, in which a figure referred to as the 'beloved disciple' is affirmed as the one testifying and having written down the events described, although the picture is confused by the introduction of perhaps an editorial voice in the first person plural, confirming 'we know his testimony is true'. At this remove it is impossible to know who wrote the text, and perhaps other aspects of the Gospel matter more. What I want to stress here is that it is not straightforward for us as readers to assume that this Gospel is based on an eye-witness account, with its main purpose being to convey historical and reliable information about the life of Jesus. As we will discover, such an assumption is hard to maintain when John's Gospel is compared with the Synoptics, or its details are scrutinized from the perspective of historical plausibility.

If the authorship of the Fourth Gospel is disputed, so too is the date of its composition. For the majority of scholars, the Gospel is later than the others, which are usually grouped under the title Synoptic Gospels. Matthew, Mark and Luke, while each with their own distinctive features, share many features in common, and may be read 'alongside' each other, or synoptically. There is an obvious relationship of dependence between them, although the details of this may be difficult to reconstruct. The Gospel of John, often called the Fourth Gospel, cannot successfully be mapped onto the same scheme, either in terms of its structure, content or language used. Many have read John's Gospel as more developed in its theology, language and narrative sophistication, and this has encouraged a belief that it must have been written later than the Synoptics.

Indeed, the differences are striking. The opening of each Gospel will concern us below – certainly here John's Gospel takes a very different approach from the Synoptics. In John we get few miracles of the sort we find throughout the Synoptics, no exorcisms, and few of the parables that are so much a feature of the others. John's Jesus makes quite distinct and startling claims for himself and for his relationship with God. 'I am in the Father and the Father is in me' (John 14.11) – there is no shying away from any suggestion of his divine or messianic calling such as we find in places in the Synoptics. Jesus in John is presented as theologically astute, given to long sermons and expositions of earlier actions, such as the feeding of the five thousand in John 6, an action that is made significant by Jesus' claim that he is the bread of life, and moreover that 'Those who eat my flesh and drink my blood have eternal life, and I will raise them up on the last day' (John 6.54). This Johannine Jesus is described in detailed and lengthy conversation with individuals who are given characters, in contrast to the one-dimensional individuals often found in the Synoptics. The Passion stories in John begin not with a description of the last meal at Passover, as we might have expected, given the significance accorded to this event in the other Gospels, but with a scene of foot-washing on the day before Passover. In his trial and crucifixion, Jesus is in control of everything, with no scene of Gethsemane agony or cry of dereliction (for example Mark 14.32–42; 15.34). Rather, he calmly prays for his disciples and even those who will believe in him through their word (John

17.20–1), and he proclaims at the last, 'It is finished', before giving up his spirit (John 19.30).

Just as the picture of Jesus offered in John's Gospel is more detailed and theologically explicit than that offered in the Synoptics, so too the way the events are narrated suggests a rather different sort of narrative perspective. One example is the scene of the cleansing of the temple, which in John comes near the beginning of Jesus' ministry, rather than in the final week as in Matthew, Mark and Luke. In John, the Jews are described as responding to Jesus' assertion, 'Destroy this temple, and in three days I will raise it up', with the incredulous 'This temple has been under construction for forty-six years, and will you raise it up in three days?' (John 2.19–20). There is then an explanation from the narrator that 'he was speaking of the temple of his body. After he was raised from the dead, his disciples remembered that he had said this; and they believed the scripture and the word Jesus had spoken' (John 2.21–2). Here, and this is not the only place where this happens in John (see also John 12.14–16), the narrator highlights to the reader that the event has been reflected upon at a later date, and a fresh meaning given to it in light of subsequent experiences. This self-conscious reflection lends itself to the sense that John's Gospel has arisen from a period well into the life of the early Church, quite removed from the more immediate retelling of the story of Jesus offered by the Synoptics.

Of course, the reality of these Gospel texts is much less straightforward than the above summary of some of the differences suggests. The differences between the Synoptics themselves should not be downplayed, and some commentators have argued that in structure and narrative flow at least, there are more similarities between John and the Synoptics than generally assumed. Others have highlighted the theological and narrative sophistication of the Synoptics; and there is certainly a movement towards validating the historical reliability of John's Gospel, rather than its theological emphasis. Furthermore, the equation of reflection on events with length of time span is not an inevitable. How long did members of the early Church need to make the connections described in John? Few suggest that even the generally assumed earliest Gospel, Mark, was written immediately after the events it describes. How many extra decades had to pass before the distinctively Johannine emphasis might plausibly be arrived at? Does it have to be several? Given that the earliest manuscript fragment of any New Testament text that we have comes from the Gospel of John, and can be dated to around 125 CE, having been found in Egypt, the Gospel must have been composed some time before this. It is at least possible that the four Gospels, or certainly Matthew, Luke and John, were written within a short space of time.

As we have seen, it is difficult to know much with certainty about the context in which John's Gospel was written. More could be said, especially about the relationship between Jesus, his followers and 'the Jews' in John, which is anachronistic in terms of the life of Jesus, himself a Jew, although this anachronism is not limited to that one Gospel. A complex relationship between Jesus, the early Church and whoever 'the Jews' represent, seems to be presupposed by John (see especially chapter 9), and we need to bear this in mind as we turn now to the opening section of the Gospel, and in particular to the echoes of the creation stories to be found there. Whereas Matthew and Luke begin with (different) stories from the time of the birth of Jesus, and Mark, after announcing that his is a story of 'good news', plunges in with Jesus' baptism by John, the Fourth Gospel opens with a poetic, theological reflection on the meaning of the incarnation.

The opening phrase of John 1, 'in the beginning', repeated in the next verse, of course situates the passage firmly in a significant relationship to the first creation story with which Genesis begins. And as books of the Hebrew Bible were often referred to by their opening phrases, it could be argued that the whole of the book of Genesis is being alluded to here. John 1.51, in which Jesus says to Nathanael he will see 'heaven open and the angels of God ascending and descending upon the Son of Man', of course brings to mind the story of Jacob's dream at Bethel from Genesis 28. The claim is being made that in the coming of Jesus something new is happening, but built on firm and familiar foundations. It has often been remarked that the opening section of John's Gospel may be compared to an overture to a symphony or a musical. In it, themes that will be picked up later are introduced, but it is only after the whole piece has been experienced that the overture is fully appreciated, and repays repeated listenings. New creation will indeed be a thread working through the Gospel to come, from Nicodemus in John 3, to the man born blind in John 9 and most dramatically the healing of Lazarus in John 11. However, I suggest that these verses are both overture to something new that will be developed in the chapters to come, and fully satisfying conclusion to something that has gone before, picking up familiar themes from a performance that has been heard many times. 'In the beginning' is the hinge that takes the listener/reader from one into the other, from the sense of conclusion and fulfilment into the new creation of possibilities and experiences. Certainly this passage has all the hallmarks of a piece of music or poetry – tightly constructed, full of balanced phrases, big ideas and words pregnant with meaning. 'In the beginning' immediately brings its own weight of poetic and theological resonance into any reading of this opening chapter, pointing both forward into what is to come and back towards that which is known and still hoped for.

If the opening phrase is intended to make the reader pause and expect the significant and dramatic, the description of what was 'in the beginning' is equally powerful. 'The Word', in Greek the *Logos*, is a deliberately chosen phrase that brings together many levels of meaning available to many different readers. We should be aware here that this section of the text is describing a state of affairs that is out-with time and creation, beyond the human realm and shrouded with mystery that perhaps only poetic language may penetrate. *Logos* was one of those crossover terms that meant something to Jew and Gentile. In Greek philosophy, it was used to describe the principle of rationality behind the universe. In contemporary Jewish writers, such as Philo, it described the means by which God governed his creation, his plan or divinely directed creative force. Although tempting, we must try to resist the urge to rush into telescoping ideas of divine father and son, or even worse, God as father of Jesus, into this opening statement. That move will be made by the poem itself in a later stanza. Here the scope is much wider and more abstract, and much closer to the tone and thrust of the creation story of Genesis 1 than Genesis 2. There God creates by his word alone: the *Logos* is God's creative force, and continues to be the way in which he is known in creation. The law given at Sinai and the work of the prophets of Israel all emanate from the power of God's Word. + Leviticus 25 sadus

By the time of Jesus, a tradition centred on the figure of Wisdom had become associated with this creative power of God. As the Book of Proverbs states, Wisdom is with God 'before the beginning of the earth', and is part of the creation process. This tradition is clearly evoked in the ideas that follow the opening statements. The eternal co-existence of the Word and God, and their respective roles in creation, both point to an echo of the popular Wisdom tradition, and link the *Logos* to the creation story. But the suppleness of the idea of the Word means that it need not be restricted or contained by that specific tradition. God has chosen to express himself as the Word, itself a metaphor for communication that reaches out to make sense of itself to others.

As we move to consider John 1.3–5, we move from the abstract and cosmic to the created order of things that all readers of these verses have experienced. Significantly, themes of light and darkness are introduced here, just as they are in Genesis 1. The shadowy darkness of *tehom*, with its underlying threat of primordial seamonster, continues to cast its shadow, and light and darkness will be themes throughout the Gospel. An assurance is given that, just as God's word brought light out of darkness in the very first beginning, so in the new beginning spoken of here, life-giving light will not be vanquished by the continuing presence of darkness. If the pervasiveness and persistence of light is perhaps less assured in John than it was in Genesis – a reader is drawn to think of the light of a candle flickering in a threateningly dark room rather than the rays of the sun piercing the dawn – nevertheless its continuing existence is assumed.

These first five verses speak of another reality, beyond that of the world of their readers, in language that points to ideas that have accumulated over centuries. Just as the first, abstract story of creation in Genesis leads into the second, more human-focused account, so this opening chapter of

44

John leads into a story of God's action in the world through history and human face. And that change is signalled in verse 6 by the appearance of 'a man sent from God, whose name was John'. By giving John the Baptist such a prominent role in the thick of the theological scene-setting, the author of John's Gospel echoes the opening of the Gospel of Mark. In both Gospels, that Jesus is witnessed to, and appears in a fixed time and place, and comes from a recognized, grounded tradition, is significant. Here the cosmic and the earthly intersect, and the moment needs to be recognized.

Verses 9–13 refocus the earthly moment of the coming of 'the light' with further reference to creation themes. 'The world came into being through him' – and yet, echoing the tension of both creation stories – 'the world did not know him' (v. 10). Worse, 'his own people did not accept him' (v. 11). There is also a new and positive note, however, expressed in terms of a new creation: 'all who received him . . . he gave power to become children of God' (v. 12). Rebirth and recreation as children of God remain key themes throughout the Gospel. Throughout, as here, the experience depends on the right response to the new and momentous occurrence that the coming of the Word into the world signifies. The closing verse of this poem or overture (vv. 14–18) grounds this occurrence in the language of the father-son relationship, and the enfleshing of the Word in the person of Jesus Christ. These theological metaphors attempt to convey a new understanding about the nature of God's relationship with the man Jesus, and through him, those who respond positively to him. This is new creation struggling to be expressed, using language that is familiar and yet raised to another plane of understanding. The creative God and the creative writer of the Prologue share in the same endeavour – to make the significance of the person of Jesus known and understood so that an appropriate response may be made. Like the unknown authors of the Genesis stories, the writer of John's Gospel seeks to explain something that he believes to be beyond human comprehension, belonging to the cosmic rather than the earthly world. Both share a common story of cosmic struggle between dark and light, and both affirm the ultimate victory of light over darkness. The story of how that victory comes about is complex – indeed, the second story of creation waits to be completed by John's story – but the opening chapters of Genesis and the Prologue of John's Gospel, in their close literary relationship to each other, are the beating heart, or the explanatory key, of the stories that follow. In the terms introduced by Marx, it would not be unhelpful to call John 1 a midrashic reading of the Genesis creation stories, not in the technical, rabbinic use of the term 'midrash' that we will discuss in Chapter 8, but in the sense that the Gospel text freely re-writes and re-interprets the Genesis stories for its new context.

While the explanatory power of the Genesis creation stories has often been invoked by later literature, it is most often the story of the Fall and its aftermath that has formed the specific biblical and imaginative back-drop to literary endeavour. Space only permits a reading of two examples: W. B. Yeats's 'Adam's Curse' and Edwin Muir's 'Adam's Dream'.

Creation themes in Yeats and Muir

Born less than 25 years apart, Yeats (1865–1939) and Muir (1887–1959) may both be classed as poets of the Modernist period. Imagery, symbolism and myth are key elements of much of their poetry, with biblical myths and stories very much part of their poetic vocabulary. While Yeats's 'Adam's Curse' was written in the poet's early middle age (1903), Muir's poem comes from near the end of his life, from a collection entitled *One Foot in Eden* (1956). Each brings the consequences of the Fall to bear upon human life, and each takes a different message or mood from the same story. Thus Yeats' poem speaks of disappointed hopes and failed dreams; for Muir, the potential for growth and change transforms the pathos of the Fall. Let us now consider each poem in more detail.

William Butler Yeats

William Butler Yeats was born in Dublin in 1865, and spent time in both Ireland and England. As an adult, his interests were wide and varied, including Irish folklore and mythology, the occult and magic, Irish nationalism and theatre. His unrequited love for Maud Gonne, a famous Irish actress and nationalist activist, inspired much of his poetry, as did a love of the countryside and a sense of the history of place. Perhaps his best known poem is 'The Lake Isle of Innisfree' (1893), which captures his longing for a simpler yet idealized and eternally significant past life, and which we considered in Chapter 1. Symbolism and myth are key forms throughout his poetry, including ancient thought patterns from many different cultures.

The setting of the conversation dramatized in 'Adam's Curse' immediately places it in a time of endings and regret, at 'one summer's end'. The sense is given that what is to come is a cold contracting of the warmth and companionship that allowed the speakers to sit outside and 'talk . . . of poetry'. As they sit, by the third stanza, they 'saw the last embers of daylight die', and the moon appear. The passing of time from day to night, the movement of the heavenly bodies, the 'waters' and the 'stars' evoke the first creation story and the cosmic dimension of the scene. From Maud Gonne's autobiography, we are given the suggestion that the poem is based on a conversation that took place after dinner in the late summer between herself, her sister and Yeats in 1902. Each agreed that both men and women are involved in the effort needed after the Fall and that beauty, like the creation of poetry, needs to be worked at if it is to appear effortlessly inspired.[6] The contrast is drawn between hard, heavy manual work ('scrub a kitchen pavement, or break stones/Like an old pauper' [ll. 8–9]), echoing God's Genesis injunction to Adam that 'in the sweat of thy face shalt thou eat bread' (3.19) and 'cursed is the ground for thy sake' (3.17); and the 'stitching and unstitching' necessary to bring forth 'a line' (ll. 4, 6). Beauty, poetry and love are quietly and gently brought together as things that the 'noisy set' of 'bankers, schoolmasters and clergymen' deem only the task of the 'idler' (ll. 12–13). The motif of idleness reappears in stanza 2 when the speaker asserts that those lovers who thought that 'high courtesy' and the quoting out of 'beautiful old books' would be sufficient, now see such behaviour as 'an idle tale enough' (ll. 25–8). Idleness is an illusory and shifting concept that brings no rewards whether it is real or imagined. The only alternative is endless effort – a curse indeed.

In the final stanza, there is little sense of hope or potential in humanity's post-Fall existence. The moon appears 'worn as if it had been a shell/Washed by time's waters as they rose and fell/ About the stars and broke in days and years' (ll. 32–4). The perspective of the poem stays with the speaker, but from consideration of the universal at the beginning of the poem, he now expresses a thought 'for no-one's but your ears' (1.35), presumably Maud Gonne: that he had loved her and her beauty in the 'old high way of love' (37) and had 'seemed happy', but they had both grown 'As weary-hearted as that hollow moon' (ll. 38–9). From inhabiting a timeless eternity, they are now at the mercy of temporal existence that seems empty and repetitive in comparison. 'The old high way of love' echoes the innocent existence of the first man and woman of Genesis 2, or the pre-Fall harmony of Adam and Eve. The use of the verb 'to strive' (l. 36) in connection with this state turns the thesis of earlier in the poem upside down. Effort had not been enough to sustain the mythic state, and has led to weariness in the face of the reality of passing time. Just as idleness, real or perceived, leads nowhere, so striving in love, and in particular the attempt to reclaim a state of innocence, brings no sense of fulfilment. The poem is deeply pessimistic and downbeat, seeing in the human situation as it exists in time little escape or respite from ongoing and fruitless toil. While a line of poetry and the beauty of a woman may be possible if worked at, transcendent love is unattainable.

Many commentators have pointed out that this poem was written just before Maud Gonne married John MacBride. Whether Yeats knew this was going to happen cannot be determined, and the poem as it stands was published after the marriage, but a sense of hopelessness in their situation is hard to avoid positing. While Gonne had promised herself in

---

6 Maud Gonne MacBride, 1994, *A Servant of the Queen*, A. Norman Jeffares and Anna MacBride White (eds), Gerrards Cross: Colin Smythe, pp. 317–18.

'mystical marriage' to Yeats, whom she had met in 1889, she had refused his several offers of marriage on a more physical level. While she became more involved in political intrigue and activism on a revolutionary and highly dangerous scale, Yeats had little appetite for such political tactics, and preferred to idolize her on an elevated plane of idealism. A sense of enduring personal loss pervades his middle age. While in his youth the hope of transcendence following self-sacrifice and of revelation for the martyred hero remained real, in the period in which 'Adam's Curse' was written there is deep weariness and regret. As Terence Brown writes in his biography of Yeats:

> They are the poems of a man who has found himself confronted by the challenges of life's ineluctable ambiguities when he had expected a transcendent consummation in a spiritual renewal of Ireland and the world with which his own destiny and that of Maud Gonne were united.[7]

The intertextual use of the creation stories in Genesis give symbolic weight to this sense of disappointment and failed dreams, situating Yeats as poet within a wider and deeper matrix of meaning. It highlights the interconnectedness of one person's situation with that of humanity's, giving his experience a mythic quality while suggesting the constraints within which individuals in time must live and love. This poem powerfully, and in the terms of Marx's reading, midrashically, brings to the fore the pathos of the myth of the Fall.

Edwin Muir

Edwin Muir was born on a farm in the Orkney Islands in 1887. After that rugged and pre-industrial landscape, the move to Glasgow in 1901 due to his family's financial problems was a huge shock, compounded by the deaths of his parents and two of his brothers within the space of a couple of years. Muir left Glasgow in 1918, after enduring a desperate series of jobs, and came to London, where he was influenced by both psychoanalysis and the literary scene of the time. A series of books of poetry followed, there was extensive travel throughout Europe and the translating, with his wife Willa, of several key German texts. Time spent in Italy gave Muir a new sense of connectedness to an incarnate Christianity of a very different sort from the pared down Calvinism of his childhood. Throughout his work, there is concern for the recovery of a fruitful relationship between myth and modern humanity, a desire to find meaning in ancient patterns.

---

7 Terence Brown, 2001, *The Life of W. B. Yeats*, Oxford: Blackwell, p. 145.

In contrast to Yeats's 'Adam's Curse', Edwin Muir's 'Adam's Dream' is a much more positive and hopeful reading of the creation story. The poem, describes the first dream of Adam after he and Eve have been expelled from Eden. The first creation story is invoked by the opening of the poem, which refers back to the 'daydream' of Adam's time in the Garden, with its 'heaven and sun', the 'hills and woods and waters' of the earth, the 'friendly' vegetation and animals and 'earth's last wonder Eve' (ll. 3–6). Eve's status as 'the first great dream', the 'ground of every dream since then' (ll. 6–7), echoes her creation from the sleeping Adam's rib, as well as a romantic notion of the place of women in the lives of men post-Fall. The break from that idyllic time is signalled by the picture of Adam 'lying on the naked ground/The gates shut fast behind him as he lay' (ll. 8–9). Both he and Eve are 'fallen', literally and spiritually, on the ground: 'terror', drowning and the 'abyss' await them, although even in this extremity there is 'comfort', as no 'further fall' is possible (ll. 11–12). This seeking a positive outcome from desperate times will run through the poem and picks up the ongoing narrative thrust of the biblical creation story.

The dream itself shifts the perspective from the 'naked ground' to a high, mountainous position from which Adam is given a new perspective. He sees increasing numbers of figures on the plain below, their movements erratic, 'identical or interchangeable' (ll. 21, 32), 'a mechanical/Addition without meaning' (ll. 25–6). And yet the characteristic that is given most prominence is their falling and rising again, 'And rising were the same yet not the same' (l. 20). In seeking to make sense of this apparently random activity, Adam calls out to them with the universal question, 'What are you doing there?', and while the echoing crags offer him no answer, he comes to realize that what he is experiencing at first remove is 'time' (ll. 46, 52), 'strange/to one lately in Eden' (ll. 53–4). With this realization comes a desire to see these people more closely, not as part of a 'story-book', but to be integrated 'among them' (ll. 65, 67). When he sees their faces and realizes they are like him, he has to restrain himself from calling them 'sons of God' (l. 69): the 'Fall' means that this connection to divinity is no longer obvious, although this realization brings 'Promise', and 'peace' to Adam, and an ability to 'turn again/In love and grief in Eve's encircling arms' (ll. 74–5).

The movement of the poem is from the impersonal ('they say' [l. 1]), the strange and the horrifically unknown ('gates shut fast' [l. 9]) and Eve's 'fallen arms' (l. 10), to the integrated and hopeful: Eve's arms are 'encircling' (l. 74), there is community and hope through the taking of his children's hands. Meaning is to be found in the experience of living with others, more real even than the 'daydream' that was life in the 'Garden' (l. 2). In the falling and rising motif that runs throughout the poem there is also an echo of the hope of the resurrection through the son of Adam who may be called the Son of God without restraint. But the overwhelmingly positive mood of the poem, although tempered and shadowed by regretful melancholy, comes from the drive of humanity to move on and forward, 'tense with purpose' (l. 37), although 'in no mode or order' (27).

By expanding the story of the Fall into Adam's experience after his expulsion, giving Adam feelings and motivations while firmly situating his role in the drama in the context of the earlier, priestly version of the creation myth, Muir manipulates his reader's attitude towards the opening chapters of Genesis. The reader is swept, like Adam, from the majesty of the creation of the universe through the devastation wreaked by the sin of Adam and Eve to a more hopeful and individual possibility on a human level. God is almost totally absent from this narrative: it is Adam who is 'our father' (l. 1); our status as children of God is uncertain (l. 69) and yet there is a solidarity in the new relationships made possible by recognizing that Adam is in our midst. Just as Adam finds peace in his vision, so the reader, after experiencing the vision with him, is left with a sense of being within 'Eve's encircling arms' (l. 74). As Muir writes in his *Autobiography*, 'there are times in every man's life when he seems to become for a little while a part of the fable, and to be recapitulating some legendary drama. The Fall is one of those events, and the purifications which happen in one's life belong to them too'.[8] This poem asks the reader to recognize his or her part in the legendary drama, as it presents that drama as offering hope from within an individual's common experience. The effect of the midrashic intertextuality of this poem is the drawing together of the creation myth and the life of individuals into a profound unity, an insight Muir had come to after deeply disturbing life experiences, reflective psychoanalysis, including dream therapy, and a spiritual awakening that involved a fresh understanding of the meaning of the incarnation in human terms.

Contextual intertextuality brings new meanings to texts. The creation myths in Genesis have a prehistory that goes some way towards explaining their contradictory messages. The Prologue to John's Gospel presents the coming of Jesus as an event as significant as the creation of the world, through the use of phrases and ideas first drawn together in Genesis 1–3. Later creation concepts, of Wisdom and *Logos*, are woven into this poetic assertion of the meaning of the life of Christ. Muir and Yeats play with similar elements of these foundational myths, each reading them according to their own experience of life and religion, and coming to very different conclusions. Later in this book, the images of apocalypse at the end of the world will be followed from their biblical roots through later literature. Creation will be shown to be a dominant image as writers strive to describe the unknown, the creation of something beyond human imagination. In all cases, the opening chapters of Genesis play a significant role

---

8 Edwin Muir, 1954, *An Autobiography*, 1993 edn, Edinburgh: Canongate Press, p. 105.

in defining and influencing literary attempts to situate humanity in its wider context in time. But it should also be noted, as Marx suggests, that these later texts, midrashic commentaries on the Genesis stories, have the power to influence the way the creation stories themselves are read and re-read in new contexts. And this two-way influence has been revealed by the insights of literary criticism.

Questions

1. Consider the significance of the creation stories in any literary examples you can think of. Does one or other of the creation myths predominate in literature in your experience?
2. Assess the interconnectedness of John 1 and Genesis 1–3. Give examples of creation themes recurring in later chapters of John's Gospel.

Further reading

Terence Brown, 2001, *The Life of W. B. Yeats*, Oxford: Blackwell.

Stephen Marx, 2000, *Shakespeare and the Bible*, Oxford: Oxford University Press.

Margery McCulloch, 1993, *Edwin Muir: Poet, Critic and Novelist*, Edinburgh: Edinburgh University Press.

Edwin Muir, 1954, *An Autobiography*, 1993 edn, Edinburgh: Canongate Press.

Edwin Muir, 1984, *Collected Poems*, London: Faber & Faber.

J. J. M. Roberts, 2002, *The Bible and the Ancient Near East*, Winona Lake: Eisenbrauns.

Alexander Rofé, 2002, *Introduction to the Composition of the Pentateuch*, trans. Harvey N. Bock, Sheffield: Sheffield Academic Press.

D. Moody Smith, 2001, *The Theology of the Gospel of John*, Cambridge: Cambridge University Press.

Laurence A. Turner, 2000, *Genesis*, Sheffield: Sheffield Academic Press.

W. B. Yeats, 1981, *The Collected Poems of W. B. Yeats*, 2nd edn, London: Macmillan.

4

Intertextuality: Methods and Limits

The relationship between texts is of central importance to literary and to biblical studies. In biblical studies, the relationship between the Hebrew Bible and the New Testament clearly has theological implications. Traditional source and redaction criticism considers issues of interdependence, of certain Hebrew Bible books such as Chronicles, Kings and Samuel, and of the Gospels too. Questions of which biblical books used which other, earlier texts, and how and why, are the stuff of all mainstream commentaries. In literary studies, the tracing of quotations and allusions, of the Bible often but of other texts too, is a common pursuit. In the previous chapter, we considered the ways in which the creation stories of Genesis relate to later biblical and literary texts. In this chapter, I argue that theories of intertextuality have something to add to both areas of study and offer an important bridge between the two fields. Here we will consider some of the implications of intertextuality as a critical approach and read Nathaniel Hawthorne's short story, 'Young Goodman Brown', for its relationship with biblical texts, in particular the First Epistle of John.

In 1969, in an essay on Mikhail Bakhtin, Julia Kristeva famously brought the word and the concept 'intertextuality' to prominence, proclaiming that 'any text is constructed as a mosaic of quotations; any text is the absorption and transformation of another', so that 'the notion of intertextuality replaces that of intersubjectivity'.[1] Although it was not a new word or idea, from this point it became a topic of debate and reassessment. Those who apply the notion most rigorously, such as Christopher Johnson, stress the resulting loss of the idea of the organic text in favour of the text as 'the product of intersections of a whole corpus of texts which may be broadly defined as our "culture" . . . [A] given text is a function of its "predecessors"'.[2] Not only textual sources but the thoughts and expressions of a wider culture are all assumed to leave

---

1 Julia Kristeva, 1969, 'Word, Dialogue and Novel', in L. S. Roudiez (ed.); transl. T. Gora, A. Jardine and L. Roudiez, 1980, *Desire in Language: A Semiotic Approach to Literature and Art*, New York: Columbia University Press, pp. 64–91, here p. 66.

2 Christopher M. Johnson, 1988, 'Intertextuality and the Psychic Model', *Paragraph*, 2 (March 1988), pp. 71–89, here p. 71.

traces in later texts, which are themselves in continual internal dialogue. The absorbed sources do not cohere naturally, but rub against each other creating friction and sparks. An intertextual reading seeks to assess the significance of these internal struggles rather than the more traditional analysis of genre, structure, character and so on.

In biblical studies, Richard B. Hays has been an influential figure in the creation of a dialogue between such theories and exegesis, in particular with regard to the use of Old Testament references in Pauline Epistles. While his key text, *Echoes of Scripture in the Letters of Paul*, is theological in its intent, it also firmly shifts the emphasis of the study of the Old Testament in the New into a literary sphere. Rather than quotations being regarded as add-ons to Paul's theological arguments, in Hays's work, published in 1989, the dialogue between Old Testament texts and Paul's writing is part of an ongoing interaction, with the potential for unpredictable outcomes. This idea that there might be literary friction between these texts was a new one in biblical studies, and opened up new reading possibilities.

Richard B. Hays and Scriptural Echoes

Hays's work on the place of the Old Testament in Pauline Epistles brought literary critical ideas firmly into mainstream biblical criticism. Drawing on the insights of John Hollander's *The Figure of the Echo: A Mode of Allusion in Milton and After*, Hays introduced several new concepts into the way references to the Old Testament in the New were understood. In addition to quotation and allusion, Hays suggested that 'echo' might be an appropriate category of reference, less obvious or certain than the former categories, but with its own 'revisionary power . . . to generate new figuration'.[3] He also argued that when an echo links two texts, the literary and semantic effect of the echo may lie in the unstated or even suppressed points of contact between them. For Hays, 'the interpretation of a metalepsis entails the recovery of the transumed material'.[4] In other words, the correspondence may be faint, but even then it may include reference to the material surrounding the echoed material in its original context; or it may refer to material as it has echoed in other places in the Hebrew Bible. Paul is to be read in 'the cave of resonant signification'[5] in which he existed, the whole of scripture as he knew it. The reader should be open to hearing correspondences echoing through the whole of that scripture, some weak and some strong, depending on the amount and the significance of the original text that is to be found in the later text.

---

3 Richard B. Hays, 1989, *Echoes of Scripture in the Letters of Paul*, New Haven: Yale University Press, p. 19.
4 Hays, *Echoes of Scripture*, p. 20.
5 Ibid.

Famously for Hays, the location of the meaning, even the existence, of the correspondence echoing between texts is to be held in 'creative tension' between the reader, the writer and the text: he asserts 'there is an authentic analogy – though not a simple identity – between what the text meant and what it means'.[6] He is open to the possibility that echoes may be present that were not necessarily intended by Paul, but he resists any move to give the reader complete freedom to posit a correspondence, instead offering seven tests to guide the reader towards a decision about the plausibility of an echo.

In its time, Hays's *Echoes of Scripture* offered a new and liberating way to read the Bible intertextually. Criticisms of his approach have been made – see the contributions to the discussion in Craig A. Evans and James A. Sanders's edited work, *Paul and the Scriptures of Israel*, and Hays's rebuttal of them in that volume.[7] However, the book remains an important milestone in the ongoing sharing of insights between literary and biblical criticism, crucially from the centre of biblical studies, and pointed the way towards further interaction between the two.

Even without taking into account the intention of the author, itself an exercise fraught with difficulty, intertextual quotations and allusions may function either to lend the weight of authority to the new text, or to assert the independence of the later text from the world of the original. There may even be a struggle or uncertainty between these two options, to which the reader must be sensitive. The old is to be accepted, but the new may also be clamouring to be introduced. The old system of meaning, which the Hebrew Bible in the work of Paul or the Christian Bible in later literature may be taken to represent, may be considered foundational, but in the act of being reshaped and re-written in these narratives, the earlier texts are shown to be springboards to something new, rather than teachings to be accepted without comment. If intertextuality introduces us to the notion that texts are woven from a wide cultural heritage, then the repetition of biblical images in new contexts through the ages offers an insight into a wider realm of meaning than the simply textual. The combination of the recognizable and the new, dependence and liberation, which biblical echoes invite us as readers to consider, draws in the literary and religious milieu in which the texts were written and in which they are read. The engagement of writers with biblical texts of all kinds allows later readers to discuss something of these writers' historical, cultural and spiritual understanding. Intertextuality is thus a powerful

---

6 Hays, *Echoes of Scripture*, p. 27.

7 Craig A. Evans and James A. Sanders (eds), 1993, *Paul and the Scriptures of Israel*, Sheffield: JSOT Press, pp. 70–96.

hermeneutical lens with which to read all texts that appropriate the Bible in any way.

Of course, as Steve Moyise has carefully argued recently,[8] inner-bible exegesis,[9] the use of an earlier scriptural reference in a later biblical text, poses particular theological issues for many biblical scholars, and the theological stance they take affects their ensuing interpretation. For some, the intertextual relationship between the two Testaments is an example of a wider literary phenomenon, in which new meanings are created in later readings of any text. For others, inspiration or canonicity is what allows and directs the process to happen in the case of scripture alone. On this view, the meanings expressed by New Testament readings of the Old are those which have been intended by God in the light of further revelation. Moreover, those who take the view that there is a unity within Scripture, either because of the unifying influence of God or because all of the later writers were operating within the same Jewish framework, read continuity and smooth transition into the relationship between the Old and the New Testaments. Those who see a wider gulf between the covenant of law open only to the Jews and the covenant of grace open to all, find a more complex and critical relationship between the two Testaments. Theological and literary perspectives interact with each other and affect the readings that are offered.

Further and related issues to be considered include those of intentionality and the role of the reader in assigning meaning. Some quotations from the Old Testament are signalled explicitly in New Testament texts. In the Sermon on the Mount, Matthew's Jesus asserts, 'You have heard it said' then goes on to quote from scripture before reinterpreting the saying in a more stringent way (for example Matthew 5.21–2). Paul apparently self-consciously quotes Isaiah with the tag-line, 'As it is written' at Romans 10.15, and again in the next verse introduces a quotation with 'for Isaiah says'. Other apparent allusions are much less obvious. Staying in Matthew's Sermon on the Mount, is it valid to assert that 'Blessed are those who mourn, for they shall be comforted' (5.4) is alluding to Isaiah 61.2, in which it is promised that the one on whom the Spirit of God rests will 'comfort all who mourn'? In the Pauline corpus, Hays offers the example of Philippians 1.19 ('through your prayers and the help of the Spirit of Jesus Christ this will turn out for my deliverance'), as an equally uncertain allusion to Job 13.16 (LXX) ('Even this shall turn out for my deliverance,

---

8 Steve Moyise, 2008, *Evoking Scripture: Seeing the Old Testament in the New*, London: T & T Clark, pp. 125–41.

9 The term and the concept are explored in Michael Fishbane, 1985, *Biblical Interpretation in Ancient Israel*, Oxford: Clarendon Press, particularly in relation to the echoes of early texts in later Hebrew Bible texts.

for deceit shall not enter in before him.'). As Hays notes, 'the echo is fleeting, and Paul's sentence is entirely comprehensible to a reader who has never heard of Job'.[10] What are the grounds for saying an intertextual relationship between these texts exists? The situation is further muddied by examples such as those found earlier in Romans 10. In verse 13, Paul explores various aspects of Moses' words about the practice of righteousness, including a direct quotation from Deuteronomy 30.14 at verse 8 – 'the word is near you, on your lips and in your heart'. However, the way Paul interprets the original text is very different from its apparent original intention: 'the word' refers, in his reading, not to the immutable Law, but to his preaching of the 'word of faith' (10.8b). As a reader of the Hebrew Bible, Paul has apparently taken a giant hermeneutical leap away from the original intention of the earlier text and its immediate context. This is worth exploring in itself – but to what extent does this liberate later readers in their reading and use of biblical texts such as this? What are the constraints on readings, and do they come from the text itself or from reading communities or elsewhere?

The issue of authorial or original intent is of course particularly tricky in texts from centuries earlier and cultures far removed from our own. The evidence that is available is extremely limited and open to multiple interpretation – even if a reader assumes a theology that includes divine intention as a guiding hermeneutical force. In that case, what Moyise calls the communicative intent of the New Testament writer may be considered to be the same as that of the writer of the alluded-to Old Testament text, although it may be a very different message from the text its immediate context.[11] A fuller, broader meaning across the centuries thus falls within the overarching purpose of God. However, even those interpreters who rely less on such divine watchfulness, and who focus more on the role of the reader in the creation of meaning, might want to place constraints on reading intertextual echoes into biblical texts. For Moyise as for Hays, these include historical constraints such as the availability of the earlier text and the likelihood that the first hearers of the later text would have been aware of the earlier one. Even then, the control of intertextual readings does not lie with the author. As Moyise comments, 'every quotation is a bridge to another text, but what travels across is not limited to the author's intentions'.[12]

---

10 Hays, *Echoes of Scripture*, p. 21.

11 Moyise, *Evoking Scripture*, pp. 128–35.

12 'Intertextuality and Historical Approaches to the Use of Scripture in the New Testament', in R. B. Hays et al. (eds), 2009, *Reading the Bible Intertextually*, Waco, TX: Baylor University Press, pp. 23–34, here p. 32.

Reader-response theories such as that offered by Wolfgang Iser endeavour to shift the focus of interest away from the context out of which the quoted to or alluded to text has come, and place it on the context in which the text has been and is being read.[13] Iser regards reading as a process of filling gaps and completing meaning. In the new context in which Paul finds himself, he 'actualizes' Old Testament texts in a specific way, making sense of the potential of those texts according to his needs and interests. On this understanding the reading process is deeply contextual and, as biblical texts are read by communities who believe themselves to be divinely created, the readings of these communities are assumed by them to be divinely authorized by the text itself. However, if texts are understood to be incomplete until they are read and interpreted by specific readers and communities, then multiple interpretations are possible and to be expected. As Moyise points out, this explains variations in the way the same Old Testament texts are used by different New Testament writers: Genesis 15.6 appears both in James 2.24 and in Romans 4, but with completely different interpretations, due, on this reading, to the different debates in which the two writers were involved.[14] Both fall within the range of meaning 'implied' by the text, nevertheless. For Iser, there is no sense that readers are completely and legitimately free to read whatever they like into a biblical or any other text. Readings are controlled or at least constrained by literary and rhetorical convention. A text's communicative intent, although not necessarily linked with its authorial intent, is still important and not to be wilfully over-ridden by later readers. However, meaning lies not in the text itself, or in some theoretical implied reader, but only in the actual reading of individuals. Later critics of Iser have questioned his emphasis on the isolated nature of activating readers, and have stressed instead the influential role of convention and community expectation in any reading of a text. All of this, of course, sheds a new light on the readings of New Testament writers of Old Testament texts. Reader-response theories also focus attention on the activity of readers today as they attempt to find meaning in biblical texts, particularly in the intertextuality of those texts. Unhooking meaning from the text itself and placing the responsibility of completing meaning on anyone who reads that text brings a certain freedom of interpretation but also forces readers to consider where the boundaries should lie. Reader-response theories will be considered in more detail in Chapter 6.

Taking insights from reader response-theories such as that of Iser encourages a present-day reader to see intertextual references or echoes in

---

13 Wolfgang Iser, 1974, *The Implied Reader: Patterns of Communication in Prose Fiction from Bunyan to Beckett*, Baltimore: Johns Hopkins University Press; and 1978, *The Act of Reading*, Baltimore: Johns Hopkins University Press.

14 Moyise, *Evoking Scripture*, pp. 136.

the Bible as examples of specific readers' responses to earlier biblical texts, and to ask questions about his or her reading of those later texts. The more culturally focused theories of Kristeva and Johnson invite speculation about wider issues of influence and control of meaning. All of this invites fresh readings of literary and other texts through the centuries that continue the process of reading and echoing words, phrases and ideas from the pages of the Bible. Just as Hays found inspiration in the writing of John Hollander on allusions in Milton, so both literary and biblical critics may find common cause and new significances in reading literature for its biblical echoes, whether strong or weak. The remainder of this chapter will focus on the example of Nathaniel Hawthorne's short story, 'Young Goodman Brown', and the way the Bible echoes within it.

Intertextuality in practice: 'Young Goodman Brown' and 1 John

A short epistle such as 1 John shares with a classic short story such as 'Young Goodman Brown' a sense of spare brevity and tight form. While a Gospel, like a novel, may have space to include detail and discursion, a short epistle, like a short story, is more likely to have a structure that focuses on driving home a particular purpose, and may tend to exclude anything that does not contribute to that goal. Edgar Allan Poe identified the essential qualities of a nineteenth-century short story as a unity of purpose, a moment of crisis and a symmetry of design. The extraneous and everyday are excluded; the particular and their moment of drama are given a brief, carefully crafted and formed literary treatment that the reader may enter and experience in a particularly intense way in the hour or so it takes to read the story. Like the form of lyric poetry, the short story form encourages a belief that nothing is wasted in the work. As a literary experience, the short story takes a shape proper to itself, the shape and experience working as functions of each other. A reader is drawn to consider not just the content of the story but the way the material is organized to create a specific effect. Image and symbol in the short story are of key importance, giving the work texture and pointing to something outwith itself, engaging something of value in the wider world. 'Young Goodman Brown', as we shall see, uses imagery and symbolism in a concentrated and careful way, as a device that offers a key to the story's form, and offers a pattern that leads the reader to appreciate the larger implications of the story. A reader of 'Young Goodman Brown' may have something to share with a reader of 1 John in his or her understanding of form and symbolism, and vice versa, and this may be argued to be one aspect of intertextuality. More obviously, it will be argued that Johannine themes are picked up and explored in Hawthorne's short story, in a way that challenges the Puritan Calvinism of both Goodman Brown and Hawthorne's day.

'Young Goodman Brown' by Nathaniel Hawthorne

First published in 1835, when Hawthorne was a young writer of 31, at its simplest 'Young Goodman Brown' is a story of a naïve young man who at first accepts individuals and society as they present themselves, is confronted with a vision of human and devil-inspired evil, and is for ever after a sad, distrustful and gloomy man. The narrative framework for this psychological and spiritual journey is based on a literal journey, set in the 1690s – Young Goodman Brown leaves his new wife, Faith, and the safety of Salem, spends the night in the forest and returns a changed man. The detached, rather cynical narrator describes Goodman Brown's experience in the wood as a pre-arranged meeting with a shape-shifting devil figure, who tries to persuade Brown to be baptized into the 'mystery of sin'. Drawn along the dark path by the sight of figures he has assumed were saintly, making their way to the ceremony, and finally by the presence of his wife Faith about to undergo the same initiation, at the altar he has a change of heart and urges her to 'Look up to Heaven, and resist the Wicked One!'.[15] Immediately, he finds himself alone in the forest, from where he returns to Salem, unable thereafter to participate in worship or family life without suspecting those around him of hypocrisy. He 'shrinks from the bosom of Faith' and, after his death, 'they carved no hopeful verse upon his tomb-stone; for his dying hour was gloom'.[16]

'Young Goodman Brown' is an example of a particular short story form, often called a sketch or a tale, perfected by Nathaniel Hawthorne and lauded by Poe. While more realistic sorts of short stories were also popular at the time it was written, these sketches or tales were characterized by a tendency towards allegory, a focus on stylized rather than realistic characters and a detachment from the norms of social behaviour. The opening paragraph of this story carefully establishes the pattern of what is to follow, and is worth considering in detail, as a demonstration of the concentrated interplay between meaning and form that characterizes the short story:

---

15 Nathaniel Hawthorne, 1835, 'Young Goodman Brown', in L. S. Person (ed.), 2005, *The Scarlet Letter and other Writings*, Norton Critical Edition, New York: W. W. Norton & Co, pp. 178–88, here p. 187.

16 Hawthorne, 'Young Goodman Brown', p. 188.

> Young Goodman Brown came forth, at sunset, into the street of Salem village, but put his head back, after crossing the threshold, to exchange a parting kiss with his young wife. And Faith, as the wife was aptly named, thrust her own pretty head into the street, letting the wind play with the pink ribbons of her cap, while she called to Goodman Brown.[17]

The paragraph immediately sets out the boundary markers that will be crossed as the story progresses, the liminal position from which Goodman Brown begins and to which he will return, changed. He steps out of the safety of the home and into the public place that is the street of the village, at the turning point between day and night. But after the threshold has been crossed – breached, perhaps – he puts his head back to make fleeting contact with his wife. A division between his head and his heart is already established – although his later words will deny this, his actions indicate indecision, struggle perhaps between his conscience, his head, and his body. The next sentence affirms and sharpens this, as we learn his wife is 'aptly' called Faith. 'His' Faith stays at home while he crosses the threshold, first into the street and then beyond even that, into the darkness of the forest. Faith is attractive, fresh and young, willing to 'thrust her own pretty head' out into the street. Later, the reader will wonder, with Goodman Brown, if she in fact is also drawn to the danger and excitement of the forest. The pink ribbons of her cap will reappear in the story, crucially at the point where Goodman Brown must decide whether or not to push onwards into the forest – he both hears her call, again, and sees a pink ribbon, 'fluttering lightly through the air'. 'My Faith is gone . . . There is no good on earth; and sin is but a name. Come, devil! for to thee is this world given' is his response, and he apparently abandons himself to the devil's cause.[18] When he sees her on his return, 'Faith, with the pink ribbons', rushing out into the street to kiss him, he looks 'sternly and sadly into her face, and pass[es] on without a greeting'.[19] The opening scene, with its tender interaction between the two, is precisely reversed in the closing scene. The colour pink itself may be read as having a symbolic quality. It is neither red nor white, an ambiguous, inbetween colour, potentially emblematic (as Hester Prynne's scarlet letter is of her) of love and innocent good; or of hypocritical evil; or of an ambiguous, slippery blend of the two? Equally the pink ribbons could symbolize feminine sexuality; or Christian faith, which Goodman Brown apparently loses, although it, in the form of Faith and her pink ribbons, follows him to his grave. Perhaps their function within

---

17 Hawthorne, 'Young Goodman Brown', p. 178.
18 Hawthorne, 'Young Goodman Brown', p. 184.
19 Hawthorne, 'Young Goodman Brown', p. 188.

the story is their objectification of ambiguity – certainly their introduction in the opening paragraph is significant. As are all aspects of this opening paragraph, each playing through the rest of the story in a highly intricate manner. The extraneous is excluded – only the significant remains.

What makes the story so compelling, or one of the things, is this combination of tragic ambiguity and clarity of form and structure. The story itself asks its readers at its end – 'Had Goodman Brown fallen asleep in the forest, and only dreamed a wild dream of a witch-meeting? Be it so, if you will. But, alas! It was a dream of evil omen for young Goodman Brown.'[20] Brown seems to resist temptation to join the ranks of the devil – but seems not to be saved, unable to listen to the holy Psalm sung on a Sunday, 'because an anthem of sin rushed loudly upon his ear, and drowned all the blessed strain'.[21] Throughout, few interpretations of events are fixed; characters shift and change, as Goodman Brown battles with himself and his understanding of the world. However, this is expressed through carefully developed patterns of images and symmetrical forms, repaying that old practice of close reading.

An example of this ambiguity of interpretation, in which no definite answers are given, yet within a tight, controlled structure, is the recurring appearance of a staff or walking stick. The devil-traveller's staff 'bore the likeness of a great black snake, so curiously wrought, that it might almost be seen to twist and wriggle itself, like a living serpent. This, of course, must have been an oracular deception, assisted by the uncertain light.'[22] The staff is offered to Goodman Brown, but he refuses it. Later it reappears, defining his companion, who is the 'traveller with the twisted staff', who laughs at Goodman Brown's scruples and willingness to take the goodness of others at face value, so that 'his snake-like staff actually seemed to wriggle in sympathy'.[23] Brown's ignorance is apparently proved when Goody Cloyse, who had taught him his catechism as a child and was still his 'moral and spiritual advisor', appears and recognizes the touch of the devil when the traveller 'put forth his staff, and touched her withered neck with what seemed the serpent's tail'.[24] He gives her the staff, in lieu of her broomstick, which has been stolen, throwing it at her feet where, 'perhaps, it assumed life, being one of the rods which its owner had formerly lent to the Egyptian Magi'[25] – a clear echo of Exodus

20 Hawthorne, 'Young Goodman Brown', p. 188.
21 Ibid.
22 Hawthorne, 'Young Goodman Brown', p. 179.
23 Hawthorne, 'Young Goodman Brown', p. 180.
24 Hawthorne, 'Young Goodman Brown', p. 181.
25 Hawthorne, 'Young Goodman Brown', p. 182.

7.9–12 and Aaron's rod, which becomes a serpent. Staff and Goody are seen no more. The traveller picks another branch as a walking stick, stripping it of leaves and twigs, which wither and dry up at his touch. This maple stick he throws to Goodman Brown before vanishing into the wood, 'to help [him] along'.[26] On being convinced that Faith is heading towards the gathering in the wood, he grasps the staff and sets off 'at such a rate, that he seemed to fly along the forest-path, rather than to walk or run'.[27] At this point, he is described as 'the chief horror of the scene', identifying himself with witch and wizard, 'brandishing his staff with frenzied gestures . . . giving vent to an inspiration of horrid blasphemy'. As the narrator comments, 'The fiend in his own shape is less hideous, than when he rages in the breast of man.'[28] The staff does not feature in the fire-lit scene of devil worship, but afterwards, when Goodman Brown awakes alone, 'a hanging twig, that had been all on fire, besprinkled his cheek with the coldest dew'.[29]

The appearance and description of the staff are carefully constructed and controlled. Little is asserted, much is suggested. It seems to have supernatural powers; it perhaps oscillates between a fixed form and the beguiling serpent. Handling it seems to bring about a change in the self-understanding of the person, a diabolic change that fades when it is no longer being held. But in the cold light of day, its power is reduced, even reversed, potentially offering a cleansing, life-giving alternative to the fiery heat of the night before. A baptism not in the uncertain contents of the rock-basin – 'Did it contain water, reddened by the lurid light? Or was it blood? Or, perchance, a liquid flame?'[30] – but 'coldest dew'. Within a few pages, the repeated yet ambiguous mention of the staff affirms the strangeness of the story, develops a question mark against the tale as it is given, tantalizingly, by its narrator. Its unstable form, open to multiple interpretation, punctuates the stable, symmetrical structure of the story, inviting the reader to make a choice between a natural and supernatural reading of its significance. Mention of its biblical echo, from the story of the Exodus, adds to the uncertainty. In the biblical story, the Egyptian magicians follow Aaron, and their rods too become serpents – only to be swallowed up by Aaron's. Who then is the 'owner' of the rod, who lent it to the magicians, claiming to be? The devil is not mentioned in the Exodus story – the power to change inanimate objects into animate ones comes only from God. The reference to the Bible puzzles rather than illuminates or confirms.

26 Ibid.
27 Hawthorne, 'Young Goodman Brown', p. 184.
28 Ibid.
29 Hawthorne, 'Young Goodman Brown', p. 188.
30 Hawthorne, 'Young Goodman Brown', p. 187.

1 John

1 John, the first of three short letters traditionally ascribed to one writer, seems to have been written at a difficult time for one part of the early Church, which was facing disputes of both a theological and ethical nature. The letter seems to assume that there is a group, which has arisen out of the original set of believers, who were denying the very nature of Jesus Christ: that he was the Son of God, that he came in the flesh or that his death was necessary for salvation. While this group was winning new converts, the original believers are understandably concerned both by this betrayal, and by the threat this poses to their own beliefs. The Epistles of John, particularly the first of them, were plausibly written to reassure this original group that the message they had been taught is the correct one. While the structure of 1 John is far from clear, it appears that the letter's rhetorical thrust is not to impart new teaching but to deepen and affirm values already held. Against the teaching of the opponents, the readers are to be assured that only those who truly know God act in accordance with his will, showing love for fellow believers in a way that demonstrates their true belief. Jesus was both fully human and the Son of God, offering an atoning sacrifice through his blood on the cross. The Holy Spirit testifies to Jesus and his divinity. Right action, in particular the living out of the command to love one another, separates those who follow the true way of this Christ from those, the 'antichrists', whose actions reveal their dangerous doctrinal folly.

We find a similarly complex and, I will argue, sophisticated structure in the First Epistle of John. The text is well known for having a difficult to fathom structure. Often explanations and diagrams of a suggested structure take more space than the epistle itself. Colin Kruse comments: 'In seeking to understand 1 John . . . it is important to appreciate the type of literature it is (genre), to understand what sort of communication it is (rhetorical form), and to be able to describe how it hangs together (structure). In the case of 1 John none of these matters is straightforward.'[31] In generic terms, it lacks the standard markers of a letter, yet its references to writing also seem to suggest that it should not be regarded as a sermon or homily first designed to be read aloud. Some have called it a 'commentary' on John's Gospel[32] written to refute the appropriation of the Gospel by the secessionists; others a 'paper' on the Fourth Gospel, written to correct erroneous views on it by members of the community.[33] Kruse himself plumps for 'circular letter', written to a group of churches with similar problems, as this would account for the lack of an opening and

---

31 Colin G. Kruse, 2000, *The Letters of John*, Grand Rapids, MI: Eerdmans, p. 28.
32 Raymond Brown, 1982, *Epistles of John*, New York: Doubleday, pp. 90–2.
33 Stephen S. Smalley, 1984, *1,2,3 John*, Waco, TX: Word Books, p. xxvii.

closing salutation to particular addressees, or to any naming of particular people or incidents.[34] Structurally, the letter's lack of structure seems to be one of its defining features. Themes are visited several times, amplified and reworked in what some have called a spiral pattern. Certainly a developing argument seems to be missing, as themes are introduced then dropped in favour of others, then picked up again from a different angle. A reader – certainly this reader – feels her or she has never quite grasped I John and all it might mean. Each reading brings something new, demands concentrated attention. One might even say that I John shares with a short story such as 'Young Goodman Brown' some of the features of lyric poetry, from a formalist point of view. That in its concentrated, pointed unity, form and meaning are related, and that reading one, form, for its inter-relatedness to meaning, might prove illuminating. And that an attention to imagery and symbolism might reveal a pattern or a lack of a pattern that both adds texture to the text, and points to a significance that lies beyond or outwith it.

What I have begun to argue with 'Young Goodman Brown', I want to argue with I John, and that is that ambiguity may be considered a formal device, used here to create in the reader a feeling of the immediacy of the situation described, and to hint at the chaos of experience. This approach to the biblical text relieves the reader of the burden of traditional biblical criticism that focuses on the recovery of the identity and theology of the opponents mentioned in the letter, or the letter's recipients. Instead, it concentrates on the internal dynamics of the text – or the lack of them.

To do this, we will trace the images of light and darkness in I John. It will be argued that these are controlling images in the text, although only mentioned at its beginning. They enable or trigger other images that scatter through the rest of the text, and may make symbolic connections with other biblical texts and themes. In Chapter 2, the same set of images reappear. Light and darkness are part of a story, or narrative, told to be passed on, linking with other references in the text to the creation story, to events and knowledge existing 'from the beginning' (1.1); the fathers of 2.13, 14 have known him that is 'from the beginning'; at 2.24, the hearers are told to let abide in them that which they have heard 'from the beginning'– if so, it is promised that they shall also 'continue in the Son, and in the Father'. At 3.11, it is asserted that 'this is the message that ye heard from the beginning, that we should love one another'. Light is the first creation of God in the darkness. It, and its separation from darkness, is the first thing God calls 'good'. In I John, being in the light signifies a purity of connection with the God of creation, and with his son, and with others in the same existential place, in fellowship. But it is not a place with boundaries that welcome and then contain – the Fall is always also present, not fully past. The act of speech, claiming to be in the light, is

---

34 Kruse, *Letters of John*, pp. 28–9.

not sufficient – it is possible to claim you are walking in light, while actually walking in darkness, if you continue to hate your brother. The light is offered as an image of reassurance for those who act 'as he (God) is in the light' (1.7): for those who do not, whatever they claim, as Adam and Eve, or Cain (mentioned at 3.12), find out, the darkness of separation is real and devastating. Love and light are the foundational messages – 'this is the message that ye heard from the beginning' – but darkness and hate are equally causally connected and present, as much part of the image-story of the text as they are of the opening chapters of Genesis.

The images of light and dark in the opening section of 1 John connect with echoes of Genesis in 'from the beginning' markers throughout the text. These images also make structural links with dynamic notions of walking offered throughout 1 John, and with those of abiding. Light enables walking, which seems to enable meeting in fellowship with those also walking in the light. In the first chapter, this connection is not stumbling into one another, but pure walking with others, sin-free, as if interpersonal boundaries are gone. In the second chapter, being in the light is more static, involving abiding in contrast to the blind stumbling, going here and there, of those who are in darkness. Dwelling or abiding in God, allied with God dwelling in the believer, is a frequent image throughout the text (3.6; 3.24; 4.12). Those who are in darkness are those who move around, to no effect, a theme developed later in Chapter 2, where, at verse 19, the 'antichrists' are described as those who 'went out from us, but they were not of us; for if they had been of us, they would no doubt have continued with us; but they went out, that they might be made manifest that they were not all of us'. Blind, stumbling movement away from the light, where the true believers abide, is a sign of exclusion from the light, even when its possession is claimed. Love of God and fellow-believer is a firm message in the text, and assumes activity – but the more passive abiding and dwelling in him is referred to more frequently, in contrast to more active yet futile activity. The first reference to light, and to walking confidently in it, without stumbling, in Chapter 1, is not picked up strongly in the rest of the text. There is a fracture in the pattern, perhaps reflecting forward to the fear that seems to cast a shadow over the perfect love experienced by those who know they are in the light in 4.18. 'There is no fear in love; but perfect love casteth out fear: because fear hath torment. He that feareth is not made perfect in love.' Images of dwelling and abiding in light and love invite ideas of fearfulness, of avoidance of walking, striding out, unafraid of stumbling. Such fear, at the end of the text, is invoked as a sign of imperfect love. Dwelling and abiding, where fear is involved, is undercut as a perfect way to be in the light. The ripples of the images of light and dark are not evenly spaced and regularly patterned in the structure of this text. Perhaps the form, or uncertainty of form of the epistle, does indeed reflect something of its meaning, as the careful but shifting patterning of images in 'Young Goodman Brown' reflected something of its meaning too. The images of light and darkness play throughout 'Young Goodman Brown' too, and would be worthy of further exploration, as Hawthorne critic, Richard Harter Fogle, has already pointed the way. As he writes, 'The light in Hawthorne is clarity of design . . . The 'dark' in Hawthorne . . . is his tragic complexity. His clarity is intermingled with subtlety, his statement interfused with symbolism, his affirmation enriched with ambiguity.'[35] It has been argued here that 1 John offers a similar combination of light and dark.

We move now into the more classically reception-critical issue of interdependence and allusion between texts. Many literary critics have considered the relationship between 'Young Goodman Brown' and Calvinism. Goodman Brown either realizes that the Puritan Calvinism of his time is right, that humanity is depraved and one never can tell who is saved, and becomes the Calvinist extraordinaire – or he misses the central point of Calvinism, that hope should be placed in the grace of God alone, whereas he attempts to place his trust first in the institutions of the Church, and then loses all sense of hope or of trust. It will be argued here, however, that the engagement of Hawthorne's text is not with that theological doctrine per se, which finds its natural home in other New Testament texts, but with the rather different assertions of 1 John. While in Calvinism faith and works are related, but not necessarily and causally connected, the outward appearance and inner reality of faith in the Johannine epistles are closely and necessarily allied, although at times ambiguously described. It is this idea that 'Young Goodman Brown' explores and questions. Ultimately for Goodman Brown, the relationship between outward demonstrations of faith and the underlying motivation of those he observes is under constant suspicion and doubt. The same relationship is scrutinized by 1 John.

In response to the devil-figure's statement that Goodman Brown's father and grandfather were his companions, Brown asserts, 'We are a people of prayer, and good works, to boot, and abide no such wickedness'.[36] He might have made the same point with an assertion from 1 John 3.7: 'Little children, let no man deceive you: he that doeth righteousness is righteous, even as he (Christ) is righteous.' Or, from 2.3, 'hereby we do know that we know him, if we keep his commandments'. Calvin had struggled with 1 John, and had resorted to interpreting it through a Pauline lens, in which faith rather than holy living was primary. On 2.3, Calvin writes:

[W]e are not to conclude from this that faith rests on works. For although everyone has a witness to his faith from his works, it does not

---

35 Richard Harter Fogle, 1952, *Hawthorne's Fiction: The Light and the Dark*, Norman: University of Oklahoma Press, p. 4.

36 Hawthorne, 'Young Goodman Brown', p. 180.

follow that it is founded on them, but they are a subsequent proof added as a sign. The certainty of faith dwells only in Christ's grace. But godliness and holiness of life distinguish true faith from a fictitious and dead knowledge of God.[37] *or with schism?*

In the same chapter, he denies the possibility of sinless perfection that 1 John seems to envisage, translating 1 John 2.1 'and when any man sin, we have an advocate with the Father', rather than 'if any man sin'; he also asserts that while the author states Jesus is 'the propitiation for our sins: and not for ours only, but also for the sins of the whole world',[38] he means that the effect of the atonement is only for those who believe. Whereas Calvin had struggled with 1 John, Goodman Brown, at the beginning of the short story, seems to agree with it. Works demonstrate saving faith. The religious figures of the Church establishment are to be trusted as righteous because they act righteously.

However, as Michael Colacurcio argues, the story does not end there, and grapples with the issue of appearance and reality in a way that a closer reading of 1 John suggests it too was grappling. Goodman Brown initially assumes that the orderly hierarchy of the Puritan community embodies moral reality, thus he is especially shocked when the devil shows him good and bad consorting together. His own piety is questioned when it is revealed that he has pre-arranged the meeting in the forest with the devil, and that he presumes he will 'after this one night', 'cling to [Faith's] skirts and follow her to Heaven'.[39] Faced with the evidence the devil presents him with, that even Faith is willing to join his side, he despairs, but still manages to resist the temptation himself. What he, and the reader, is never certain of, is whether or not Faith also resists. Or indeed whether or not the incident is a dream. Colacurcio suggests that Hawthorne offers his reader a dramatically credible version of what it would have felt to be a Puritan in the 1690s from his own perspective of the 1830s – like Goodman Brown, he too had forefathers who had participated in the witch-hunts of the 1680s. He raises the real question, live in his time as it had been in the 1680s and 1690s, about the reliability of spectre evidence – whom to trust for information about the invisible world; can the devil impersonate the saints; on what basis should witchcraft be assessed and judged? Colacurcio writes, 'From Hawthorne's cautiously Arminian point of view, Calvinist Brown is habitually making simple judgements about settled moral realities in a world where only the most flickering

---

37   John Calvin, 1959, *The Gospel According to St John 11–21 and The First Epistle of John*, D. W. Torrance and T. F. Torrance (eds); trans. T. H. L. Parker, Grand Rapids, MI: Eerdmans, p. 246.

38   Calvin, *Gospel According to St John*, p. 244.

39   Hawthorne, 'Young Goodman Brown', p. 178.

sorts of appearances are available as evidence . . . Moral and spiritual status is . . . an invincible interior and a radically invisible quality.'[40] Goodman Brown lives in the moral gloom of one who is fully convinced of neither his lostness nor his salvation, or that of others, and who has discovered that evil is not to be played with or goodness assumed. The delights either of the company of Satan, or of the communion of saints, are denied him. He judges without love or sympathy for others, consumed by suspicion. Perhaps Hawthorne's purpose is to suggest that it is better not to ask ultimate questions about the evidence for faith, but rather to accept that all are engaged in a common moral struggle. A healthy scepticism about the appearance of morality, allied to a belief that others on the whole seek good rather than evil, would lift Goodman Brown from the gloom of his dread of the possibilities of pervasive evil. By leaving the events of the story uncertain, Hawthorne encourages the reader to question the possibility of making moral judgements of others, including of Goodman Brown.

As I have argued, the dominant message of 1 John is that actions demonstrate moral and spiritual states. However, this is not the only message in the text. The ambiguity comes from the apparent contradiction between 1.8–10 and 3.6–10. The latter section continues with the claim that the identity of those who are children of God and those who are children of the devil is 'manifest' by whether or not they do righteousness and love their brother. Manifestation, the act of disclosing that which is secret or dark, is a central concern of the text. The letter opens with a strong claim to have experienced in the most real and direct way the manifestation of the Word of Life, and to have borne witness to it. The purpose of this manifestation, in Chapter 3, is the destruction of the works of the devil. The struggle in the text is centred on the question of what actions manifest. How to work out what actions signify or make manifest in terms of light and darkness, spiritual allegiance? What reality lies behind the appearance, and whether that reality can change if the appearance of action changes. Sin is both stated as inevitable, and a remedy is offered, through the agency of the manifested reality of the word of life; but sin is also claimed as an impossibility for those who are in reality born of God and abide in him. Appearances both do matter, as manifestations of eternal categories, and they do not, as God has made manifest a way to change the significance of sinful actions. Despite the attempts of various commentators, this contradiction is not resolved within the letter. Outward markers, love of brother and doing what is right from the perspective of the text, should be taken as trustworthy signs of reality, and yet those to be judged as born of God will still display signs of sin, but the reality of their status should not be questioned.

---

40 Michael J. Colacurcio, 1984, *The Province of Piety: Moral History in Hawthorne's Early Tales*, Cambridge, MA: Harvard University Press, p. 299.

Indeed, what should be questioned are the claims of those who deny their potentially reality-changing actions. 1 John may seem at first to endorse the initial view of Goodman Brown, that outward appearance signifies salvific reality – and yet it does not leave that simple, comforting message as it stands. The complexity of life and the impossibility of making moral judgements are also acknowledged, going some way towards explaining Brown's compromised flirting with danger at the beginning of the story, and the situation he finds himself in at the end – unable to accept the piety of others at face value because he mistrusts the evidence of appearance. Where 1 John offers a positive alternative to the experience of Goodman Brown is in its command to love one another – an alternative we know from his Notebooks that Hawthorne himself believed went some way towards living in community with others with acceptance and an avoidance of paralysing gloom. In 1844 he wrote:

> The Unpardonable Sin might consist of a want of love and reverence for the Human Soul; in consequence of which, the investigator pried into its dark depths, not with a hope or purpose of making it better, but from a cold philosophical curiosity, – content that it should be wicked in whatever kind or degree, and only desiring to study it out. Would not this, in other words, be the separation of the intellect from the heart?[41]

Hawthorne's 'Young Goodman Brown' is a short story that has been carefully crafted and formed to focus the reader's concentration on its sophisticated, ambiguous spiritual and moral significance. 1 John does not share the short story's narrative tightness, but does mirror its concentrated, repetitive structure, and its thematic struggle to reconcile appearance with reality. This chapter has argued that the short story form of 'Young Goodman Brown' has highlighted some aspects of the form of 1 John that may not have been considered sufficiently before; and that the short story struggles with the same spiritual and moral issues as does 1 John. The two texts are not in a conventional intertextual relationship, and no claim has been made to support the idea that the short story is in any straightforward way dependent on the biblical text. The echo is fainter than any Richard Hays suggests in his exegesis of Paul's readings of the Old Testament. However, the argument of this chapter has taken seriously the aim of this book to read biblical and literary texts fruitfully alongside one another, and invokes intertextuality as a concept in its broadest sense. It may be a step too far for many biblical scholars, and

---

41 From *The American Notebooks,* vol. 8 of *The Centenary Edition of the Works of Nathaniel Hawthorne,* C. M. Simpson (ed.), 1972, Columbus: Ohio State UP, quoted in L. S. Person (ed.), 2005, *The Scarlet Letter and other Writings,* Norton Critical Edition, New York: W. W. Norton & Co, p. 215.

some literary critics too. Nevertheless, I suggest it demonstrates a way to read the Bible and literature that takes both sides of that conjoined phrase seriously and positively.

Questions

1. Consider the idea of 'inner Bible exegesis'. What examples of stories and references echoing throughout both Testaments of the Bible can you think of?
2. Compare the use of Genesis 15.6 in James 2.24 and Romans 4. What explanation may be given for the differences in the way the Old Testament text has been read by the two authors?
3. Trace the images of light and dark in 1 John, and the play of daylight and night-time in 'Young Goodman Brown'. In what ways do these symbols contribute to a reading of both texts?
4. Is intertextuality a useful umbrella concept for understanding and discussing the relationship between the Bible and literature?

Further reading

Raymond Brown, 1982, *Epistles of John*, New York: Doubleday.

John Calvin, 1959, *The Gospel According to St John 11–21 and The First Epistle of John*, D. W. Torrance and T. F. Torrance (eds); trans. T. H. L. Parker, Grand Rapids, MI: Eerdmans.

Michael J. Colacurcio, 1984, *The Province of Piety: Moral History in Hawthorne's Early Tales*, Cambridge, MA: Harvard University Press.

Craig A. Evans and James A. Sanders (eds), 1993, *Paul and the Scriptures of Israel*, Sheffield: JSOT Press.

Michael Fishbane, 1985, *Biblical Interpretation in Ancient Israel*, Oxford: Clarendon Press.

Richard Harter Fogle, 1952, *Hawthorne's Fiction: The Light and the Dark*, Norman: University of Oklahoma Press.

Nathaniel Hawthorne, 1835, 'Young Goodman Brown', in L. S. Person (ed.), 2005, *The Scarlet Letter and other Writings*, Norton Critical Edition, New York: W. W. Norton & Co, pp. 178–88.

Richard B. Hays, 1989, *Echoes of Scripture in the Letters of Paul*, New Haven: Yale University Press.

Wolfgang Iser, 1974, *The Implied Reader: Patterns of Communication in Prose Fiction from Bunyan to Beckett*, Baltimore: Johns Hopkins University Press.

Wolfgang Iser, 1978, *The Act of Reading: A theory of Aesthetic Response*, Baltimore: Johns Hopkins University Press.

Christopher M. Johnson, 1988, 'Intertextuality and the Psychic Model', *Paragraph*, 2 (March 1988), pp. 71–89.

Julia Kristeva, 1969, 'Word, Dialogue and Novel', in L. S. Roudiez (ed.); transl. T. Gora, A. Jardine and L. Roudiez, 1980, *Desire in Language: A Semiotic*

Approach to Literature and Art, New York: Columbia University Press, pp. 34–61.

Colin G. Kruse, 2000, *The Letters of John*, Grand Rapids, MI: Eerdmans Publishing Company.

Steve Moyise, 2008, *Evoking Scripture: Seeing the Old Testament in the New*, London: T & T Clark.

Steve Moyise, 'Intertextuality and Historical Approaches to the Use of Scripture in the New Testament', in R. B. Hays et al. (eds), 2009, *Reading the Bible Intertextually*, Waco, TX: Baylor University Press, pp. 23–34.

Stephen S. Smalley, 1984, *1, 2, 3 John*, Waco, TX: Word Books.

5

Narrative Criticism and the Role
of the Reader
Part 1

In Chapter 2, when we considered what it meant to read the Bible as literature, we introduced a way of reading John's Gospel that took seriously the narrative unity and design of that text. In this chapter, we examine such narrative criticism in more detail and in particular how it has developed in biblical studies over the past 30 years. In the next chapter, we will discuss its near relation – reader-response theory – as it has been applied to biblical and literary texts.

Narrative criticism as applied to Gospel exegesis is a good example of the contentious place literary critical methods have had in the field of biblical studies as, in various forms, it has sought to read against the prevailing historical trend of much biblical scholarship. The history of the way biblical scholars have sought to use this method is also typical of the interaction between the two disciplines: just as narrative criticism was losing popularity in literary studies, in some circles it was becoming the new 'key' to Gospel scholarship. However, as often happens, over time the insights it has brought to biblical studies have tended to be absorbed into more mainstream but much less theoretically aware biblical commentary. In this chapter, we will trace the development of narrative criticism in biblical studies, and then seek to read both the parable of the Prodigal Son and Charlotte Brontë's novel *Jane Eyre* according to some of its guiding principles. As part of these readings, the particular sub-genre of parables and their reception will be examined, and the parabolic aspects of *Jane Eyre* will be highlighted. Here we will find that the relationship between the reader, the text and both the implied narrator and the world of the actual author will be central to our discussion. In the next chapter, we will consider more avowedly reader-centred readings of literary texts, and discover the role of narrative criticism in the assimilation of that approach within biblical studies.

Narrative criticism: history and terms

In the late 1970s and early 1980s, there was a move in literary studies to explore and describe the autonomous unity and internal coherence of a literary work, which came to be labelled as 'narratology' or narrative studies. Originally a heavily structuralist approach, later proponents of this line of enquiry used the term to cover any theory of narrative and narrativity. These studies asked what assumptions a text made about its narrator and its reader; what did the way the story was told imply about who was telling the story and who was reading it; in what ways did a text seek to elicit a response from its reader? As this approach was taken up within biblical studies, it was combined with the ongoing influence of the New Criticism of the 1950s, which placed an emphasis on 'objective' analysis of a piece of literature, rather than on any consideration of the author's intention. In its purest form, narrative criticism of the Bible – most usually applied to the Gospels and to the Book of Acts, as the most obviously story-like texts there – disregards issues of historicity or later reception, and seeks to understand the text as a closed story completely on its own terms as literature. Such narrative critics focus on the narrative of each biblical text as a whole, and seek to offer an interpretation that takes into account all of the elements of the narrative. To do this, they assume the coherence and unity of the text under discussion, an assumption that is not always made by more traditional biblical scholars.

Before looking more closely at points of friction between narrative criticism and other interpretative approaches to the Bible, let us first define some key terms. Theories of narrative most often read texts as communications between an implied author and an implied reader. The *implied author* is constructed in the text from the totality of the values, the view of the world and the dominant point of view offered throughout the story. The *implied reader* is the constructed interpreter of the story that the story itself assumes, in terms of his or her knowledge, action or emotion. Both of these narrative reconstructions may be very different from the actual author and any real-life reader, and should not be confused with either. A modern reader, if he or she is following the principles of narrative criticism, will aim to read the text in the way the implied author intends: in other words to be the best implied reader as possible. This will involve reading it (or hearing it) in the form the author assumed, for example, as a play or in one sitting; and finding out everything the author would have expected the reader to know and believe but not to bring in any other prior knowledge or beliefs. Furthermore, interpreters must be aware of the difference between *story*, the characters, settings and events that make up the plot; and *discourse*, which is the way these aspects of the story are used, how they are presented to the reader. The characters, events and settings that make up the plot, in terms of both story and discourse, are the stuff of discussion and analysis for narrative critics.

If we take the example of character in a text (and characterization in the Gospels has become a popular field of study for biblical scholars), we can tease out the difference between story and discourse as an approach to analysis. On the level of story, narrative critics ask what type of characters appear in the text, what distinguishes them from each other in terms of their thoughts, actions and types, how consistent is the characterization throughout the text and, most importantly, what is the point of view of each character. Characters may be grouped together, as the disciples are in the Gospels, and given no distinguishing features; or characters may be drawn in great detail as individuals. They may change over the course of the story, or stay the same. The level to which a reader identifies with a character, and the nature of that identification, is often in line with the point of view of the protagonist. On the level of discourse, a narrative critic asks about the methods and strategies used to convey to the reader the types and points of view of various characters. Often the distinction is noted between the narrator telling the reader something about the character, from the point of view of the implied author ('The rich man went away sad'); and the reader being shown something about a character, from the reported point of view of other characters (when Jesus commands the children not to be turned away, and comments that the kingdom of heaven belongs to such as these (Matthew 19.13–14), he is revealing rather than asserting something about children as a group character, but also something about himself). The speech, actions, thoughts and beliefs of a character are all aspects of characterization that are of interest to a reader at the level of discourse, and where conflict between any of these aspects occurs, the reader is called upon to decide which is the most reliable.

While these distinctions and levels of interpretation may all be categorized and exemplified in this way, at times in the practice of narrative criticism they are not so easy to distinguish. In a narrative reading, the construction of the implied reader may be very far from the response of any actual reader, whether ancient or modern, and this lack of congruity raises questions about the effectiveness of the literary text – or the plausibility of the interpretation. The construction of the implied author, particularly in biblical studies, is often less easy to keep separate from the actual author as the narrative critic conceives him or her, and it is in this area that the peculiarities of biblical narrative criticism may be distinguished from the more purely literary approach. The need for this adaptation may be understood within the context of the development of literary studies of the Bible in general and narrative criticism in particular, which has been out of the context of interpretation firmly rooted in historical criticism: looking through a biblical text in order to seek to understand more about its genesis and the world to which it refers. Any reading that sought to read the text on its own terms, with the assumption of its unity and coherence, commonly seemed to go against the genre of the Gospels themselves; the intention of the author, whose role, at least in redaction criticism, was key; and the history of the interpretation of the Gospels, which had been based on the pericope rather than the literary whole.

One of the biblical critics who first championed the application of narrative criticism to Gospels interpretation was David Rhoads, who, in the early 1980s and along with Donald Michie, a literary critic, sought to investigate formal aspects of narrative in the Gospel texts, in particular Mark's Gospel, focusing on the world of the narrative alone, and those rhetorical strategies used to tell the story. Their book, *Mark as Story: An Introduction to the Narrative of the Gospel*, was first published in 1982, and will be reissued for the second time (with Joanna Dewey as co-author), in 2012. In this seminal book, it was the closed world of the story that was to be considered, rather than the history or theology behind the text (echoing the concerns of New Criticism noted above), and the emphasis was to be on the unity of the narrative, rather than the way small pieces of tradition were brought together (thus entering the ongoing debate about whether Mark's Gospel was the work of an artistic hand, or a clumsily stitched together compilation). This approach assumed, at its core, that the Gospels were good literature, and therefore the sort of 'close reading' demanded by narrative criticism was a worthwhile pursuit. Its followers then set about demonstrating how the Gospels work as literature, although its critics continued to assert that the Gospels should not and could not be considered literary art. Mark's Gospel will be considered from this perspective in more detail in the next chapter.

At least in part to defend their approach, many biblical narrative critics have conflated the idea of the actual author with that of the implied author in their writing, seeking to justify their claim that there was deliberate artistry behind the Gospel texts. In their article, 'Reconceiving Narrative Criticism', Petri Merenlahti and Raimo Hakola highlight a significant quotation from Rhoad's and Michie's early and influential book on the narrative criticism of Mark:

> the writer [of Mark] has told the story in such a way as to have certain effects on the reader ... The author has used sophisticated literary techniques, developed the characters and the conflicts and built suspense with deliberateness, telling the story in such a way as to generate certain emotions and insights in the reader.[1]

As Merenlahti and Hakola note, a purely text-centred approach would not be concerned with the historical author at all. Rather it would be the narrator, the storyteller as inscribed in the text itself, which would be of interest.

---

1 David Rhoads and Donald Michie, 1982, *Mark as Story: An Introduction to the Narrative of a Gospel*, Philadelphia: Fortress Press, p. 1, quoted in Petri Merenlahti and Raimo Hakola, 'Reconceiving Narrative Criticism', in David Rhoads and Kari Syreeni (eds), 2004, *Characterization in the Gospels: Reconceiving Narrative Criticism*, London: T & T Clark, pp. 13–48, here p. 22.

If the actual author's role is invoked, then historical considerations have to be brought into the discussion, which narrative critics of the Gospels have sometimes been reluctant to do. Nevertheless these same narrative critics continued to ask similar historical questions to those of the redaction critics who had gone before them. And while redaction critics stressed the episodic, fragmented nature of the Gospels, and sought to explain their bringing together, finding seams and gaps in the narrative to prove their point, narrative critics stressed the inherent narrative unity of the Gospels, brought about by the artistry of the literary hand that created them. This has led to attack both from historical critics who have been unconvinced by arguments of literary cohesion; and from postmodern literary critics, who are also interested more in gaps and textual fissures than in the discovery of overarching narrative design. Indeed, critics following the latter approach specialize in demonstrating ways in which narratives resist any attempt to mould them into one unified whole: the internal logic of a text is always constructed rather than intrinsic, and the contingent influence of the reader is central to this construction. Here is one place in which traditional literary reader-response criticism and the narrative criticism of the Gospels are in tension.

Developments in literary theory, and the ongoing insights of historical criticism, including genre studies, have all highlighted the importance of the role of the actual reader across time in the creation of meaning out of texts. The social and ideological context in which a text was written has also become more important in both literary and biblical studies. Narrative biblical criticism, at least in its early incarnation, swam against this tide in its belief in the intrinsic and discoverable unity of Gospel texts, which has meant it has been open to criticism on several fronts. However, it continues to offer tools for the interpretation of texts that are useful, for example highlighting the difference between the showing and telling of character types, and the importance of point of view in a text. These tools of analysis have been integrated into many readings of literary and biblical texts that would not label themselves as narrative critical, but that take seriously the way in which a text is constructed to have an effect on the reader. With these tools in hand, we turn now to our two texts. In the next chapter, we will look more closely at reader-response criticism, the more radical cousin of this approach.

Charlotte Brontë's novel, *Jane Eyre*, responds well to a reading that is sensitive to its narrativity. Point of view, the role of the implied author, and characterization are all issues that repay careful consideration in the novel. Rather than compare *Jane Eyre* with a whole Gospel, I offer a reading of a very famous parable, the parable of the Prodigal Son. A narratological reading of a parable avoids the complicating factors of historicity that a reading of a Gospel would involve. A parable may have been told to make a theological point or points, but in itself it claims no reference to historical events. While some of the Gospels claim to have been written to provoke belief in a historical character and so anchor themselves in a particular time and with a particular purpose, parables

may be read as free-floating narratives: their contexts, literary and historical, need not be considered as integral to their meaning (although some
would argue that they should be). The Gospels struggle to be considered as
fiction, but parables do not, and the distinction is helpful for narrative critics. Merenlahti and Hakola comment: 'While communication in fictional
narratives can be described as a game of make-believe, in non-fictional
narratives we meet a game of commitment and belief.'[2]

They go on to explain that the implication of this distinction is that in
non-fictional narratives, the narrator represents the author, while in fictional narratives the notion of the implied author comes into play, who
may or may not be identified with the actual author. While this distinction
explains the difficulty narrative critics have faced when interpreting the
role of the author in the Gospels, in the parables this difficulty is at least
partially dissolved. Point of view and implied authorship again become
issues to be wrestled with, released from the constraints surrounding the
Gospels as a whole.

Moreover, in both texts, characterization and character types and traits
may be explored in similar ways. At times this way of reading the parables
has led to very fixed and formulaic typological interpretations, but in both
Jane Eyre and many of the parables, characters do seem to invite identification with wider ideas and references. I will suggest that the novel may be
read as a parable of sorts, with a similar use of stock characters as is found
in the parables of Jesus: but also that the novel invites participation by the
reader, and makes use of the element of surprise and even shock in a way
that is similar to the rhetorical strategy of the parables. Using some of the insights offered by narrative criticism as it has been applied to both literary and
biblical texts, we will discover that a comparative reading of the parable of
the Prodigal Son and *Jane Eyre* highlights significant features of both texts.

Charlotte Brontë (1816–55)

The daughter of an evangelical clergyman, Charlotte grew up in a rectory
in Haworth in Yorkshire, one of six children. She was educated first at
a Clergy Daughters' School at Cowan Bridge, where conditions were so
harsh that she blamed them for the death of two of her sisters at an
early age – many have argued that this school was the model for Lowood school in *Jane Eyre*. After this unfortunate experience, the remaining
children were educated at home, and developed a rich imaginative and
literary world of their own. In her early twenties, Charlotte worked as a

---

2 Merenlahti and Hakola, 'Reconceiving Narrative Criticism', p. 36.

teacher and then as a governess in various families, then in 1842, she went with her sister Emily to study languages in Brussels. She fell in love with the owner of the school, M. Heger, although this was apparently not reciprocated, and she returned to Haworth in 1844. With her sisters, she made an attempt to break into the publishing world, using the male pseudonyms Currer, Ellis and Acton Bell and, in 1847, her novel *Jane Eyre* was published. By 1848, with their novels receiving much critical and popular attention, the sisters made themselves known, but due to the deaths first of their brother, and then of Emily that year and Anne the next, Charlotte was unable to enjoy her success or respond to the many invitations that she received. She married her father's curate in 1854, and died the next year. While during her lifetime she was the most admired of all of the Brontë sisters, her work was criticized for its unseemly depth of passion and feeling.

Jane Eyre is a classic text for narrative critics as it has a clearly defined implied author, the Jane of the title. The point of view, whether shown or told, is exclusively hers, and it transpires at the end of the book that the story has been told many years after the eventual marriage of Jane to Rochester, which forms the climax of the novel. Jane explains:

> My tale draws to its close: one word respecting my experience of married life, and one brief glance at the fortunes of those whose names have most frequently recurred in this narrative, and I have done. /I have now been married ten years.[3]

The implied reader, who has been directly addressed throughout the novel (not just in the famous 'Reader, I married him' line),[4] is drawn into the story with skill, almost as if he or she were being read to by a patient and kindly teacher. As she is bringing her story to a close, Jane asks, 'You have not quite forgotten little Adèle, have you, reader? I had not.'[5] While gently chiding the reader, who is assumed to be more interested in Jane's fate than that of Rochester's irritating ward, Jane presents herself as a caring stepmother who is in control of the narrative and of all of the characters who are in need. However, a slight note of discord is introduced in the way she continues. Jane explains that she felt that the school Adèle had been sent to was too strict, and so:

> I took her home with me. I meant to become her governess once more: but I soon found this impracticable; my time and cares were now required by

3 Charlotte Brontë, 1847, *Jane Eyre*, 1973 edn, London: Granada, p. 479.
4 Brontë, *Jane Eyre*, p. 477.
5 Brontë, *Jane Eyre*, p. 478.

another – my husband needed them all. So I sought out a school con-
ducted on a more indulgent system; and near enough to permit of my
visiting her often, and bringing her home sometimes ... As she grew
up, a sound English education corrected in great measure her French
defects.[6]

There is something grudging about this: Adèle remains a problem to be
solved, and her needs are viewed as secondary to those of Rochester.
Jane, who had longed for a home as a child, brings Adèle back to her
home only 'sometimes'. Adèle's perceived French defects are corrected
'in great measure', rather than fully: there is no sense that she was accepted as she was, as Jane has found acceptance of herself by Rochester;
and some stain or defect remains. While it is tempting to associate Jane
as narrator with Brontë herself, and many have found biographical elements in the novel, a consideration of the narrative strategy employed
highlights a potential distance between the actual and the implied author. Jane's point of view is not presented uncritically, a point that is
reinforced by the revelation that the story is told from a much later perspective, with much time having passed to allow for reflection. While the
implied reader is being invited to collude in Jane's narrative, drawn in by
its direct address and gentle chiding, it could be argued, from the conflict
between Jane's experience as she has presented it, and her later thoughts
and actions as she has described them, that Jane's point of view is not to
be accepted without question. With no other point of view offered, the
reader is nonetheless shown that Jane may not be as completely reliable
or innocent of prejudice as she portrays herself.
    A good example of this is the incident that leads to Jane's imprison-
ment in the red room, from near the beginning of the novel. The first–
time reader is presented with the events as if they are being described
at the time; the point of view is assumed to be that of Jane as a young
child. At the end of the novel, the narrator reveals to the reader that the
perspective was in fact that of a woman, married and with a child of her
own. Jane has been sent to the room because she has been accused of
hitting the son of the family, who is presented as odious and cruel. She
comments: 'There were moments when I was bewildered by the terror he
inspired, because I had no appeal whatever against either his menaces or
his inflictions.'[7] With the hindsight of the end of the novel, this assessment is revealed to be that of someone who has stereotyped the boy as a
monster, and herself as innocent victim. As she admits, 'I really saw him
as a murderer'[8]: given that the action against her was the throwing of a
book, this is more the reaction of an adult who has built up the incident

---

6 Brontë, *Jane Eyre*, p. 479.
7 Brontë, *Jane Eyre*, p. 14.
8 Brontë, *Jane Eyre*, p. 15.

with significance, than that of a young child who is used to the physical knocks of a Victorian family. In the red room itself, Jane describes her mental state:

> 'Unjust! – unjust!' said my reason, forced by the agonizing stimulus into precocious though transitory power; and Resolve, equally wrought up, instigated some strange expedient to achieve escape from insupportable oppression.[9]

The effect on a first-time reader is to perceive Jane as a classic victim of universal persecution; a child with insight into the wrongs of the world, rather than as a young girl with a naughty reputation in an extended Victorian family. While the narrator goes on to hint that she has reflected on this scene, and concluded that there were wider forces at work, this hint is not developed any further until the end of the novel:

> I could not answer the ceaseless inward question – *why* I thus suffered; now, at the distance of – I will not say how many years, I see it clearly. /I was a discord in Gateshead Hall; I was like nobody there.[10]

By refusing to divulge information, and yet offering an interpretation that gives herself a unique and special status, Jane as implied narrator is asserting and retaining control over the narrative, and building herself up as privileged and significant. The reader is given enough clues in the way the narrative is told to be able to question this perspective, particularly once he or she has reached the end of the novel, but the text demands alert reading in order to distinguish between the various layers of narrative strategy. Such an alert reading offers the possibility that Jane's narrative of her experience is not to be taken at face value, and her interpretation of events is not to be accepted without critical appraisal.

Many narrative critics of the Gospels assert that a similar alertness is needed to read these texts, and some argue that their approach has paved the way for the introduction of reader-response criticism, which places an even greater interpretative role on the reader. All stress, in a way that literary critics of novels do not have to, that the autonomous narrative world of the text is a valid locus of enquiry, and that the unity of the Gospels makes such readings possible. The shifting points of view in a Gospel, particularly obvious in John's Gospel (see, famously, John 21.24–5; and also the Book of Acts), which redaction critics read as evidence of a multiplicity of sources, for the narrative critic point to literary strategy. When a narrator interrupts the flow of his story to explain something, as in Mark 5.41, where the narrator translates the Aramaic 'Talitha

---

9 Brontë, *Jane Eyre*, pp. 19–20.
10 Brontë, *Jane Eyre*, p. 20.

kumi', and then in verse 42 comments that the girl who was healed was 12 years old, a redaction critic, trying to glean historical information from the text, argues that Mark's readers, and perhaps the editor of Mark himself must not have been Aramaic speakers, although these words of Jesus were treasured and remembered by that early Church community. He or she would go on to discuss the significance of a girl being 12 years old, and the puzzle that exists between the child being called a 'little girl' by Jesus and yet, in that culture, being of marriageable age. He or she might suggest that the redactor of Mark must have got the story wrong, or mixed it up with another story. A narrative critic would be more interested in the way in which the implied narrator of the text puts himself in a position of privilege over events by both including the Aramaic and offering a translation, and would want to consider the pattern created by other examples of such breakings-in to the narrative. He or she would also want to explore the significance of the number 12 in the rest of the Gospel, and the role of children as a stock character in the text, and what his interaction with children reveals about Jesus in comparison to other characters.

For our purposes, Gospel parables offer a convenient introductory point of comparison with literary texts. Parables have come under intense hermeneutical scrutiny over the years, and as self-contained fictive units they have demonstrated a remarkable tolerance to being read with profit from many literary critical, and other, methodological perspectives. While the literary context in which they are found may be of interest, particularly to those readers who seek to understand the redactional peculiarities of each Gospel editor, they may also be read as independent literary creations. There is an ongoing debate between those who argue that 'any interpretation which does not breathe the air of the first century cannot be correct';[11] and those who find the parables speak as well to contemporary situations as they did to their original ones, arguing that the reading of someone with no knowledge of the context in which Jesus taught may be as valid as a more traditionally historical one.[12] While this debate speaks more directly to issues raised by reader-response criticism, as we have noted and as we discuss in the next chapter, it may be argued that narrative criticism initiated and prepared the way for that approach in biblical studies. What is important to note here is that the parables as narrative discourses are effective beyond their settings in the Gospels or

---

11 Klyne Snodgrass, 2008, *Stories with Intent: A Comprehensive Guide to the Parables of Jesus* Grand Rapids, MI: Eerdmans, p. 25.

12 See, for example, the reading of the Parable of the Prodigal Son from the perspective of someone who had run away from an abusive situation in childhood, offered by Mary Ann Beavis in '"Making up Stories": A Feminist Reading of the Parable of the Prodigal Son (Luke 15.11b–32)', in M. A. Beavis (ed.), 2002, *The Lost Coin: Parables of Women, Work and Wisdom*, London: Sheffield Academic Press, pp. 98–122. This reading will be considered in greater detail in the concluding chapter of this book.

in their historical contexts. I will argue that the tools of narrative criticism may give us a way to explain why this is.

The parable of the Prodigal Son (Luke 15.11–32) is one of the longest of the parables of Jesus, and undoubtedly one of the best known and loved. Much commentary has been offered on its historical background: how shocking, in its context, would be the request of the younger son for his inheritance before his father had even died; the extent to which he had fallen, that he had resorted to looking after pigs; the wantonly undignified response of the father, running towards his son, who had broken the kinship ties which bound together members of village society; and the understandable but equally socially inappropriate response of the older son to his father's joyful actions. Many have read the parable as a response to the historical situation of Jesus and the first disciples, who were being called upon to justify to other groups, such as the Pharisees, their practice of eating with those who were regarded as sinners.

However, the parable also speaks powerfully as literature, addressing human needs that are universal, as the way in which it echoes in later literature, and the prevalence of the term 'prodigal son', often without an understanding of its original meaning, suggests. Its narrative structure is classically simple, with three main characters who are always shown in various forms of dialogue, never all three together. The implied narrator is detached at the start, in the KJV translation commencing the story in a traditionally folkloric way: 'A certain man had two sons' (Luke 15.11). However, as the story continues, the point of view changes and, unusually for biblical narratives, something of the motivation and emotions of the characters is revealed. The cool narrative detachment lasts until the younger son is far from home. The reader is given no indication of the reason behind his desire to leave the family, and this lacuna has been of compelling interest to modern interpreters. But after the son's money has been 'wasted . . . with riotous living' (v. 13), a judgemental perspective from the implied author worthy of the older son himself, as the reader will come to realize later, the younger son is described as being 'in want' (v. 14). The reader is given a poignant insight into the depth of his desperation with the observation that he 'would fain have filled his belly with the husks that the swine did eat' (v. 16). From the narrative detachment of the beginning of the story, there is now a shift of point of view: the reader is given access into the mind of the younger son, and any lack of sympathy for him that the beginning of the story might have encouraged is dispelled. The very modern-sounding phrase, 'when he came to himself', which leads to the internal monologue in which the younger son plans what he will say to his father, signals a sense of reintegration of his character, the beginnings of a new attitude that will literally lead him home. His worthy intentions are clearly signalled and a set of expectations is constructed that the reader is drawn into. However, just after the reader is given access to the character of the younger son, the focus shifts to the perspective of the father. The distance between them is closed by the father running to embrace the young man, and the reader is told of his feelings of compassion and shown evidence of it in his command to the servants to honour his son and prepare a lavish party. The expectation that has been set up, that the son will have to ask to be re-admitted into the house as a servant, is turned upside down by the overwhelming nature of his father's response to his return.

The exaggerated nature of this response has led some modern commentators to question the motives of the father, finding his eagerness to re-integrate the son into the family with public rejoicing somewhat sinister.[13] Certainly the introduction of the older son adds a discordant note to the description of the celebrations, although he also attracts the sympathy of the reader by the way in which his entry onto the scene is described. Again, spatial dimensions are used to signal narrative significance. The older son was absent when the younger son returned – he was 'in the field' (v. 25), presumably working dutifully. His distance from the centre of the action is highlighted by his hearing the 'music and dancing' in the house, his refusal to enter, and his initial approach to a servant for information. His anger and refusal to join the party may seem petulant, more like the action of a young and jealous child than a grown man, but when he speaks and reminds his father of the many years he had served him, with no reward (and the mention of the friends with whom he might have celebrated with a 'kid' (v. 29) shows the reader that he is a man with his own social network, and not a peevish recluse), the reader's sympathy is provoked. All this despite the disparity between his interpretation of what his younger brother has been doing while in the far country ('devoured thy living with harlots' (v. 30)) and what the implied author had stated was a squandering 'with riotous living' (v. 13). His father's response is conciliatory, reassuring and moving, invoking profound categories of death and life, lostness and being found to describe the change in his younger brother. But in narrative terms this perspective is neither explicitly validated nor challenged, beyond the father's voice being the last one to be heard. The response of neither son to this repeated assertion of the father is given, and his is certainly the dominant voice in the text. The younger son has moved far away but is finally situated at the centre of the home and the celebration; the older son remains on the periphery, in an ambiguous place not only spatially, but in the family, for while he has been told that everything the father has is his (v. 31), the younger son's return leaves the new workability of the family dynamics in disarray. What will the younger son do; what will he live off; where

---

13 For a full discussion of the disfunctional nature of this family, and in particular the motives of the father, from both ancient modern perspectives, see Beavis, '"Making Up Stories"', pp. 98–122.

does this leave the older son? None of these questions is answered and the older son remains within earshot of the party, but not a participant.

Perhaps the father holds the narrative key. The story begins with him and ends with him. We hear the voices of the two sons only briefly, but his voice is the one that makes things happen (the fatted calf is killed, presumably the ring is brought, certainly the dancing begins). While the younger son goes through a change of perspective, and the older son is called on to change his understanding of events, the father's point of view is consistent throughout. From the moment the reader is given an insight into his mental attitude (one of 'compassion' (v. 20)), and shown that attitude in his lavish actions, going out to both sons, rather than waiting for them to come to him, to the statement that closes the narrative, the father is accepting and welcoming. The reader has been led through the narrative from the impersonal ('A certain man had two sons' (v. 11)) to a new, constant and warmly surprising understanding of this man as a father with sons who push him away. The characters are universal, the intra-family relationships of distance and closeness speak to people across time, but it is the father to whom the main characters are shown to have to relate and find a way of being with. Reading the parable alert to its narrative, such as its structure, characterization and point of view, suggests that it might more accurately be called the parable of the constantly compassionate father, rather than the prodigal son. It is his perspective the reader is called to share, and for him the reader is asked to have sympathy.

There is a final issue of comparison that might be made between this parable and *Jane Eyre*, and that is the way both texts have been read such that characters have a representative function beyond their role within the closed world of the story. Allegorical readings of the parables have been common since the time of the early Church, giving theological meaning or significance to many or all aspects of a parable. And so, famously, in Augustine's interpretation of the parable of the Good Samaritan, among other correspondences, the attacked man is Adam, the priest and the Levite are the priesthood depicted in the Old Testament, the Good Samaritan is Christ himself and the oil and wine are the comfort brought by hope and the impetus to work for the kingdom, the donkey is the incarnation and the inn is the Church; even the innkeeper is given significance as the Apostle Paul. While not all allegorical readings are as contrived or as comprehensive as this, some commentators argue that this way of reading is more meditation on the biblical text than interpretation of it, and warn that it replaces the intention of Jesus as teller of these tales with the teaching or ideology of the Church.[14] For such scholars, these readings bring presuppositions to the text that fail to allow the parable to speak

---

14 See, for example, Snodgrass's caution against allegorical readings in his *Stories with Intent*, pp. 4–7.

as it was originally intended. While literary criticism of the sort we have been considering here tends to emphasize the role of the reader in the creation of meaning, in fact traditional narrative criticism of the Gospels would uphold such an attempt to read the text on its own terms, without presuppositions. More critical literary readings, however, question whether such value-free readings are ever possible, although they would also recoil from the notion that the recovery of the author's intention was possible or desirable. Perhaps, therefore, into the complexity of this relationship between author, reader and text, the role of allegorical readings of both the parable of the Prodigal Son and the novel *Jane Eyre* might briefly be considered with interest.

Nearly all commentators on the parable of the Prodigal Son implicitly or explicitly assume that there is an association between God and the father, sinners and the younger son, and those who consider themselves 'righteous' and the older son. This correspondence between the image and reality of the world of Jesus and of the parable is hard to avoid, even for the most ardently anti-allegorical parable reader. Some have gone further, however, and have identified the robe, the ring and the shoes with the Holy Spirit, the gift of God to repentant sinners; for others, the feast represents the messianic banquet; modern and early Church readers have understood the father's going out to the younger son as an allegory of the incarnation; for others, taking this idea to its conclusion, Jesus is identified with the Prodigal, who leaves and then returns to the father. The role of the atonement in the parable remains contentious, and springs again from an attempt to correlate the theology of Jesus, or the early Church, or later interpreters, with the details offered in the story. In the costly action of the father, who runs to meet his son, or even in the death of the fatted calf, some have found a mirror of atonement theology. Others, seeking to situate the parable in the life of the Lukan community to which it was read and for whom it was included, find the Gentiles or Gentile Christians lying behind the figure of the younger son, and the Jews or Jewish Christians represented by the older son. Some suggest the parable speaks of conflict in the community between those who accepted Gentiles into the Church, and those who did not; or between the Church community and the synagogue. Such readings, for traditional commentators such as Klyne Snodgrass, are 'gratuitous assumptions', which place too much theological weight on the parable. Rather, they would argue, the story moves at a fast pace, evading such associations, and instead offers a straightforward and 'powerful presentation of the saving grace of God', not a picture of the whole Gospel.[15]

When we turn to *Jane Eyre* we find there have been similar, although perhaps not so comprehensive, attempts to find associations between characters and events in the novel and the religious views of Charlotte

---

15 Snodgrass, *Stories with Intent*, p. 139.

Brontë or at least of her time. Mr Brocklehurst, the headmaster of Lo-wood School, is often described as a character who embodies, negatively, the evangelical tradition in the Victorian Church. With its emphasis on conversion, the Bible, activism in the social sphere and a stress on the atoning sacrifice of Christ on the cross, aggressive evangelicalism stood in contrast to the more gently intellectual direction of the Oxford Movement and its followers, who sought signs of transcendence in the sacraments and in poetry. Brocklehurst may be read as a critique of a perverted version of evangelicalism. He runs the school for children who have been abandoned, but there is no compassion behind his philanthropy, merely hypocrisy: his own daughters are dressed in extravagant fashions, including, Jane tells the reader, a 'false front of French curls', while a schoolgirl with naturally curly hair is accused of being 'in defiance of every precept and principle of this house ... conform[ing] to the world so openly – here in an evangelical, charitable establishment'.[16] Brocklehurst's use of the Bible is also mocked for its literalism. When he berates the headmistress for allowing the girls to have replacement food after a burnt breakfast, Brocklehurst reminds her of the words of Christ:

His warnings that man shall not live by bread alone, but by every word that proceedeth out of the mouth of God; ... 'if ye suffer hunger or thirst for my sake, happy are ye.' Oh, madam, when you put bread and cheese, instead of burnt porridge, into these children's mouths, you may indeed feed their vile bodies, but you little think how you starve their immortal souls![17]

The characterization of Brocklehurst and his association with a particular type of evangelicalism is not hard to see. Strikingly, no mention is made by him of the redemptive hope that was such a feature of the evangelicalism of the time. More subtle is the identification sometimes made between Helen Burns, the girl Jane befriends at Lowood, and the Oxford Movement. Helen's calm acceptance of her fate is in contrast to the judgemental activism of Brocklehurst. She is aware of, and seeks, that overflow of immanence into a glimpse of the knowledge of God that the Oxford Movement so prized, telling Jane:

The sovereign hand that created your frame, and put life into it, has provided you with other resources than your feeble self ... Besides this earth, and besides the race of men, there is an invisible world and a kingdom of spirits: that world is round us, for it is everywhere ... and

---

16 Brontë, *Jane Eyre*, pp. 71–2.
17 Brontë, *Jane Eyre*, p. 70.

God waits only the separation of spirit from flesh to crown us with a full reward.[18]

For Helen, reality exists unseen, religious knowledge is hidden to all but the faithful; reserve rather than militant evangelism will draw others to God, as she draws Jane to a new way to be amid the deprivations of the school. Her passion burns, as her name suggests, but it is contained within a controlled and accepting frame and framework. Helen may be read as offering a contrasting approach to God, with references to the Oxford Movement of the time, but she is not presented uncritically. Her presence in the novel and in Jane's life is brief, and her controlled acceptance of her fate is shown not to be a way that Jane, who is more spirited and independent, is able, or should, follow.

Finally in *Jane Eyre*, the character of St John Rivers has puzzled many readers who have sought to find in him an analogy or even allegory of an aspect of Brontë's religious context. As with both Helen Burns and Brocklehurst, Jane is shown to be unable to submit to his version of authority, but that version is not easily categorized. Rivers is shown to be driven by ambition, glory, self-importance as well as a deep sense of moral duty. When Jane suggests he might give up his plan to become a missionary in order to marry Rose, his response is emphatically focused on his own eternal destiny, with the benefit he perceives he will bring to his converts very much a secondary product of his own devotion to his calling:

> Relinquish! ... My great work? My foundation laid on earth for a mansion in heaven? My hopes of being numbered in the band who have merged all ambitions in the glorious one of bettering their race – of carrying knowledge into the realms of ignorance ... Must I relinquish that? It is dearer than the blood in my veins. It is what I have to look forward to, and to live for.[19]

However, Rivers, with his cold beauty and singularity of purpose, is an ambiguous character in the novel in a way in which Brocklehurst is not. Jane is shown to be unable to bend her will to his; is repelled by his attempt to overpower her into marriage to him out of duty, and the reader is drawn to taking Jane's perspective. And yet it is Rivers's words that close the novel, in the form of an excerpt from what Jane assumes will be his last letter to her. She comments 'his hope will be sure; his faith steadfast' as he writes:

---

18 Brontë, *Jane Eyre*, p. 77.
19 Brontë, *Jane Eyre*, p. 398.

My Master ... has forewarned me. Daily he announces more distinctly, – 'Surely I come quickly!' and hourly I more eagerly respond – 'Amen; even so come Lord Jesus!'[20]

Although Mr Rochester's conversion following his experience of the fire, in Jane's perspective, is miraculous and enabling of a new, Edenic life together, it is the energy and vision of St John Rivers's own words that the reader is left with. Some critics have found this ending uncomfortable, its ecstatic use of the Bible here incongruous with the more nuanced approach taken by Jane and Rochester elsewhere. Certainly St John Rivers resists any attempt to cast him in an allegorical light, and his presence at the end of the novel reminds the reader that there is power in the Bible without any mediation of literary or historical context. And perhaps the signalling of that effect of the Bible on its readers is what Rivers may be understood to stand for: as a man who embodies the starkness and strangeness of the Bible's message.

We have ended up at some distance from the narrative critical aims we described in the opening section of this chapter, and have yet to come to any conclusion about the placing of meaning in the spectrum of the reading process, whether of a biblical text such as a Gospel or a parable, or a novel such as *Jane Eyre*. But narrative critical tools of characterization, point of view and in general terms the *way* the story is told have proved useful in this comparative reading of the novel and of the parable. An awareness of narrative in its broadest sense has offered new ways to approach both texts, reading both as unified and coherent pieces of literature. In the end, we have noted that characterization pushed into allegory brings the reader's role in the creation of meaning into the forefront of the discussion. While this role for the reader is generally accepted in literary circles, it is less widely accepted with reference to the Bible. However, when we come to reader-response criticism in its most pure form, and the response of more postmodern critics, we will find that the issue of place of the reader cannot be ignored.

Questions

1. Consider the differences between showing and telling in a biblical episode, such as the Feeding of the 5,000 (see the different versions of the story in Matthew 14.13–21; Mark 6.32–44; Luke 9.10–17; John 6.1–14). What do the categories of implied author and implied reader add to your reading of an episode such as this?

---

20 Brontë, *Jane Eyre*, p. 481.

2. Suggest examples of novels that share narrative features with the parables of Jesus in terms of their ability to refer to wider issues and concerns.

Further reading

Charlotte Brontë, 1847, *Jane Eyre*, 1973 edn, London: Granada.

Petri Merenlahti and Raimo Hakola, 'Reconceiving Narrative Criticism', in David Rhoads and Kari Syreeni (eds), 2004, *Characterization in the Gospels: Reconceiving Narrative Criticism*, London: T & T Clark, pp. 13–48.

Mark Allen Powell, 1990, *What is Narrative Criticism?*, Minneapolis: Fortress.

James L. Resseguie, 2005, *Narrative Criticism and the New Testament: An Introduction*, Grand Rapids, MI: Baker Academic.

David Rhoads and Donald Michie, 1982, *Mark as Story: An Introduction to the Narrative of the Gospel*, 2nd revised edition, with Joanna Dewey, 1999, Minneapolis: Augsburg Fortress Press.

David Rhoads and Kari Syreeni (eds), 2004, *Characterization in the Gospels: Reconceiving Narrative Criticism*, London: T & T Clark.

Klyne Snodgrass, 2008, *Stories with Intent: A Comprehensive Guide to the Parables of Jesus*, Grand Rapids, MI: Eerdmans.

6

Narrative Criticism and the Role
of the Reader
Part 2

In the last chapter, we began to consider ways in which the text and the reader might be understood to interact with each other. Narrative criticism, in its slightly different forms in literary and biblical studies, was introduced and examples offered of readings taking this approach. In this chapter, we will look in greater detail at literary theories that take the role of the reader seriously, tracing something of the history of reader-response theory and offering examples of readings of a text from this perspective. In recognition of the fact that narrative criticism rather than reader-response criticism probably remains the most influential approach to have come into biblical studies from literary criticism, the chapter will conclude with a reading of Mark's Gospel using insights from this interpretative field. A critique of such readings will then be offered from biblical critics who argue that they fail to take on board the radical challenge to the possibility of objective interpretation that reader-response criticism inevitably throws up.

Of critical concern to both literary and biblical studies is the issue of the importance of the reader in the assigning of meaning to a text. On one level, it could be said that without a reader, or a reading, a text remains a collection of squiggles on a page. But equally many would want to argue that the reader is not free to make the text mean whatever he or she wants it to: the text constrains the possible range of meanings, at the very least. And then there is the influence of the context or reading community in which a reading is made: how important is this in the reading that results?

The role of the reader only became of explicit concern in the latter part of the last century. In the 1950s, the reader's importance was stressed in contrast to Formalism's emphasis on the literary work as an independently existing object, freed from the influence of its author, reader or context. For many, such a high view of the text seemed to fly in the face of the evidence that the reader's influence, across time and context, resulted in radically different interpretations of the same literary work. For those in the first wave of reader-response criticism, while their starting points were all different, it was the reader who created the text just as much as the author: it was in the interaction between the reader and the text that meaning was arrived at, and in which scholarly interest should be placed. While this was a rejection of everything Formalism stood for, which was the attempt to make objective that which was always in danger of sliding into subjectivity, such critics were in fact standing in a developing tradition that included scientific enquiry itself. The frame of reference of the observer, whether in the study of science or literature, was coming to be understood as crucial to the resulting reading.

A second unifying theme among the early reader-response critics was the recognition of the place of rhetoric as the means by which a text affects the reader. Rhetoric, with its long history in the field of literary criticism, is usually defined as the art of persuasion. While, in classical times, the term referred to the formal elements in a literary work, and not directly to the effects these might have on the reader, more recently it has been used to describe the way in which the author directs the reader. Most famously, perhaps, Wayne Booth, in his *Rhetoric of Fiction*, explored the concepts of the implied narrator and reader as aspects of the rhetorical strategy of the author. As was argued in the previous chapter, this strand of reader-response criticism in literary studies has proved most amenable to mainstream biblical studies, spawning a movement more or less of its own, namely narrative criticism. Booth took seriously the evidence of the text itself, which both implied and directed a reader's involvement, understanding and knowledge. The actual reader, like the actual author, is less important to this interpretation than the reader and narrator constructed by the text.

Booth uses Jane Austen's *Emma* to demonstrate the rhetorical strategies employed to guide the reader to take Emma's perspective on events, whether accurate or not. As we noted earlier, in the famous interventions in Charlotte Brontë's *Jane Eyre*, the narrator, the now middle-aged Jane, directly addresses the reader – 'Reader, I married him' – in a way that creates intimacy and implies a relationship of trust based on the sort of truth-telling blunt speaking for which Jane is noted. Just as Jane is not to be conflated with the actual author, Charlotte Brontë, so the actual reader should not be assimilated with this implied reader: the actual reader may choose to read against the rhetorical strategy employed, and to question what he or she is being encouraged to accept. Jane's revision of her story, particularly of her childhood, from a much later perspective, may be unreliable in notable ways.

While early critics who took an interest in the role of the reader were still maintaining the importance of the stable text in the act of interpretation, more recent writers on reader-response criticism have given the text much less of a role to play. One such critic is Wolfgang Iser, for whom the reader's perception or experience of reading the text cannot be separated from a text as independent meaningful entity. Rather than explaining the text as a thing 'out there', to be objectively discussed, for Iser the critic's role is to consider the effect of the text on the reader. While Iser continues to maintain that the structure of the text still has some role to play in the creation of the reading, specifically in the influencing of the implied reader, he moves away from the essentially Formalist view that there is one 'correct' interpretation of a text, to which all readings aspire. Each reader, coming to the text with his or her own experiences, will find that the text will produce different effects on them. Indeed, for Iser, no text provides all the answers, and there are gaps or blanks in every text – their 'indeterminacy' – that readers must fill in in order to make meaning for themselves. Readers share in the creativity of the author in this way. In his use of the idea of the implied reader, Iser posits a sophisticated reader who is aware of literary conventions and has the ability to decode what the text is telling him or her: but this is not the only possible and plausible reading for Iser, whose phenomenological approach demands that all experiences of a text are of interest. The text remains the work of the author, but the range of its interpretations is inexhaustible.

Hans Robert Jauss maintains a similar interest in the rhetoric of a text, although his focus is on the history of the reception of a text in a particular period. It is public reception that is key here, and the mode of exploration is the comparison of reviews, diaries and letters. Jauss tries to establish what he would call the 'horizon of expectation' of a reading community, the prior knowledge of such a community about the conventions of a genre. This horizon more or less determines what will be the reaction of readers from a particular context to any given text – and is likely to vary over time. The classic Scottish novel, James Hogg's *The Private Memoirs and Confessions of a Justified Sinner*, was considered to be too confusing, and even blasphemous, when it was published in 1824. More than half of its first editions went unsold. It was not until it was republished in 1947, with an Introduction by the French novelist and critic André Gide, that the novel gained critical recognition, mainly due to the 'discovery' of its strong psychological resonances. Jauss's work stresses that there is nothing universal about any literary text. No one horizon of interest establishes a final meaning. A verdict about a literary text may only be established if interpretations from different time periods are brought together in conversation, and horizons self-consciously fused in some way.

Finally, we should consider the influential, and developing, work of the critic Stanley Fish as an important voice in reader-response interpretation. For Fish, who coined the phrase 'affective stylistics' to describe his approach, Formalism's insistence on a poem as a static object with one overall meaning to be grasped at once is open to question. In his first foray into the world of reader-response, *Surprised by Sin*, Fish argued that meaning is negotiated by individual readers as the act of reading a text progresses. Rhetorical strategies may surprise readers, and make them change their minds about the text's meaning as they read. The act of informed reading, a sequential and dynamic act demanding awareness of literary conventions, is the focus here. In his later work, Fish placed even more emphasis on the reader, and less on the role of the text in controlling meaning. In *Is There a Text in This Class?*, he argues that both meaning and the literary text itself are created in the act of reading. The text's role as autonomous controller of interpretation is no longer allowed. Rather, readings create meaning when they are carried out within interpretative communities. When common reading strategies, informing expectation and understanding, are pooled, a meaningful literary text is created.

While most critics will generally accept that many readings of a particular text are possible, because of the wide variety of experiences brought to bear on the text by individual readers, few would agree that literary criticism is a completely relative field, with all possible readings equally valid. However, reader-response criticism, in its many forms, has highlighted the various ways a text might affect its readers, and it has robbed the text per se of some of its authority, giving it instead to the reader. It has also highlighted that the cultural heritage of readers inevitably plays a part in the creation of meaning, and here wider examples of literary theory are valuable too, as they inform readings from particular periods. Wherever an interpreter stands in the debate about the relative importance of the reader, it may be argued that reader-response theories have changed the way the reader is regarded, whether in literary or biblical studies. In this chapter, interpretations of two texts are compared, which give the reader a considerable amount of influence and authority: Mark's Gospel and Robert Louis Stevenson's novella, *The Strange Case of Dr Jekyll and Mr Hyde*.

Reading *The Strange Case*

The Strange Case of Dr Jekyll and Mr Hyde is a short text with a wide echo and a presence in the common imagination that goes far beyond the number of people who have read it. This is likely to affect a reading of the text itself and, indeed, in the Introduction to the Penguin edition of 2002, Robert Mighall advises that '[n]ew readers will . . . find the experience more rewarding if they forget all their preconceptions, and put themselves in the position of Stevenson's first readers who knew nothing about "Jekyll and Hyde"'.[1] Later we shall see in what ways a first-time, 'innocent', reading might differ from one influenced by prior

---

1 Robert Mighall, 2002, 'Introduction', in Robert Louis Stevenson, 1886, *The Strange Case of Dr Jekyll and Mr Hyde*, London: Penguin, p. x.

expectations. First, it will be useful to set the text in its historical context, if only to draw a contrast between the author's potential and plausible intentions and interpretations that have gone beyond this.

The novella was written when Stevenson was in his mid-thirties, living with his wife and stepson in Bournemouth, and still financially dependent on his father. Written with a commercial market in mind, the tale was conceived as a 'shilling shocker', as requested by the editor at Longmans. It was to appear at Christmas 1885, the traditional time for such spooky tales although, as it happened, the tale was not published until January of the following year. Placed firmly in the tradition that included Charles Dickens's 'A Christmas Carol', *Jekyll and Hyde* was to conform to the genre of Gothic sensation fiction while offering something much more sophisticated and demanding of the reader. While Gothic fiction tended to be set a time long ago and in places of decay and degeneration far away (think of Mary Shelley's *Frankenstein* from 1818, or Bram Stoker's *Dracula*, which would appear in 1897), *Jekyll and Hyde* is set in present-day London. The horror resides within an apparently respectable individual, making the everyday seem infused with threat. And the supernatural element is downplayed in favour of a more scientific explanation. Finally, the use of collected and varied testimony evidence rather than a straightforward narrative demands more of the reader, and invites him or her to participate in the detective work of the central character, Utterson.

This final point about narrative strategy and its effect on the reader is not unique to this text in the Gothic tradition. Hogg's *Memoirs and Confessions of a Justified Sinner* offered equally ambiguous and multiple perspectives on the true nature of its protagonist. Although not a particularly popular text at the time, Stevenson had read it and commented to his friend that it was a 'real work of imagination' which had 'haunted and puzzled' him.[2] Wilkie Collins in the 1860s, a master of 'Sensation' fiction, used diaries and testimonies to construct early forms of detective stories involving murder and intrigue. When Stevenson offers individual documents written by different characters, a quasi-newspaper report of a murder plus an explanatory letter by Dr Jekyll himself, he builds up a sense of veracity while extending suspense – for none of these witnesses offers the full story, not even Jekyll's final 'Full Statement of the Case'. The use of the term 'Case' highlights the respectable milieu in which the events occur – a world of lawyers and doctors, although their expected expertise is undercut by their eventual inability to solve the case or deal with its implications. This is a 'strange' case indeed.

Where a contemporary reader and an original reader of this novella might have different views and experiences of the text is in the understanding of the two characters of its title: Dr Jekyll and Mr Hyde. Few

---

2 B. A. Booth and E. Mehew (eds), 1995, *The Letters of Robert Louis Stevenson*, vol. VII., New Haven and London: Yale University Press, pp. 125–6.

people coming to the story today would be unaware that these two characters are one and the same person, two opposed aspects of a single personality. However, an original reader has no grounds on which to make this assumption. The relationship between Hyde and Jekyll is the issue to be resolved by Utterson and by the reader. On the surface, two less likely companions are hard to imagine. Jekyll is an apparently clean-living, respectable bachelor in his fifties; Hyde is a repellent and violent young man who inhabits the shadows of the night. And yet the reader discovers, with Utterson, that Hyde has access to Jekyll's money and his house, and to his estate after his death. As Mighall comments, Jekyll's stated 'very great interest' in Hyde, who is not his son, is very likely to have aroused suspicion in his first readers that they were in an illegal sexual relationship, despite Jekyll's reassurance to Utterson that 'It isn't what you fancy; it is not so bad as that'.[3] Stevenson understandably might draw back from describing the possibility of such a relationship in what was to be a popular text, but by suggesting the subject in this way, he manipulates his reader to make an assumption about an 'unnatural' relationship, only to turn such expectations completely around when he reveals the extent of the 'unnatural' relationship between the two men. This moment comes in Lanyon's doctor's surgery, expressed in the language of a medical examination by Dr Lanyon himself. As Lanyon experiences the transformation of the repulsive Hyde into the respectable Jekyll, the revolution of all he had understood in medical, psychological and epistemological terms is such that it leads to his death, apparently from shock. The shaking of the foundation on which he had built his life, that scientific explanations could be found for all that he experienced, is too profound when appearances and reality are revealed to be so fundamentally at odds. The modern reader misses the shock of such a revelation.

However, modern readings bring much to the text that Stevenson's original readers are unlikely to have considered. Stevenson's contemporaries commented on the age-old theological issues presented in the story, some seeing it as a form of allegory based on the dual nature of humanity, as described in Paul's Epistle to the Romans and elsewhere. The text was the basis of contemporary sermons and religious writing, used to illustrate humanity's ultimate depravity and deep need for Christ's salvation and redemption. A modern reader is more likely to see Freudian theories of repression exemplified here. Jekyll's severe repression of his desires, due to his extreme sensitivity to the opinion of others and need to maintain a respectable appearance, leads to a fundamental split in his personality. Jekyll comments in his 'Full Statement of the Case' that 'all human beings, as we meet them, are commingled out of good and evil': but the creation of his alter ego, Hyde, is 'pure evil'.[4] The aspect of his

---

3 Mighall, 'Introduction', p. xix.
4 Stevenson, *Strange Case*, p. 58.

self that he has attempted to control for so long, under the influence of the mysterious combination of drugs, grows in power until, as Jekyll describes it, it was 'knit closer to him than a wife, closer than an eye; [and] lay caged in his flesh, where he heard it mutter and felt it struggle to be born; and at every hour of weakness, and in the confidence of slumber, prevailed against him and deposed him out of life'.[5] Jekyll's psychological equilibrium is altered:

> I had voluntarily stripped myself of all those balancing instincts, by which even the worst of us continues to walk with some degree of steadiness among temptations; and in my case, to be tempted, however slightly, was to fall. Instantly the spirit of hell awoke in me and raged.[6]

The notion of unstable subconscious forces at war within Jekyll's psyche, which he has attempted to control but that threaten to overpower him, speaks clearly to anyone familiar with the work of Freud and later psychologists. Such a reader might want to explore more deeply the sexual nature of these forces – and find it significant that Jekyll describes Hyde as being 'knit closer to him than a wife', in a text filled with men and their various degrees of closeness. Even Stevenson's contemporary readers were aware of some sexual element at play here, and not just the suggestions of an erotic relationship between Jekyll and Hyde. Gerard Manley Hopkins, writing to Robert Bridges, commented that 'the trampling scene [Hyde's collision with the young girl in the dead of night] is perhaps a convention: he was talking of something unsuitable for fiction'.[7]

Pushing such readings further, Richard Dury reads much into the hand that Jekyll looks down upon, and by which realizes he has involuntarily turned into Hyde. The hand was 'corded and hairy'.[8] For Dury, the hand is a reference to the story of Jacob and Esau in Genesis 27, in which Jacob deceives his blind father Isaac into giving him the precious paternal blessing by putting a goatskin over his hand and arm. This makes him seem more like his hairier and older twin, Esau. Although Isaac recognizes that it is Jacob's voice, he accepts the evidence of the hairy hand he holds, and gives Jacob his blessing, believing him to be Esau. Dury comments:

> Psychologically, we could see this tale (*Jekyll and Hyde*) as the effective rejection by the individual of the hands, body, instinctive nature, and sexuality (the disinheritance of Esau and his 'hairy hands') and

---

5 Stevenson, *Strange Case*, p. 69.

6 Stevenson, *Strange Case*, p. 64.

7 Paul Maixner (ed.), 1981, *Robert Louis Stevenson: The Critical Heritage*, Routledge & Kegan Paul: London, p. 229.

8 Stevenson, *Strange Case*, p. 66.

the granting of pre-eminence of the mind and soul (Jacob, the 'voice'), thanks to the collaboration of the super-Ego, Isaac.[9]

Such a reading depends on knowledge not just of Freudian theories of the subconscious but also of the Hebrew Bible. Reader-response criticism would accept the validity of this interpretation as meaningful, although it is unlikely to have been intended by Stevenson himself – or, as an interpretation of the Jacob, Esau and Isaac story, to have been intended by the writer of Genesis. Allowing readings of texts from different periods to influence and reflect on each other, as we discussed with regard to the issue of intertextuality, is an important aspect of reader-response criticism, especially if 'text' is taken in its widest sense. For a discussion of such a reading to take place, of course, a shared pool of knowledge is at least a useful, if not a critical, prerequisite. This is where Fish's interpretative community notion comes in, both in the creation of readings, and in their evaluation. All readers stand in a tradition of reading, which changes over time but affects any reading at any one time – and *Jekyll and Hyde* has shown that a first reading may well produce a very different understanding from a later one; or from the one that was influenced by a common idea of what the text is about. A reading of the Gospels is likely to be influenced by such common ideas about the content of these well-known texts, which a reading of one of them may or may not bear out. Similarly, the issue of a first-time reading compared with repeated readings may well be of interest.[10]

Reading the Gospel of Mark

As was noted in the previous chapter, the Gospel of Mark was the first Gospel to be the subject of interpretations that took the role of the reader seriously, perhaps in part because it throws up a number of puzzles that such methods are adept at handling and explaining. Narrative gaps and characters that are not fleshed out psychologically, aspects of the text with which Mark's Gospel abounds, leave many opportunities for the reader to create meaning for him or herself, or to be guided to create, in narrative critical terms. Iser's textual indeterminacies, which each reader

---

9 Richard Dury, 'The Hand of Hyde', in William B. Jones (ed.) 2003, *Robert Louis Stevenson Reconsidered: New Critical Perspectives*, Jefferson, NC and London: McFarland, pp. 101–16, pp. 103–4.

10 Larry J. Kreitzer considers the ways in which what he asserts is the modern obsession with sex has influenced modern interpretations of both *Jekyll and Hyde* and Romans 7. See Larry Kreitzer, 1993, *The New Testament in Fiction and Film*, Sheffield: Sheffield Academic Press. As an example of a specific reading of readings of earlier texts, Kreitzer's chapter 'Dr Jekyll and Mr Hyde: Re-reading the Pauline Model of the Duality of Human Nature' (pp. 88–126) is extremely useful.

must resolve, are much in evidence when Mark's Gospel is read from beginning to end – not something that a hearer of the Gospel in a liturgical setting often attempts. Wayne Booth's notion of the implied author and reader also plays well with regard to Mark's Gospel, a text whose genesis is uncertain. While many suggestions have been made about who the actual author was, and who was his intended audience, no conclusions can be made with any certainty or consensus. An interpretation based on the theories of Booth offers a way to work around this difficulty for more traditional historical-critical interpretations. If there is an implied author and reader within the text itself, this is all that is needed to understand the literary meaning and significance of the text. Even if the text is anonymous and the original readers are unknown, all texts have an implied author and reader, which may be identified and considered. While this is 'soft' reader-response criticism indeed, with its focus technically more on the text than on the reader, it provided a way for New Testament scholars to start to consider the Gospels apart from historical-critical concerns, and in particular to ask *how* the text affected its reader. Mark's Gospel, with all its difficulties for traditional criticism, proved to be a fruitful place to start such a task.

The literary critic Frank Kermode first took Booth's categories of implied reader and author and straightforwardly and in a groundbreaking way applied them to a reading of Mark's Gospel (as he had done with John's Gospel in *The Literary Guide to the Bible* from 1987, discussed in Chapter 2). In his *The Genesis of Secrecy* (1979), the way meaning is created from narrative in literary texts is compared with readings of Mark's Gospel as a narrative text. The same issues of gaps in information needing to be filled, the use of rhetoric and point of view to direct the reader's sympathy and textual expectation of the pre-knowledge of the reader are considered in the cases of all of the texts. Earlier, in 1966, in the first edition of *The Sense of an Ending*, Kermode had explored the way readers seek order and design in literature, as in life. The Gospels, the poetry of T. S. Eliot and other literature are all read for the way in which the reader may find in them a gratifying conclusion. While Kermode's work, with its focus on the relationship between the reader and the text, literary or biblical, was influential in the field of literary studies, it was less well-read by biblical scholars. For them it was not until late in the 1970s that more reader-focused literary criticism became an approach to be considered seriously. The biblical scholar David Rhoads collaborated with his colleague in English Literature, Donald Michie, to produce *Mark as Story* in 1982. In the following years, scholars such as J. D. Kingsbury, R. Alan Culpepper and Robert C. Tannehill produced readings of the four Gospels and Acts using a text- and reader-focused approach, in contrast to the author-focused readings of traditional historical criticism. As we have noted, this 'narrative criticism' is rather different from any specific approach taken within literary studies, but it has influenced biblical studies, in particular the study of the Gospels, widely. It would be a rare Gospel commentary today that did not mention narrative strategy of the text as a whole or the characterization of, for example, the disciples in the text.

As was detailed in the previous chapter, narrative biblical critics are interested in the text on the level of story, its plot in terms of its characters, settings and events; and on the level of discourse, how the plot is developed and how the characters, settings and events are conveyed to the reader. And so, the significance of what happens in a story is considered alongside the significance of the way in which the events are presented. The use of rhetorical devices such as irony, suspense, symbolism and the ordering of events are all considered in so far as they affect a reading of the text. The point of view of characters is of interest, but also the way in which point of view is presented and may change through a narrative, affecting the sympathy and understanding of the implied reader. Further the distinction may be drawn between what a reader is told by the implied author directly and what a reader is shown by the implied author through an event being reported by a character's words or thoughts. Where the narrative of a text is set is also important to this approach: in social and in temporal terms, but also symbolically, with places such as wilderness and sea all carrying their own connotations for an implied reader aware of, for example, the significance of these places in the Hebrew Bible. On the level of discourse, whether readers are left to assume much about a story's setting, create a setting for themselves, or there is a wealth of detail given, may all affect an interpretation of the text. Not all narrative critics will place equal emphasis on all of these possibilities for comment, but the range offered here, including plot, point of view, characterization and setting in terms of both story and discourse, gives a flavour of the areas of interest to those taking this approach.

Some biblical commentators stress that their work is more based in reader-response criticism than in narrative criticism, although I would argue that even in the work of these critics, the implications of reader-response criticism are not taken fully on board. A good example of this is Bas M. F. van Iersel's *Mark: A Reader-Response Commentary*, which, despite its title, focuses almost entirely on the reader implied in the text, and the text's first readers (often conflated). Later readings, including of modern readers, might be mentioned briefly, but with little sophistication. For example, with reference to Jesus' teaching about the coming Kingdom of God in Mark 1.15, van Iersel rather states the obvious in closing his section on Mark 1.1–15:

> The readers of later generations, including our own, are confronted with the considerable problem that the interval between the moment these words were written and the moment of reading becomes greater and greater, so that it will be increasingly difficult to understand the nearness of God's kingdom as something that can be measured

in hours, days, years, generations and centuries. Accordingly, those readers will understand and experience the nearness of God's kingdom differently.[11]

The specific implications of this modern-day reading, or even any examples of actual contemporary readings, are not offered or discussed. The focus remains on the constructed response of the first readers. With regard to this verse, van Iersel asks 'how [did] the first readers respond to the coming of God's kingdom and the call for repentance and faith'? He confidently answers his own question thus: 'As the book does not seem to be written for outsiders, they will generally have regarded themselves as having already answered the call.' The circularity of this argument does not seem to strike van Iersel as strange.

Mark's Gospel

Mark's Gospel is usually considered to have been the first of the Gospels to be written because of its simpler style and less developed theology in comparison with the others. Its author is unknown, although traditionally associated with someone with a connection to Peter, possibly the John Mark mentioned in Acts 12.12, 25; 15.37–39. The Gospel speaks of the persecution of followers of Jesus, which may place it in the 60s CE, when Nero was actively persecuting Christians; given the evidence of Mark 13, it is hard to state with certainty whether the Gospel is predicting the cataclysmic fall of Jerusalem that occurred in 70 CE, or reflects this as having happened. A conservative suggestion is that the Gospel was written between 65–75 CE. Once the relationship between Matthew, Mark and Luke began to be a focus of scholarly interest (the 'Synoptic Problem'), the majority view came to be that Matthew and Luke depended on Mark as at least one of their sources. Written in Greek, Mark is usually considered to have been written for a Gentile, possibly Roman readership – Jewish matters such as what Sadducees believe have to be explained (12.18) and Aramaic words translated (3.17), although Latin terms such as *praetorium* (15.16) are not. It is often suggested that the Gospel was intended for those who shared the author's belief in Jesus as Messiah (8.29), in the Hebrew Bible as the word of God (7.8) and understood what it means to say that Jesus died as a ransom for many (10.45). Rather than aiming to persuade those who do not believe, Mark's Gospel is usually described as written to comfort and encourage Christians from a different culture from the first disciples.

---

11 Bas M. F. van Iersel, 1998, *Mark: A Reader-Response Commentary*, Sheffield: Sheffield Academic Press, p. 108.

Many aspects of Mark's Gospel could and have been considered from the perspective of reader-focused narrative criticism. Here we will focus on two: the characterization of Jesus and the ending of the Gospel in narrative terms.[12]

The Gospel opens with a statement full of theological importance: the reader is told that what follows is 'the gospel (good news) about Jesus Christ, the Son of God' (1.1). This states the belief of the implied author, and becomes part of what the implied reader is expected to know and take into consideration as the story continues. Much of the irony of what follows, stemming from the reader knowing more than the characters in the text, is enabled by this opening assertion.

Further important signals are given to the reader in the verses that follow: in preparation for the appearance of John the Baptist, the implied author offers an explanatory quotation from Isaiah 40.3. John will be sent from God as 'a voice . . . calling: In the wilderness prepare the way for the LORD'. Immediately the setting of the story is placed within an existing running narrative, that of Israel with its shifting experience of sin and repentance, hearing and ignoring prophetic calls to return to God. The implied reader is now aware that Mark's story they are about to read/hear of Jesus is part of a pre-existing story, of which Isaiah's text is also a part. Traditional biblical interpretation would now go on to explore the theme of prophecy in the Gospel: the significance of Jesus' apparent self-understanding as a Jewish prophet (6.4); what this meant for those who heard him and understood he was a prophet (6.14–16; 8.27–28); also the relationship between Jesus' actions such as the feedings in the wilderness and the cleansing of the temple and the pattern of prophetic behaviour already established in the Hebrew Bible. The focus would be on the historical implications of this connection for an understanding of who Jesus was (or at least who he was understood to be by the Gospel writer).

Narrative, reader-based criticism is more interested in the effect on the implied reader of this placing of the narrative of Jesus' story within the wider context of the story of the Jewish people. And on the basis of this quotation from Isaiah, the reader is led to anticipate the arrival, heralded by John the Baptist, of the Lord himself. Having prepared the reader in this way, the low-key arrival, at 1.9, of Jesus in Galilee, not even a town associated with kingly rule, is a shock. The raising of expectation followed by such a humble appearance forces the reader to reconsider her or his understanding of the nature of God and of the one already introduced as the Messiah and the Son of God. However, the narrative goes on to

---

12 For a fuller discussion of issues such as these in Mark, from this perspective, see Morna Hooker's contribution, 'Good News about Jesus Christ, the Son of God', in Kelly Iverson and Christopher Skinner (eds), 2011, *Mark as Story: Retrospect and Prospect*, Atlanta: Society of Biblical Literature, pp. 165–80.

show in graphic ways that the status of this newly appeared figure is divinely established and confirmed: at Jesus' baptism a heavenly voice proclaims 'Thou art my beloved Son; with thee I am well pleased' (1.11).

In Mark's Gospel, narrative time moves swiftly in the first chapter. The temptation narrative is much briefer than in the other Gospels, focusing on the Spirit's role as Jesus' guide and on the way that the temptation follows so quickly after the moment of affirmation. Jesus states his purpose and demands a response: 'The time has come: the Kingdom of God is at hand. Repent and believe in the good news' (1.15). He goes on to call his disciples, teach in the synagogue, heal many and exorcize demons. This teaching, healing figure is full of energy and purpose. Most significantly, as the narrative progresses, his divine status is clearly demonstrated to any reader with a knowledge of the presentation of God in the Hebrew Bible. While traditional commentators might examine the use of titles ('son of God' and 'son of man') in Mark's Gospel to try to work out the Christology of the author, a narrative critic will focus instead on the way the text presents Jesus, not necessarily directly stating who he is.

A straightforward example is the healing of the paralysed man in Mark 2.1–12: Jesus first forgives his sins, and then only heals him in order to demonstrate that he does indeed have the (divine) power to forgive sins. As his opponents, the scribes, assert, 'Who can forgive sins but God alone' (2.7): here Jesus assumes divine authority and everyone watching him, including the reader, is made aware of it.

In the episode of the stilling of the storm in Mark 4.35–41, we have another important narrative clue to the implied identity of Jesus. The disciples, safe after Jesus has calmed the waves that had threatened to engulf them, ask in amazement, 'Who is this? Even the wind and the waves obey him' (4.41). Anyone committed to the message of Genesis 1 or to the Book of Job would answer – God alone. In this way, the implied author communicates on a narrative level with the implied reader, revealing rather than stating important information about his central character.

A modern reader might miss an important aspect of the claims being made, which the 'original' implied reader might have been expected to pick up, and this is in the area of Jesus' challenge to imperial power. Whenever Jesus is recognized as 'Lord' by, for example, the demoniac of 5.19 or the Syro-Phoenician woman in 7.28, there is the suggestion that this language challenges the 'lordship' of the Caesars. Jesus himself redefines his understanding of 'lordship' in contrast to the Gentile definition: 'You know that those who are supposed to rule over the Gentiles lord it over them, and their great men exercise authority over them. But it shall not be so among you' (10.42–43). Jesus goes on to overturn the expected order of service and lordship: both his followers and he himself have come to serve. Perhaps this implicit criticism of imperial overlordship is clearest in the confession of the Roman centurion as he watches Jesus die on the cross. When he asserts, 'Truly, this man was the Son of

God' (15.39), he is not only in ironic contrast to the disciples who might have been expected to realize the significance of Jesus' death, who have all fled the scene, but he is also highlighting a challenge to unquestioning loyalty to the Empire and all it represents. The implied reader, well aware of the reach of Roman rule, knows this, while a later reader might miss this narrative emphasis.

The hectic narrative pace of Mark's Gospel stops abruptly after Chapter 10. Up until this point, years have been covered in ten chapters. From Chapters 11–16, it is the final few days of Jesus' life that are described, suggesting that while Jesus' teaching and ministry are important to an understanding of his story, the events leading up to his death and resurrection have key narrative power. In many places in this second half of the Gospel, irony is used to establish a connection between the implied author and reader, which the characters within the story fail to understand. Jesus predicts that Peter will betray him three times (14.27–30); as he is beaten in 14.65, his guards mock him and demand that he prophesy for them; in the very next verse the story of Peter's betrayal, as Jesus predicted, is begun. Similarly, a placard is mockingly placed on the cross, announcing that this is the 'King of the Jews' (15.26): but the implied reader is aware from the baptism scene that this announcement is true, and Jesus is the Son of God, the legitimate king of the Jews. Into this double-layered scene of mockery and yet, for the reader, expression of truth about Jesus, comes the centurion's confession (15.39), which brackets all that has happened in the narrative with the assertion made at the very beginning of the Gospel, that Jesus is 'truly' the Son of God (1.1). Significantly, however, it is only in the context of Jesus' death that the centurion is able to grasp this truth. Jesus' death makes sense of all that has gone before, for both this character and for the implied reader. Jesus' opponents, in contrast, never come to this realization. The implied reader is in a privileged position, which affects every reading of the Gospel as a narrative text.

A final narrative point may be made about the ending of this Gospel. A glance at any modern translation of the text will reveal that there is some doubt about where the Gospel should finish. The earliest and most reliable manuscripts close with a group of women coming to the tomb to anoint Jesus' body. They find a young man, perhaps an angel, sitting beside the tomb, who tells them that Jesus is risen and they are to tell Peter and the other disciples that Jesus will go before them to Galilee, where they shall see him again. The women are overcome with fear and flee (16.8a). Later texts add that they 'said nothing to anyone, for they were afraid' (16.8b). Later texts still add a much more extensive resurrection account, very much in line with those found in Matthew and Luke (16.9–20). Historical enquiry has focused on the question of whether Mark intended the Gospel to end at verse 16.8a, later verses having been added to bring the text into line with the other Gospels, or whether a part of the original text itself has been lost, resulting in the enigmatic and incomplete ending of the earliest manuscripts. A narrative approach to the text accepts it as it is, and argues that such an ending is designed to make a powerful impression on the implied reader. Such an approach might suggest that the implied author has brought the implied reader to this point for a purpose. Jesus as central character has been demonstrated to have huge theological importance, and the faithful dedication of his life and revelatory power of his death has been contrasted with the fickleness of his disciples. The implied reader might be expected to realize both that these same disciples were empowered by the resurrection to lead the Church of which they are a part, and that they have a role to play in carrying the story forward. The story did not in fact end with the fearful silence of the women, for, as the reader is aware, the Church was born and has spread through the known world. Something must have changed the disciples from being weak and uncomprehending (see, for example, their ironic ignorance about where the food will come from to feed the multitude in 8.4) to having the power and motivation to convince others of the claims of Jesus. And so, while the immediate after-effects of the resurrection are not described by the implied author, the implied reader is aware of the ultimate effects of whatever the resurrection represented for Jesus' first followers, and is encouraged to consider what it might represent for him or her. As a narrative device, this abrupt ending is potentially sophisticated and rhetorically powerful.

A critique of readerly readings

In this chapter and in Chapter 5, we have explored the various potential roles of the reader in the creation of meaning in literary and biblical texts, offering two examples from each category. Some criticisms of these various approaches were offered in the previous chapter, particularly with regard to biblical texts, such as those of Merenlahti and Hakola, who noted the conflation in many narrative studies of Mark's Gospel of the 'actual' and implied author.[13] Before leaving a consideration of these approaches, we should also take note of much more strident criticisms that have come from more theoretically rigorous biblical critics. One such example is the chapter on reader-response criticism in *The Postmodern Bible*.[14] While agreeing that biblical reader-response criticism, such as that of Rhoads and Michie, 'may provide an important first step toward

---

13 Petri Merenlahti and Raimo Hakola, 'Reconceiving Narrative Criticism', in David Rhoads and Kari Syreeni (eds), 2004, *Characterization in the Gospels: Reconceiving Narrative Criticism*, London: T & T Clark, pp. 13–48, here p. 20.

14 The Bible and Culture Collective, 1995, *The Postmodern Bible*, New Haven & London: Yale University Press, pp. 20–69.

consciousness raising about our own reading experiences',[15] this chapter goes on to argue that it fails to 'expose the ideology or psychology that has led generations of biblical scholars to suppress their responses to their own reading experience . . . It is but a first step toward a self-conscious, self-reflexive critical praxis.'[16] The predominance of the belief that the historical experience and situation of the implied (and for this, read 'original') reader is recoverable and objective sits uneasily with any approach that is suspicious of the possibility of this as a goal.

The Postmodern Bible argued that while, for these critics, narrative criticism, and indeed much of the early reader-response criticism, continued to view the text and the reader as objective and separate, in fact, focusing on the reader erodes the idea of the text as objective object of study. When the text, and any historical event to which it refers, is truly understood as a narrative construct in the experience of the reader, the reader as critic is called upon to reflect on the influences, particularly the ideological and psychological forces, which result in one reading rather than another. Or one group of readers' readings rather than another such group's. To try to read Mark's Gospel as the original reader is to make huge assumptions about the historical but also sociological and ideological circumstances of that literary construct. And these assumptions are driven by the ideological and psychological influences at work on the contemporary critic. Feminist and liberationist readings, for example, demand that such assumptions are challenged and new readings from completely different perspectives are to be regarded as just as valid as those attempting to ground themselves in the historically plausible. Reader-response criticism has the potential to open texts, biblical and literary, to a new and wide range of readers who have traditionally been excluded from the debate. But to allow that to happen, the realization that all readings, including those of the 'academy', are constructed and contingent, needs to be reflected upon and acted upon. These ideas will be taken up in the next chapter, when we turn to feminist readings of the Bible and literature.

While narrative criticism, as used in biblical studies, may not be as reader-centred as many reader-response critics in literary studies would expect or demand, it has changed the way the Gospels in particular are read, just as reader-response criticism has shifted the way literary texts are approached. Some in both disciplines have held back from following this line of interpretation, fearing its subjectivity and loss of connection to the sort of objectivity that Formalism, or historical criticism, seemed to offer. Others have found it too timid and insufficiently accepting of the implications of postmodern readings of texts. In particular, narrative criticism of biblical texts often remains tied to a notion that the historical

---

15 Bible and Culture Collective, *Postmodern Bible*, p. 23.
16 Bible and Culture Collective, *Postmodern Bible*, p. 24.

context in which a text was produced is a key factor in determining the limits of the knowledge of the implied reader and author. Actual, later readings from a different context are of less interest, although the establishment of the implied author and reader in any text is surely also influenced by the context of the reader carrying out the interpretative task. Narrative criticism is very open to critical probing by more radical reader-response approaches, as well as to the critical scepticism of those who still hold to the possibility of recovering objective historical truths 'behind' a text – still a powerful force in biblical criticism. However, there is no doubt that the (re)discovery of the rhetorical power of the Gospels as narratives has influenced biblical studies, and the reader-centred nature of narrative criticism has had a key role to play in this shift of emphasis.

Questions

1. Are there readings of texts that are not valid in your view? Are the boundaries different for biblical and literary texts?
2. Where is meaning to be found in the interaction between author, reader and text? Is a text's relationship to historical events recoverable and if so, to what extent?
3. What forces are at work in the changing ways texts are understood? How important is the age, context, gender of the reader?

Further reading

The Bible and Culture Collective, 1995, *The Postmodern Bible*, New Haven & London: Yale University Press.

Wayne Booth, 1961, *Rhetoric of Fiction*, Chicago: University of Chicago Press.

R. Alan Culpepper, 1983, *The Anatomy of the Fourth Gospel: A Study in Literary Design*, Philadelphia: Fortress Press.

Stanley Fish, 1967, *Surprised by Sin: The Reader in 'Paradise Lost'*, Berkeley: University of California Press.

Stanley Fish, 1980, *Is There a Text in This Class?* Cambridge, MA: Harvard University Press.

Morna Hooker, 'Good News about Jesus Christ, the Son of God', in Kelly Iverson and Christopher Skinner (eds), 2011, *Mark as Story: Retrospect and Prospect*, Atlanta: Society of Biblical Literature, pp. 165–80.

Wolfgang Iser, 1978, *The Act of Reading*, Baltimore: Johns Hopkins University Press.

Kelly Iverson and Christopher Skinner (eds), 2011, *Mark as Story: Retrospect and Prospect*, Atlanta: Society of Biblical Literature.

Hans Robert Jauss, 1982, *Toward an Aesthetic of Reception*, trans. Timothy Bahti, Minneapolis: University of Minnesota Press.

Frank Kermode, 1979, *The Genesis of Secrecy: On the Interpretation of Narrative*, Cambridge, MA; London: Harvard University Press.

Frank Kermode, 2000, *The Sense of an Ending: Studies in the Theory of Fiction with a New Epilogue*, New York: Oxford University Press.

J. D. Kingsbury, 1983, *The Christology of Mark's Gospel*, Philadelphia: Fortress Press.

Larry Kreitzer, 1993, *The New Testament in Fiction and Film*, Sheffield: Sheffield Academic Press.

Paul Maixner (ed.), 1981, *Robert Louis Stevenson: The Critical Heritage*, London: Routledge & Kegan Paul.

Mark Allan Powell, 1993, *What is Narrative Criticism? A New Approach to the Bible*, London: SPCK.

James L. Resseguie, 2005, *Narrative Criticism and the New Testament: An Introduction*, Grand Rapids, MI: Baker Academic.

David Rhoads and Donald Michie, 1982, *Mark as Story: An Introduction to the Narrative of the Gospel*, 2nd revised edition, with Joanna Dewey, 1999, Minneapolis: Augsburg Fortress Press.

Robert Louis Stevenson, 1886, *The Strange Case of Dr Jekyll and Mr Hyde*, 2002 edition introduced by Robert Mighall, London: Penguin.

Robert Tannehill, 1986 and 1990, *The Narrative Unity of Luke – Acts: A Literary Interpretation*, 2 vols, Philadelphia and Minneapolis: Fortress Press.

W. R. Telford, 1999, *The Theology of the Gospel of Mark*, Cambridge: Cambridge University Press.

Jane Tompkins (ed.), 1980, *Reader-Response Criticism: From Formalism to Post-Structuralism*, Baltimore: Johns Hopkins University Press.

Bas M. F. van Iersel, 1998, *Mark: A Reader-Response Commentary*, Sheffield: Sheffield Academic Press.

7

Feminist Readings

In the previous chapter, we began to argue for the potential importance of the context of the reader in the widest sense of the term 'context'. The influence of ideological forces such as patriarchy, socio-economics and colour, argue some literary critics, needs to be reflected upon and exposed in order that a text's meaning for all readers is allowed to be heard. In this chapter, we will focus on readings of biblical and literary texts from a feminist perspective, aiming to discover new meanings in texts that have often been used to silence the voices and views of women. We will consider two biblical texts from feminist perspectives, the Book of Ruth and the parable of the Foolish Virgins, and read Margaret Atwood's classic science-fiction novel, *The Handmaid's Tale*, as a feminist critique of the Bible.

Of course, there is no such thing as a definitive feminist reading of any text, but it may be possible to identify some key features of readings from feminist perspectives. A common assumption is that the text of the Bible, in common with many other texts, is a product of a patriarchal culture and shares the profoundly androcentric prejudices of its time. Texts arising from these contexts have influenced readers not just in literary terms but also, particularly in the case of the Bible, by legitimizing contemporary and prejudiced views about women. Most feminist readers would agree that what the Bible says, and does not say, matters. For this reason, many feminist readers seek to expose the patriarchal ideology of such texts: some then to reject them completely, others to recover what they can from the wreckage, still others to re-write or recreate the voices that have been silenced. We begin by defining what such readers mean when they accuse texts of such patriarchal bias.

Patriarchy is literally the rule of the father over some men, those younger and in a subservient position to the patriarch, and over all women, who are excluded by virtue of their sex from positions of power. Under a patriarchal system, men hold all positions of power and the views, talents and contribution of women are debased and counted as being without inherent value. It is an ideology to which the biblical texts themselves bear witness and with which subsequent readings of the text collude. An awareness of this underlying network of power relationships goes beyond noting that all of the biblical texts, we assume, were written by men:

instead, readers who approach the texts with such an awareness observe that these power relationships affect all levels of narrative, character, point of view and the construction of what constitutes gender differences between 'feminine' and 'masculine'.

Continuing to take a broad-brush approach to this topic, we might say that most feminist critics bring to their reading of a text a strong acknowledgement of the insights of socio-historical criticism, and in general the vast difference between the concerns of the period in which the text was written and the concerns of the modern, feminist reader. Focusing on the construction of women and gender in a text, acknowledging these differences leads to questions being asked of the text that an original reader would be unlikely to have considered: which characters speak and which are silent; which act and which are given no role to play; what are the implicit and explicit concerns expressed by a text with regard to the relationships between men and women, power and powerlessness, and how are these expressed? Famously, this leads to a position of 'hermeneutical suspicion', as promoted by Elisabeth Schüssler Fiorenza in works such as *Bread Not Stone: The Challenge of Feminist Biblical Interpretation*. Rather than accepting the text as objectively 'true' in any sense, or bearing authority over the reader on any level, a hermeneutics of suspicion reads against the grain of the text. It takes seriously the understanding that such texts convey only the patriarchal views of men, not the real voices of women or a willingness to deal fairly with their concerns. Even texts that allow women to speak and to act as characters within the narrative reveal only what the dominant culture, patriarchy, wants or expects them to say and do. These female characters (and male ones too) are constructs of a system that promotes and supports male dominance. The implicit motives of the authors of the Bible should, on this view, be kept at a distance and treated with critical suspicion rather than acceptance. Feminist readings, then, are very different from more traditional female-centred approaches to a text, which concentrated simply on highlighting the female characters in the Bible or the feminine imagery used in places of God, often with a view to recovering something about the actual situation of women in biblical times. Feminist criticism reminds us that biblical texts reveal only what the dominant ideology, patriarchy, deems necessary to reveal. Consciously or not, the writers of the Bible portray only a construct of both genders, in which women only say and do what men, and probably men in power, believe they should.

The Woman's Bible

Writers about the feminist movement and its relationship with the Bible often start with the work of Elizabeth Cady Stanton, who led a movement in the United States in the late 1890s to give a voice to the biblical interpretation of female scholars. Women had been denied a role in the first major translation of the Bible since the Authorized Version of 1611, namely the Revised Version published under the auspices of the Church of England in 1888. The Women's Suffrage Movement in America was gaining popular support, and the dominance of men in the field of biblical interpretation, a major influence on the lives of many, was seen as one more bastion of male power to be challenged and overcome. Cady Stanton, a well-known suffragette of the day, chaired the 'Revising Committee' set up to allow women's perspectives on those parts of the Bible that had women's concerns at their heart to be heard. The result of this intellectual endeavour was *The Woman's Bible*, a two-volume work that was published in 1895 and 1899. Ahead of her time, Cady Stanton and her fellow female interpreters realized the role the Bible had to play in the maintenance of their society, which denied women power and influence at many levels. It was used to prevent women from stepping outside biblically sanctioned roles, but it also, when given divine authority, supported men's claim to have a special relationship with God, who had chosen them to convey his message. Cady Stanton argued that the Bible was the product of human minds, rather than the unerring voice of God: the fact that it resulted in the oppression of women was for her proof of this human involvement. For her, everyone had the right to interpret and question scripture, not just the educated and mainly ordained men of the past. And so *The Woman's Bible* was the product of those who had not been trained in biblical studies but who knew the Bible, were sensitive to its literary qualities and, most importantly, were aware of the damage it could do when it was taken as historical and authoritative fact. Although it was far from a runaway success at the time it was published, and not all suffragists supported its radical religious claims, *The Woman's Bible* was an important founding document not just for feminist criticism but also for any study of the Bible that takes the rhetorical effect of the Bible on its readers seriously.

The Woman's Bible and its changing place in the history of feminist criticism of the Bible reveals something significant about this approach. For it too has been criticized for failing to grapple with the other major injustice of its day, racism and in particular slavery. In exposing one set of inequalities it perpetuated another, giving black women no voice in the interpretation of the Bible, which it was purporting to open out to all who had been silenced by it. This serious charge has weakened the status of *The Woman's Bible* as a feminist icon, but it also points to the difference between feminism and the critical approaches we have considered so far. Feminism is not a way of reading or an interpretative stance: rather it is a collection of political positions and strategies, and an intellectual movement that is contested and continually up for debate. The experience of women in their encounters with institutions such as the Church, the academy or the state led to an impulse to critique those institutions, and new ways to understand those experiences were offered by the vocabulary of feminism: notions such as patriarchy and androcentricism and the validity of women's experience. However, over time, these notions have come to be regarded as only partial and preliminary in the feminist movement, which covers a much broader spectrum of understanding of power relationships. Feminist critique questions the placing of 'man' at the centre and in the privileged, normative position of history, epistemology and discourse. For womanist critique, it is not just 'man' in opposition to 'woman' who occupies this position, but 'man' from a particular class and ethnic group: womanist criticism extends to include opposition to any discourse, including feminist, which does not take this additional element of oppression into account, and wittingly or not takes on the role of such a position. Womanist criticism, then, a movement often associated with women of colour, critiques those aspects of feminism that take as their starting point the perspective of the white middle-class. Here is the root of the modern critique of *The Woman's Bible*. For both feminist and womanist interpretation, there is a reaction against any claim to universal or objective knowledge, which leads to the domination of one reading over another. This certainly puts it at odds with biblical studies in its traditional form, although its multiplicity of outcomes and movements makes it difficult to assess in a short introductory chapter such as this one.

If we look more closely at the history of feminist interpretation of the Bible in its broadest sense, we find first a move to recover or recuperate the witness of women in the Bible. From before even the work of Cady Stanton and her 'Revising Committee', some Victorian women were discovering in the Bible female role models to bolster their own struggles to be heard, particularly in the Church. Mary Magdalene, as the first witness of the resurrection who is told to tell the others, and Phoebe, the deaconess and helper of Paul in Romans 16, were just two of the named biblical women who might be taken as authoritative examples to be followed by contemporary women readers. This approach, while it might validate the work of a small number of special women who might claim to have the same extraordinary spiritual gifts as these mould-breaking exemplars, did not challenge or offer an alternative to biblical authority, and left the majority of women voiceless and powerless.

A hermeneutics of suspicion

As already mentioned, a hermeneutics of suspicion, most often associated with the work of Schüssler Fiorenza, shifts the weight of defining authority away from the biblical text and replaces it with a conviction that '*the* litmus test for invoking Scripture as the Word of God must be whether or not biblical texts and traditions seek to end relations of domination and exploitation'.[1] The task is wide-ranging and revolutionary:

> A feminist reading of the Bible requires both a transformation of our patriarchal understandings of God, Scripture, and the Church and a transformation in the self-understanding of historical-critical scholarship and the theological disciplines.[2] *+ Why s ofan kept powers?*

Such an approach assumes the androcentric nature of the biblical text and later interpretations, and that the text was written and has been used for patriarchal purposes. Now, the experience of women is the ground for interpretation and the ethical guide. The writing of history as revealed in the text is questioned by placing such experiences, both contemporary and from the time of the writing of the text, at the centre of the hermeneutical enterprise. The theological imperative of both the reader and the text is laid bare for scrutiny in this approach – and for both, the possibility of reaching a definitive, objectively 'correct' reading is assumed. This will bring the hermeneutics of suspicion into debate with feminist and womanist readings which challenge the very possibility of such certainty. However, as an approach, this has had a strong influence on biblical studies, and we shall pause here to consider the work of Phyllis Trible, whose readings of marginalized biblical characters such as Hagar and Tamar, and of the traditional heroine Ruth, are important markers in the field.

The Book of Ruth

Unusual in the Hebrew Bible, the Book of Ruth has a woman as its central character. Much of the setting of the narrative is the world inhabited by women, and Ruth herself demonstrates her heroic qualities in an act of solidarity shown towards her kinswoman by marriage. A short book of only four chapters, the background to the story is a famine in Israel, which results in a family from Bethlehem travelling to the nearby, but Gentile, land of Moab. There the patriarch, Elimelech, dies, leaving his widow Naomi. His sons, Mahlon and Chilion, marry Moabite women, Ruth and Orpah. The sons promptly die too, leaving the three widows childless and without means of support. Naomi decides to return to her homeland in the hope of finding support there and advises her daughters-in-law to stay in Moab, where they might find new husbands. Orpah

---

1 Elisabeth Schüssler Fiorenza, 1984, *Bread Not Stone: The Challenge of Feminist Biblical Interpretation*, Edinburgh: T & T Clark, p. xviii.

2 Fiorenza, *Bread Not Stone*, p. xvii.

reluctantly agrees, but Ruth makes the famous declaration, 'Intreat me not to leave thee, or to return from following after thee: for whither thou goest, I will go; and where thou lodgest, I will lodge: thy people shall be my people, and thy God my God' (Ruth 1.16). The two women return to Bethlehem and Ruth starts 'gleaning' from the edge of the harvest fields to provide for herself and Naomi. It turns out that these fields are owned by Boaz, a distant relative of Naomi's husband, who, by the laws of the time, potentially has a duty to marry Mahlon's widow. He protects Ruth, having heard of her return with Naomi, and after coming into close contact with Ruth as a result of a scheme of Naomi's, arranges that he is in the lawful position to marry her. A son, Obed, is born as a result of this marriage, who is viewed as the direct heir of Naomi. The narrative closes with the genealogical note that Obed is the ancestor of David (and therefore, for Christian readers, an ancestor of Jesus).

Phyllis Trible's stated aim in her readings of the Hebrew Bible from an avowedly feminist and literary perspective is to reach, as she argues with regard to the Book of Ruth, 'a theological interpretation of feminism: women working out their own salvation with fear and trembling, for it is God who works in them'.[3] Trible focuses on the unusual way in which, in this text, it is female characters who act out the text's thematic purposes and, in theological terms, represent the providence of God. For her, Naomi acts as a link or bridge between tradition and innovation; Ruth, in contrast, is a paradigm for the radical. Both may be ascribed feminist motivations. Trible reads Ruth's moment of decision in the first chapter as positive and significant. Ruth may be compared with Abraham in her decision to leave her native land. She makes the radical choice to follow another woman over the option of a conventional domestic life in her homeland, in doing so choosing to follow another God. The comparison with the heroic life of the patriarch is strengthened by the comparison in chapter 4 with matriarchs such as Rachel, Leah and Tamar (vv. 11–12) (although here her divinely agreed role as a producer of children for the Israelite dynasty is stressed), and by the famine motif of chapter 1 which sets up the narrative, just as it does throughout the story of Israel's succeeding generations in Genesis. For Trible, the key to all that follows lies in the first chapter: here Ruth, on a par with the patriarchs of Israel's past, breaks with the convention for her as a woman, and chooses to commit to an elderly woman and her fate, leaving behind all the security she has known, rather than to seek a husband at home. This action is divinely sanctioned by the result of the marriage to Boaz, engineered by Naomi, and the birth of a son and heir not just for Ruth and Boaz, but

---

3 Phyllis Trible, 1978, *God and the Rhetoric of Sexuality*, Philadelphia: Fortress Press, p. 196.

for Naomi and her son Mahlon. While in no place does God intervene directly, these women have enabled God's work, from curse to blessing.

Throughout the Book of Ruth, Trible asserts, it is women who control the content and the structure of the story. They stand and act alone at the beginning, although later Boaz is shown to react to their initiative. Chapter 4, in which there is a scene between Boaz, his 'rival' for Ruth's hand, and the elders, is for Trible 'the shock of reminder'[4] that this remains a man's world that still holds the patriarchal power to overturn the concerns of women. However, the introduction of the women of Bethlehem to the scene of the celebration of the birth of Obed refocuses the story so that women's concerns are integrated into a new beginning for men and women. There is wholeness after the fear and distress of chapter 1. The challenge Ruth presents to her established world is, argues Trible, the legacy of her story for all later readers.

Of course, this is not the only way to read the Book of Ruth from a feminist perspective. Other feminist readers, such as Esther Fuchs, have stressed the final rather than the first chapter of the book as offering the key to its meaning and Ruth's motivation in particular. For them, Ruth's concern throughout was to return to Bethlehem with Naomi in order to marry a kinsman of her dead husband and produce an heir for his estate. She sees herself as an instrument of the system that places highest value on the production of a male heir in order to maintain the patriarchal line. There is no radical sisterly solidarity here, in opposition to convention, but rather an attempt to place herself in a position to maintain patriarchal expectations. With Naomi, she places herself at the mercy of Boaz, who alone can bring about the possibility of this happening. On this reading, Ruth offers little for feminist readers to applaud or emulate.

For others, however, such as Mieke Bal and André LaCoque, it is the subversive nature of Ruth and/or Boaz's actions that give this text and this character some value for contemporary readers. Here Ruth's ethnic identity is significant: Moabites were among Israel's most hated enemies, but here it is not only a Moabite woman who is the hero of the story, but the law of levirate marriage is applied to her and her steadfast loyalty is stressed. Boaz too, in his unconventional dealings with the other, unnamed claimant for Ruth's hand in marriage, may be read as a figure who bends the established rules and places charitable justice above the law. For Mieke Bal, the subversive approach of these characters is highlighted by the comparisons with other rule-breaking figures from the Bible that appear in the text: Rachel, Leah and Perez the rule-breaker in Ruth 4.11–12. More recently, finding even this level of subversion in the text is inadequate for those sensitive to colonialism and its damaging effects. Ruth assimilates to a culture that, according to the biblical account, conquered Canaan: the question is asked if a reader from such a conquered nation

---

4 Ibid.

can be as charitable to her, or read her approach in as positive a light as a reader from a dominant culture. Orpah, the daughter-in-law who returns to her homeland, is being given a voice as someone who refused to abandon her own people, unlike Ruth who chose to align herself with a culture that at the time was the dominant one. The work of Laura E. Donaldson, who is of Cherokee Indian descent, is significant here.

The Book of Ruth has proved itself to be astonishingly polyvalent, even among readers who might be termed as having broadly similar, feminist concerns. Despite having a dominant female character at the heart of its narrative, and carrying the name of a woman as its title, the text's level of, or complicity in, androcentrism is open to strong debate. The importance of the perspective of the reader informed by feminism, and the varieties of ways he or she might respond to the text, is well highlighted by the readings of the Book of Ruth that have been offered in the past 40 years.

The parables of Jesus

The conflicting approaches held under the umbrella of feminist or womanist interpretation may also be seen in various readings of the parables of Jesus. Here we will also find examples of more socially-aware feminist readings, and ones that lift the biblical text completely out of its historical context into the world of the reader alone.

Although male characters are in the majority in the parables, women are represented too, sometimes as main characters. Luke in particular at times seems to pair up the parables so that, for example, in chapter 15, one about a man (the shepherd finding the lost sheep) is followed by one about a woman (the woman who finds her lost coin). However, Daphne Hampson reminds us in her *Theology and Feminism* that there is little evidence in the parables to suggest that Jesus was some sort of proto-feminist. Rather, 'inasmuch as the parables provide us with some indication of how Jesus saw the world, it must be said that women would appear to have been marginal to his perception'.[5] Of the 18 main characters in the parables in Mark's Gospel, all are men; of the 85 in Matthew's Gospel, there are 12 women, but this includes the ten bridesmaids; of the 108 in Luke, there are nine. Of even greater significance, perhaps, is the difference between the rich variety of the roles the male characters are shown to fulfil, and the rather limited and stereotyped roles of the women. The men are builders, merchants, stewards, judges, rich and poor, thieves, scoundrels, fathers and kings. The women are bounded by convention: they are bridesmaids, a housekeeper searching for a lost

---

5 Daphne Hampson, 1990, *Theology and Feminism*, Oxford: Blackwell, p. 88.

coin, a widow persisting in the pursuit of justice and a few undifferentiated wives, mothers and daughters. For Hampson, 'the facts speak for themselves'.[6]

More recently, these 'facts' have been heard in another way. In the introduction to her edited volume, *The Lost Coin: Parables of Women, Work and Wisdom*, Mary Ann Beavis notes that the parables that do feature women suffer from a lack of scholarly interest, the significance of women's work implied in some parables, such as the sewing of a patch on a garment (Matthew 13.33; Luke 13.20, 21), is often ignored, and that even a parable that only refers to the relationships between men may imply the presence of women, for example in the parable of the Prodigal Son.[7] These issues, argues Beavis, have traditionally been neglected and deserve further discussion. Two scholars who have attempted to redress this imbalance are Luise Schottroff, in *The Parables of Jesus*, and Elisabeth Schüssler Fiorenza, in *Sharing Her Word: Feminist Biblical Interpretation in Context*. Schottroff's focus is on the feminist social history of the world of Christianity in which the parables were first read, in order to understand the subversive nature of the message of the reign of God imbedded there. For Schüssler Fiorenza, the parables, particularly those centred on female characters, are significant for feminist biblical interpretation because they enable readings that recognize the boundary-crossing activity of Divine Wisdom, seeking to recover the struggle for women's voices and witness afresh. Here, however, we will focus on one parable, the Ten Bridesmaids (Matthew 25.1–13), and compare the work of Schottroff with that of Vicky Balabanski, who in her article in Mary Ann Beavis's edited volume offers a feminist re-reading of this parable in an attempt to 'Open [. . .] the Closed Door'.

Both scholars attempt to rehabilitate the parable, and by extension, Jesus, from the apparent harshness of the ending. It seems impossible to believe that the five foolish bridesmaids deserve their punishment of being confronted with a closed door while a party goes on inside, and, worse, complete rejection by the 'Lord'. Their crime, not to have taken extra oil for their lamps, seems so trivial compared to their fate. The lack of compassion by the five wise bridesmaids, who refuse to share what they have and send their friends out to buy more in the middle of the night, is also hard to square with a modern understanding of a compassionate Christ. Finally, the advice that follows the parable, to 'watch . . . for ye know neither the day nor the hour' (25.13), is puzzling given that both sets of women slept: it was the foresight and preparedness of the

---

6 Ibid.

7 Mary Ann Beavis, 2002, 'Introduction: Seeking the "Lost Coin" of Parables about Women', in Mary Ann Beavis (ed.), *The Lost Coin: Parables of Women, Work and Wisdom*, Sheffield: Sheffield Academic Press, pp. 17–33.

wise that earned them access to the party. It is these difficulties and ambiguities that feminist readings are likely to probe and to question.

Schottroff offers a variety of interpretations of this parable as a multi-layered attempt to tease out its meanings both in its original context and for modern readers. Her expectation that these are not the same places her within the broad ambit of feminist interpretation, particularly regarding this parable and its focus on women characters. Socio-historical analysis of the parable draws in evidence from near-contemporary Jewish texts such as the Mishnah, in which 'virgins' such as the main characters in the parable are in competition with one another to secure a husband. Beauty, piety, diligence and prudence are all attributes to be prized and cultivated in order to be successful in this market place. Set in this social world, the two groups of women in the parable are in competition with one another, suggested by the less than friendly dialogue between the two groups. The contrast between them is both 'an instrument of education and also of oppression',[8] and the judgement of society on the 'foolish' women is pronounced by the bridegroom: 'I do not know you' (v. 12). Schottroff then goes on to ask a more literary question about the perspective from which the parable is narrated: is it that of the social norm, or is there a challenge to expectation? She suggests that the patriarchal perspective is established from the beginning with the separation of the ten women into two camps, the wise and therefore good future wives, and the foolish and therefore unmarriageable. The refusal to share oil is not criticized, as it demonstrates the capability of the wise women. However, Schottroff also hears an 'unspoken critique' of this position within the narrative, offered by the wider biblical witness to show love for neighbour. For her, the final scene reveals the terrible consequence of the socially acceptable competition. The exaggerated nature of the rejection of the foolish women, for whom the future has now closed in terms of the patriarchal expectation for young women, inevitably, for Schottroff, arouses critical questioning. 'The final scene reveals the ugly face, the hard reality of a society that defines women in terms of their accommodation, subjection, and marriage',[9] and as such it cannot fail to make the reader suspicious of the message the parable apparently presents.

Schottroff is critical of ecclesiological and eschatological interpretations of the parable that read the bridegroom as God passing judgement on those who have not exhibited the right behaviour before him. It is not so much the issue of God's judgement and God's justice that is difficult for her, as it is for some commentators, such as Balabanski, whose work we will consider below. Rather, the problem is that 'the parable is heard as a message about women, even when the interpreters use it only as an

---

8 Luise Schottroff, 2006, *The Parables of Jesus*, trans. Linda M. Maloney, Minneapolis: Fortress Press, p. 30.
9 Schottroff, *Parables of Jesus*, p. 31.

'image', as a quarry for material to be transferred to a different level'.[10] The reaction to the foolish women demonstrates deep social oppression and violence, and when the wise women are used as a metaphor for acceptable behaviour in response to God, this is at the expense of the foolish girls, who face very real social exclusion. Schottroff asks in what way this can be considered good news. The imagery of the message needs to be heard. And having heard it, for Schottroff there is still a positive message to be taken from the parable, which gives its readers a picture of their world, which is characterized by such injustice. This injustice is a sign that the end is near and the kingdom of God, characterized by justice, is close by. The parable makes visible the need for God's intervention and the repentance of those responsible for it. The call to action at the end of the parable is an encouragement to act according to God's will, while there is still time. The parable is not about fixing those who will be saved and those who will be on the other side of the door. Rather, 'it opens up the present and transforms it into a time of hearing and acting'.[11]

Balabanski approaches the parable rather differently but shares with Schottroff the belief that it is more about exposing and critiquing current injustices than about the righting of wrongs at the end of time. For Balabanski, the central problem of the story, from a feminist perspective, is the unwillingness of the wise women to share their oil with the foolish women, and their apparent complicity at the end of the parable in the fate of their unfortunate but imprudent sisters. While some have argued that this is part of the narrative drive of the story, and does not need to be explained or accounted for, a feminist reading attempts to expose the rhetoric of a narrative to reveal the oppression it seeks to hide. Applying Schüssler Fiorenza's hermeneutics of suspicion to the parable, Balabanski offers various responses to the fate of the marginalized and excluded foolish women, those most affected by the actions of their more 'wise' sisters.

Balabanski's starting point is a consideration of the genre of the parable, which she argues is a narrative that promotes the well-known idea of two opposing ways to follow, one of which is clearly rhetorically marked as superior. From the start, the parable seeks to establish the reader's identification with the wise women rather than the foolish ones. Such a marked binary opposition is ripe for deconstruction. Furthermore, a study of the particular word used to describe the successful women, usually translated as 'wise', reveals that this is not the wide, truth-seeking wisdom (*sophia*) found in positive ways throughout the Bible, but rather a restricted sort of prudence (*phronimos*), which promotes self-preservation above ethics – see its use in the parables of the trustworthy slave in charge of the master's household (Matthew 24.45) or, famously,

---

10 Schottroff, *Parables of Jesus*, p. 34.
11 Schottroff, *Parables of Jesus*, p. 37.

of the dishonest steward (Luke 16.1–9). This wisdom is not a relational ideal in a feminist reconfiguring of the world, which Balabanski seeks to promote, and so is open to strong critique. Both of these aspects of the parable, from her perspective, allow her to confront the rhetorical stance the parable, on first reading, seems to espouse.

Having stated the grounds of her hermeneutics of suspicion, Balabanski goes on to offer historically plausible feminist reconstructions of ways in which the parable may have been received by its first audiences. The first she terms the 'View from the Mastaba/Village Bench': the patriarchal reception of the story. Given that there is an alternative term available to refer to unmarried women (*gynē*) than the one used (*parthenoi*, virgins), Balabanski argues that the parable highlights the nubility and sexual availability of these women. By setting the scene with a reference to ten young, available girls, of whom five were foolish and five were wise, the parable in a patriarchal context would be heard as a 'comic jest'.[12] The butt of the joke is immediately set up as the group that contains the five foolish girls. There would be humour in the wild goose chase that is described in verses 7–9: both groups believe they must fulfil their function as torch bearers, seeing themselves as more important than the concerns of the bridegroom. From the perspective of the village bench, both groups are foolish, believing that the dangers of a midnight search for oil are less significant than the danger of not fulfilling their role. The particularly foolish five return too late to carry out their task, but could still expect to be welcomed back into the party. At this point the joke turns nasty, with the reaction of the host going way beyond the expectation of these hearers, who had up until now identified themselves with him. Male hearers, suggests Balabanski, would be alienated by the host's ungenerous and hard to understand reaction. Unresolved, the story for these hearers leaves them with the question: 'if the bridegroom acts in this way to these guests, who eventually made it to the wedding against great odds, might he not do so to us as well?'.[13] For these hearers, who would naturally assume they were 'insiders' in religious terms, the parable presents a world in which God is unpredictable, and generosity and justice are not ensured.

Balabanski's second historical reconstruction is from the perspective of female hearers, the 'View from the Agora/Market Place'. For these hearers, given that there is no bride to identify with, the story's rhetoric offers the possibility of identifying with either the group of foolish women, or the group of the wise. As we have already seen, the overwhelming force

---

12 Vicky Balabanski, 2002, 'Opening the Closed Door: A Feminist Rereading of the "Wise and Foolish Virgins" (Mt. 25.1–13)', in Mary Ann Beavis (ed.), *The Lost Coin: Parables of Women, Work and Wisdom*, Sheffield: Sheffield Academic Press, pp. 71–97, p. 85.

13 Balabanski, 'Opening the Closed Door', p. 86.

of the rhetorical imperative is to be counted with the wise women, and with their proper use of the oil. Solidarity with or compassion for others, even other women, is less important than showing yourself to be worthy of inclusion in the wedding banquet by virtue of what you do with your oil. Being wise in this way is the prerequisite for entry into the eschatological feast. While some women, those who fell short of patriarchal expectations, might have identified themselves with the foolish girls, for them the story offers no hope or relief from their sense of worthlessness. As Balabanski notes, both of these reconstructed interpretations of the parable are very far from the ministry and teaching of Jesus demonstrated at least in some other places in the Gospel witness. However, it is the view from the market place that becomes the dominant reading of this parable, as demonstrated in its setting in Matthew's Gospel, in which the separating out of the wise from the foolish and the placing of its emphasis on right actions conveying worth and inclusion are given prominence. The open-endedness of the view from the village bench, the reading that leaves men perplexed and unsure about where they stand and what sort of a God they identify with, is not encouraged by Matthew's placing of the parable in a narrative sequence with the coming judgement as its focus. The parable of the talents and the teaching about the separating out of the sheep and the goats that follow this parable in Matthew 25 all point to future judgement on those who fail to measure up.

Balabanski goes on to offer a contemporary feminist reading of the parable that offers a hope of justice in the present, rather than in an unspecified future time. Eschatology as promoted by Matthew's redactional interests, for theologies of liberation such as feminist theology, merely validates the maintenance of a system with patriarchy at its core: a system that has not always been concerned about the current plight of those it has excluded from power. As a feminist, Balabanski seeks meaning from the parable that may be of 'earthly use' now.[14]

In order to find such a meaning, Balabanski focuses on three aspects of the parable that have proved troublesome: the way the two groups of women interact; the way the bridegroom speaks and acts; and the meaning of the closed door. Balabanski notes that at the start of the story there is no division between the women. Even when the division occurs, over the sharing of the oil (v. 8), read against the grain of the story this may be interpreted as based on friendship and love for neighbour, rather than an unreasonable and self-centred request. Theologically it might be regarded as a request for compassion, even mercy. The response of the others has a different focus, that of fairness: they do not just refuse the request out of hand, but make a suggestion about how the others might resolve the situation. But if they gave the others their oil, it would not be fair on them. Theologically, they are concerned with what might be called 'forensic

---

14 Balabanski, 'Opening the Closed Door', p. 93.

justice', in human and divine terms.[15] In the interaction between the two groups is enacted the deep theological tension between God's justice and God's mercy. Significantly, in the story itself, it is justice that is promoted and the possibility of relationship with those outside those parameters is denied by the words of the bridegroom: 'I do not know you' (v. 12).

For this feminist reading, on this basis, this bridegroom 'cannot symbolize . . . Jesus Christ, the liberator'.[16] The story must be read alongside, and critiqued by, the wider story of Jesus of Nazareth and, when this is carried out, the bridegroom symbolizes not Jesus but all people in power who make rules and then use them to exclude others. The bridegroom is thus a negative figure, rather than one to be followed and worshipped.

Finally, the closed door is to be deconstructed and read in its widest context in Matthew's Gospel. It is not a symbol of the final word for those who have taken the wrong way, but, when read in the context of Matthew 27.60, it has the potential to be opened by the resurrection power of the Christ. The door to the tomb was shut with the body of Jesus within it; but it was not shut permanently and the new hope of God brings with it unexpected results. The parable for Balabanski brings hope to those for whom the door is closed, in the figure of Christ, not as bridegroom, but as liberator of the 'foolish' and marginalized. This Christ stands with those on the outside while the door is kept shut; only when it is opened by readings such as this is Christ the liberator glimpsed in the parable.

Balabanski's work has been considered in detail because it demonstrates well the complex hermeneutical moves that may be demanded by readings motivated by feminist concerns. Here, the perspective of the reader is foregrounded, and the rhetoric of the text, its apparent narrative direction, is ruthlessly interrogated and critiqued. The biblical material such feminist commentators have to work with is not obviously congenial to a feminist perspective, particularly if such commentators hold positions of faith that presuppose certain beliefs about God who is in some way revealed in these texts as scripture. For some, the work involved, and the hermeneutical hoops to be jumped, are not justified, and the Bible is considered antithetical to the feminist cause. For others, such as Schottroff and Balabanski, using the feminist insights of scholars such as Schüssler Fiorenza, the effort brings liberating and revealing rewards.

The Handmaid's Tale

Feminist critique of the Bible, or of biblical religion generally, is not confined to academia, of course. Margaret Atwood's classic science fiction,

---

15 Balabanski, 'Opening the Closed Door', p. 96.
16 Balabanski, 'Opening the Closed Door', p. 97.

or, as Atwood has preferred to call it, speculative fiction, novel, *The Handmaid's Tale*, may also be read as an exploration of key biblical texts from a feminist perspective. Written in 1985, it offers a dystopian vision of life under a totalitarian theocracy. A fundamentalist group has gained control of American society, which is now run according to selective Old Testament principles. An unspecified event has led to a dramatic fall in fertility, and much of the energy of the state is directed towards controlling those women who retain the potential to reproduce. Dissent and deviation are punished severely, and the state operates a terrifying system of secret police, known as the 'Eyes', to root out any threat to their control. The narrative comes to the reader through the eyes of a woman given the name Offred, which the reader ultimately realizes is a temporary patronymic: while in his house, the woman is the property of a Commander named 'Fred'. Gradually she reveals something of her past under the previous regime, in which she was married to a divorced man named Luke, and had a daughter. Under the rules of the new system, the biblical precepts about divorce led to her being removed from the home as an adulteress, her child taken from her, and her re-education as a 'handmaid'. Assigned to the patriarchal household of a Commander of the Faithful, each month she must submit to sexual intercourse with him, while lying on his apparently infertile wife, in the hope that she will conceive his child. For Offred, her situation is complicated by the Commander's desire to forge some sort of covert intimacy with her, and by his wife's plan to have her sleep with their servant in order to better her prospect of pregnancy. Finally, her compromised situation is discovered and she is taken away, whether by the Eyes or by a group loyal to the resistance is unclear. The novel closes with Offred's taped witness to the regime being discussed in a light-hearted and typically convoluted way by academics several hundred years later.

The novel may be read as a critique of many aspects of life in the late twentieth century, including religious and political fundamentalism. However, its feminist focus is confirmed by Atwood's comment in an interview that forms part of the Afterword to the 1998 (Anchor Books) version of the novel that 'This is a book about what happens when certain casually held attitudes about women are taken to their logical conclusions.' Of interest here are the potentially casually held attitudes towards the Bible and what it says about women, and the ways in which these logical conclusions are played out in a feminist context.

The biblical text from which the theocracy asserts its power over women and their bodies is Genesis 29–30. Here the two sisters, Leah and Rachel, compete with each other to produce children with Jacob. While Leah, the first although less-desired wife (married by the trickery of her father Laban), conceives with no difficulty, this proves harder for Rachel. She demands from her husband, 'Give me children, or else I die' (30.1), to which he responds that he does not have control over this, only God has this power. Rachel's solution to her desperate need is to present her maid Bilhah, and demand that Jacob 'go in unto her, and she shall bear upon my knees, that I may also have children by her' (30.3). Bilhah duly conceives two sons; Leah then presents her maid Zilpah, and she bears two more. Leah conceives further children after this, and even Rachel produces a son, the favourite Joseph. Behind this episode, too, lies Abraham's attempt to start his promised dynasty in Genesis 16: here Sarah persuades Abraham to have intercourse with her Egyptian maid Hagar, which results in the conception of Ishmael, although the outcome for both is divisive.

The connection in the novel between the later story and the justification of the regime's actions against women are clearly stated, and perhaps the disruption and dissension of the earlier story is also echoed in the sour unhappiness and manipulation of the Commander's wife, ironically given the name Serena Joy. Fertile women are removed from society by the state and placed in the Rachel and Leah Centre to be re-educated. There is sisterly solidarity here, covertly expressed, as between Moira and Offred, but weaker women, such as Janine, are encouraged to spy on the others. Here the Bible is read to the women, who are not allowed to read for themselves, and it is only faint memory that alerts Offred to its manipulation and misuse. Over lunch, the women hear a version of the Beatitudes, including the non-biblical 'Blessed are the silent'.[17] As well as the 'usual' stories concerning the command to be fruitful, they are read a long passage from 2 Chronicles 16.9, in which the constant surveillance is justified:

> the eyes of the Lord run to and fro throughout the whole earth, to shew himself strong in the behalf of them whose heart is perfect toward him. Herein thou hast done foolishly: therefore from henceforth thou shalt have wars.[18] *even heaven did*

Here the context of the passage is ignored, that these are the words of judgement of a powerless prophet against the powerful king, who promptly imprisons him for speaking the truth, rather than words to be used by the state to justify their oppression of the powerless. The language of the King James Version gives the rhetoric its ageless force. Later in her time in the Centre, Offred and the others are inculcated with a revision of a more modern, secular mantra, which she assumes 'was from the Bible . . . St Paul again, in Acts': 'From each, according to her ability: to each according to his needs'.[19] Both political and biblical rhetoric, in the

---

17 Margaret Atwood, 1985, *The Handmaid's Tale*, 1996 edn, London: Vintage, p. 100.

18 Atwood, *Handmaid's Tale*, p. 103.

19 Atwood, *Handmaid's Tale*, p. 127.

minds of these women, are granted sacred status, presumably as those in control of language intend. The reader, aware of the differences between the two, and the nuances of the biblical text, is granted a privileged status that Offred does not share, at least not securely.

However, the power of the Bible as a revolutionary text remains potent, even in the mind of those oppressed by its use at the hands of the Commanders. As Offred comments regarding the Bible kept in its locked box in the Commander's house: '[it is] an incendiary device. Who knows what we'd make of it, if we ever got our hands on it? We can be read to from it, by him, but we cannot read it.'[20]

The novel suggests that the Bible retains some authority and power by virtue of its status as scripture, and even casually held attitudes towards the Bible, such as those which read narratives about women in an innocent and uncritical way, or worse, in a way that privileges men over women, may affect current society.

The categorization of women in the novel further mirrors the characterization of women in biblical texts, taking that characterization to its logical conclusion. The biblical Rachel and Leah share the patriarchal imperative of the need to bear children, preferably sons. Their role and even their interaction with each other is defined by their desperate desire to please Jacob, and demonstrate their favour before God, by having children. Although they are ideal role models for the handmaids, these women actually embody the voiceless servant girls Bilhah and Zilpah, who have no choice but to obey their mistresses' commands. Offred's witness to this persecution, the sole voice, we are told by the academics who find her tapes, remaining from the Gilead period, contrasts her personal story with the grand narrative of her society, itself based on biblical metanarratives. In some ways it re-visions the voiceless experience of the maid servants, although it remains ultimately in the hands of the male academics who order it according to their own scheme and trawl through it for evidence of arcane details, such as the identity of the Commander named Fred.

Many of the women on the periphery of the narrative are also defined by biblical categories. The serving women, who are for whatever reason sterile but not of the ruling class, are named 'Marthas', after the sister in the story in Luke 10 who chose to prepare the meal rather than sit at the feet of Jesus. Given that it is Mary who hears the words of approval from Jesus, as having chosen the 'better way', these women's status is very low indeed, although the element of choice has been taken away from them.

The Wives, too, in their blue outfits, take their significance from a biblical figure, that of Mary the mother of Jesus: in ideal terms, elevated from the sex act itself, patiently awaiting the will of God to bring about a miraculous birth (and the birth of healthy babies is shown to be

---

20 Atwood, *Handmaid's Tale*, p. 98.

becoming more and more of a rare event). In reality, these wives, such as Serena Joy, are revealed to be deeply unsatisfied by the society they have colluded in creating, driven to using what power they have in ways that bring danger particularly to the Handmaids. The Wives lead the reader to question the biblical portrayals of Mary, fleshing out her quiet acceptance with the reality of frustration in response to the system that she has played her part in establishing.

Also significant are the women who work in 'Jezebel's', the state sanctioned brothel for men of high rank. Offred encounters the rebellious lesbian Moira here when she is taken to Jezebel's by the Commander. When she tells Moira she 'look[s] like the whore of Babylon',[21] Offred reflects the horror and the fascination of the figure from Revelation 17. Like the Whore, Moira lives under the shadow of judgement, awaiting the time when her body will no longer be considered suitable for the brothel, but while she is there she is garishly different from the rest of society, drawing the gaze of those around, transgressive and, although there to service men, she nevertheless manages moments of personal freedom.

Sexual violence is a key motif of the world of *The Handmaid's Tale*, just as it is in the Hebrew Bible, despite the claims of the state to have made society safer for women. And while Atwood is critical of radical feminists such as Offred's mother who, like the right wing, sought to restrict free speech in order to 'protect' women from pornography (a live debate in the feminist ideologies of the 1980s), it is the biblical fundamentalism of the religious right that draws her most fierce criticism. The novel suggests that when the Bible is accepted uncritically, one of many potential consequences is that women are reduced to their ability to bear children, their rights are curtailed and they are in danger of abuse at the hands of those who believe having children over-rides all other considerations. The conclusion of the novel is bleak and offers little hope beyond the assumption that Offred survived to save her story on tape. A reader who is aware of the biblical basis of the ideology of the ruling class in Gilead may read the novel as a warning against allowing such uncritical readings to stand unchallenged. In this way, the novel offers a feminist critique of the Bible itself, and of its complicity in deeply engrained and powerful patriarchy. Like Trible's reading of the Book of Ruth, and Balabanski's and Schottroff's readings of the parable of the wise and foolish virgins, *The Handmaid's Tale* brings modern concerns to a reading of the biblical text. The text is deconstructed and not allowed to speak as it has for centuries. In order for it to retain any sense of scriptural power, which is the aim of many but not all feminist biblical scholars, it must be re-envisioned according to new rules of justice and equality. The feminist ideology of these readers is clearly the driving force of these interpretations.

---

21 Atwood, *Handmaid's Tale*, p. 254.

Questions

1. How dominant a force is patriarchy in the Bible? Can you think of examples that are clearer than others?
2. Do women read the Bible differently from men, and is this a feminist issue?
3. What examples can you give of other literary texts that challenge the Bible's apparent view of the world from a modern or postmodern perspective?

Further reading

Margaret Atwood, 1985, *The Handmaid's Tale*, 1996 edn, London: Vintage.

Mieke Bal, 1987, 'Heroism and Proper Names or the Fruits of Analogy', in *Lethal Love: Feminist Literary Readings of Biblical Love Stories*, Bloomington: Indiana University Press, pp. 68–103.

Vicky Balabanski, 2002, 'Opening the Closed Door: A Feminist Rereading of the "Wise and Foolish Virgins" (Mt. 25.1–13)', in Mary Ann Beavis (ed.), *The Lost Coin: Parables of Women, Work and Wisdom*, Sheffield: Sheffield Academic Press, pp. 71–97.

Mary Ann Beavis, 2002, 'Introduction: Seeking the "Lost Coin" of Parables about Women', in Mary Ann Beavis (ed.), *The Lost Coin: Parables of Women, Work and Wisdom*, Sheffield: Sheffield Academic Press.

Harold Bloom (ed.), 2001, *Margaret Atwood's* The Handmaid's Tale: *Modern Critical Interpretations*, Philadelphia: Chelsea House Publishers.

Laura E. Donaldson, 1999, 'The Sign of Orpah: Reading Ruth through Native Eyes', in Athalya Brenner (ed.), *Ruth and Esther*, Sheffield: Sheffield Academic Press, pp. 130–44.

Elisabeth Schüssler Fiorenza, 1984, *Bread Not Stone: The Challenge of Feminist Biblical Interpretation*, Edinburgh: T & T Clark.

Elisabeth Schüssler Fiorenza, 1998, *Sharing Her Word: Feminist Biblical Interpretation in Context*, Boston: Boston Press.

Esther Fuchs, 2005. 'The History of Women in Ancient Israel: Theory, Method, and the Book of Ruth', in Caroline Vander Stichele and Todd Penner (eds), *Her Master's Tools: Feminist and Post-colonial Engagements of Historical-Critical Discourse*, Atlanta: Society of Biblical Literature, pp. 211–32.

Daphne Hampson, 1990, *Theology and Feminism*, Oxford: Blackwell.

André LaCoque, 1990, *The Feminine Unconventional: Four Subversive Figures in Israel's Tradition*, Minneapolis: Fortress Press.

David E. Nelson (ed.), 2011, *Women's Issues in Margaret Atwood's* The Handmaid's Tale, Farmington Mill, MI: Greenhaven Press.

Luise Schottroff, 2006, *The Parables of Jesus*, trans. Linda M. Maloney, Minneapolis: Fortress Press.

Elizabeth Cady Stanton, 1895 and 1899, *The Woman's Bible*, 1999 edn, New York: Prometheus Books.

Phyllis Trible, 1978, *God and the Rhetoric of Sexuality*, Philadelphia: Fortress Press.

8

Reading and Re-writing: Midrash and Literature

Midrash . . . holds together two competing truths, first, the authority of Scripture, and, second, that equally ineluctable freedom of interpretation implicit in the conviction that Scripture speaks now, not only then.[1]

We have already met the term 'midrash' when we discussed the work of Stephen Marx in Chapter 3, and noted he used the term to describe the way in which Shakespeare's plays might be read as literary commentaries on the Bible. In this, Marx was following in a literary critical tradition. In the literary criticism of the 1980s, there had arisen an interest in the rabbinic interpretative practice of midrash, exemplified by Susan Handelman's book, *The Slayers of Moses: The Emergence of Rabbinic Interpretation in Modern Literary Theory*. The apparent playful freedom of midrashic interpretation of the Hebrew Bible seemed close to the diffracted readings of other texts encouraged by deconstruction. Both approaches appeared to revel in the unending possibilities inherent in the written word. In this chapter, we will explore midrash in its original and in its later, literary, context. We will consider midrashic readings of a famously open and enigmatic text, Jacob wrestling with the angel in Genesis 32. We will also read two poems that are self-consciously based on, even interpretations of, the text of Genesis 32: Gerard Manley Hopkins's 'Carrion Comfort' and Emily Dickinson's 'A Little East of Jordan'. Throughout we will aim to assess the contribution of midrash as an interpretative lens to an understanding of the relationship between the Bible and literature.

While it is a term that is still in use in modern rabbinic and to some extent in literary circles (particularly where the influence of the Bible is under discussion), midrash traces its roots, as a meaningful way to read scripture, back to the Bible itself. It stems from the root *darash*, to search out or interpret, and is found in texts such as Ezra 7.10 and 2 Chronicles

---

1 Jacob Neusner, 1987, *What is Midrash?*, Philadelphia: Fortress Press, p. 103.

13.22 and 24.27 with reference to the study of texts about God and his laws. More generally, the Books of Chronicles, in their relationship to the Books of Samuel and Kings, exhibit what came to be called midrashic exegesis of earlier texts of scripture: the basic narrative is expanded and gaps are filled in. Later, *darash* is found frequently in the Dead Sea Scroll texts from Qumran, where the searching out and interpretation of scripture is a key activity. Post-biblical literature, such as Sirach 44–50, the writings of Philo and Josephus, and Jubilees, all offer evidence of midrashic readings of the Bible: interpretations that elaborate on the text in narrative form. In recent times, scholars have sought to show that there is much more rabbinic-style midrash in the New Testament than has been recognized in the past, in all of the genres found there. Certainly it is in later rabbinic circles that midrashic activity is most common and with which it is identified. Before we turn to consider this in detail, however, we should note that inner Bible exegesis, in other words, the way the Bible reads itself, and post-biblical, non-rabbinic, interpretation, all demonstrate a close similarity to classical rabbinic midrash. This is an ancient, widespread and well-attested way of reading and appropriating the Hebrew Bible.

The precise history of midrash as a conscious interpretative approach is difficult to establish as its roots appear to come from an oral tradition. Late rabbinic sources assert that Moses received the Torah in two forms: one, which was written and embodied in scripture; and one, which was oral and embodied in the tradition that developed alongside written scripture. Torah, properly understood, is both scripture and tradition in relationship. For tradition to be valid, it had to be developed by those sages and scribes who were in succession from Moses; beyond that, the only limit on tradition was the imagination and ingenuity of the interpreter.

The impetus for the jump from the oral tradition to classical, written midrash is unclear, but its result reaches us in various forms, stemming from between the fifth and the tenth centuries CE, including the Mishnah and the Babylonian and Palestinian Talmudim. In these texts, rabbis are mentioned, and their interpretations are engaged with, who lived many years before the period in which the collections were written, pointing to a tradition that has long-standing roots. Indeed, it has been argued that Nehemiah 10.31 is in the form of a 'rabbinic'-style midrash on Exodus 34.15, extending the prohibition on intermarriage. The interpretation of scripture, and the revision of these interpretations in a Jewish context, is an ongoing process over many centuries.

The foundation of all of this activity is the belief that Torah is unchanging, but also that it speaks to all times and all situations. The rabbis, working in a new and alien environment after the catastrophe of the fall of Jerusalem in 70 CE, sought to restore the connection between the sacred text and the people of faith. The text depended on the Temple as the centre of religious observance: when the Temple was destroyed, the rabbis recognized that the text did not meet the current needs of its readers. In response, they sought to fill in the gaps in the text to make it speak to a new situation, bringing the text and its community of readers, authority and tradition back together.

Behind their interpretative activity lay some key assumptions. One was that scripture is coherent and consistent with itself: any one verse may shed light on another. Any contradictions within it must only be apparent and not real, awaiting explanation, because scripture is never wrong. All truth may be found within it, although it may be hidden: and there are many levels of meaning available to be mined. And so, the rabbi was free to exploit any problems of consistency in the text in order to find a peg on which to hang his own theological or exegetical views; but he was also free to explain or smooth out any surface difficulty in a text for its own sake, filling up gaps with new meanings, and finding significance in every aspect of the text. All of this activity has a theological purpose, as the text of scripture is understood to be the way God relates to his people: interpretation is a religious imperative and a sacred task.

Midrash is usually divided up into two categories: *halakhah*, from the Hebrew 'to go', dealing with legal aspects of scripture and involving issues of practice and lifestyle; and *aggadah*, 'to say or tell', involving more literary texts and issues of form and meaning. While some of the more recent commentators who have sought to relate midrash to literary endeavours, such as Lesleigh Cushing Stahlberg, make much of this distinction, it is less obvious in earlier literary reflections on the subject, which tended to concentrate on *aggadah*, the more creative and apparently freer of the two approaches. Jacob Neusner, however, in his *The Halakhah and the Aggadah: Theological Perspectives*, sees both as a seamless unity reflecting God and Israel in partnership in the world. For him, the *halakhah* deals with Israel's internal, day-to-day relationship with God in terms of the way individuals run their households and deal with one another; the *aggadah* is concerned with Israel in the world, its external relationship with the nations and the story of its relationship with God as it is presented to others. Both testify to God as creator and sustainer of justice, and of Israel as having an active part to play in the second of these roles. Important for both, as most commentators assert, is that they seek 'to reinscribe, not replace, the received divine text'.[2] The end result of their labours is a fusion of interpretation and text, rather than a conquering of one by the other. While Stahlberg will go on to concentrate on the tight interpretative rules of *halakhah*, most literary critics have taken a rather less detailed approach to midrash as a genre and as a method, focusing on *aggadistic* midrash, and it is to this that we will now turn.

---

2 Lesleigh Cushing Stahlberg, 2008, *Sustaining Fictions: Intertextuality, Midrash, Translation, and the Literary Afterlife of the Bible*, New York: T & T Clark, p. 96.

Aggadah midrash comes in many forms, usually made up of a composite of paragraphs rather than a sustained narrative. Its interpretation of the biblical verse under discussion (and it is almost always a verse rather than a book or even a story) may take the form of a parable (asking 'to what may this be likened?') or short sermon; or it may clarify a difficult historical point, or show how that point is relevant to contemporary readers. It may take a more philological approach, and reveal hidden meanings in a verse or a word through wordplay, acrostics, numerology, rearranging sentences or bringing another verse into dialogue with the original one. These midrashim have no independent life of their own: their contact with the text of the Bible is secure and clearly stated, and is followed by a range of different views in close debate with one another.

An example of the philological approach, and of midrash used to exemplify a previously held theological belief, comes from a midrash on the story of the near-sacrifice of Isaac in Genesis 22. The word used to describe the knife Abraham takes with him to carry out the killing is an unusual one, occurring in scripture only in this story, in Judges 19.29 where it is used of the knife taken by the Levite to cut up his dead concubine, and in Proverbs 30.14, where it refers metaphorically to the teeth of men who exploit the poor. While the context in which it is used is particularly violent, the interpretative route chosen by R. Hanina in the *Genesis Rabbah* is to relate the word to food: the word was used because this knife makes food fit to be eaten (*Genesis Rabbah* 56.3). He makes this connection because the consonants in the knife-word reappear in the word for food. The midrash continues that 'the Rabbis said: All eating which Israel enjoys in this world, they enjoy only in the merit of that knife' (*Genesis Rabbah* 56.3). The implication of this reading is the continuing connection between Abraham and his promised descendants, based on his obedience. The Jews continue to be sustained because he was willing, at God's command, to use that knife. Thus a theological lesson is embedded within the meaning of one, obscure word.[3]

Another lexical example, this time of interpretation of a lexical puzzle, is found in the midrash on the angel's double call, 'Abraham! Abraham' in Genesis 22. While we might read this as having little significance beyond narrative urgency, R. Hiyya argues that the two calls have two different meanings. The first call is an expression of 'love' and the second of 'encouragement'. A second rabbi joins the discussion and makes a further point that the double reference indicates that God spoke both to Abraham and to future generations: 'There is no generation which does not contain men like Abraham, and there is no generation that does not contain men like Jacob, Moses, and Samuel' (*Genesis Rabbah* 56.7). The repetition supports the rabbinic belief that all future generations will

---

3 The text is found in H. Freedman and M. Simon (eds), 1983, *Midrash Rabbah: Genesis*, New York: Soncino, and is quoted in Stahlberg, *Sustaining Fictions*, p. 102.

be connected to God, who will raise up great men in each of them: the promises made to Abraham will never end.[4]

Further rabbinic midrashim argue from what the text does not say to explain the interpretative gap between the text and the contemporary reader. If Abraham was a pious Jew, why is there no mention of him observing the commandments or the religious holidays, or following the food laws that formed such a significant part of the lives of the rabbis' readers? That these were developed long after Abraham could have lived is not important: rather, Abraham of the Rabbis lived the life of a Torah-observant Jew. Genesis 26.5 was invoked to explain this claim: 'Because Abraham listened to my voice and kept my watch, my commandments, my laws and my instructions.' Each term is taken to refer to a different aspect of the law, so that one clause refers to the laws given to Moses, one to the laws given to Noah, one to the written and one to the oral Torah.[5] The apparent redundancy of the text and the problematic silence surrounding Abraham's law-abiding are both dealt with in one interpretative move, based on the underlying assumption that the Bible is consistent and without redundancy.

Midrash in literary criticism

While the actual form of rabbinic midrash is complex and not always easy to follow, the approach it appears to take was particularly attractive to secular literary critics. Its emphasis on the text alone, taken out of its context; the validity of a variety of meanings; the blurring of the distinction between text and interpretation, appealed to the literary critical world of the 1980s, which was ready to forge links beyond its traditional subject area boundaries. To this world, midrash seemed to reflect the concerns of literary theory and to be a fruitful genre of literature to be considered. The multiplicity of voices to be heard, with no hierarchy visible, for these postmodern readers, implicitly asserted that all interpretations were valid, and chimed with their deeply held convictions. Susan Handelman was one of the first to explore midrash from a literary critical perspective, and she noted with approval that in midrash 'the infinity of meaning and plurality of interpretation are as much the cardinal imperatives, even the divine virtues, for Rabbinic thought as they are the cardinal sins for Greek thought'.[6] While 'intertextual' was and remains the more common term to describe the general relationship between texts in literary criticism, midrash seemed to offer a model of a text in which there is no time distinction between the past

---

4 Quoted and discussed in Stahlberg, *Sustaining Fictions*, p. 103.

5 *B. Yoma* 28b, quoted in Stahlberg, *Sustaining Fictions*, p. 104.

6 Susan A. Handelman, 1982, *Slayers of Moses: The Emergence of Rabbinic Interpretation in Modern Literary Theory*, Albany: State University of New York Press, p. 21.

and the present and free association seems to lie behind the generation of new readings: 'texts echo, interact and interpenetrate. In the world of the text, rigid temporal and spatial distinctions collapse.'[7] For Handelman, compared to the monologic readings of scripture by the Church Fathers, midrash plays with the text's infinite possibilities, turning the reader into a producer of texts in a way that accorded closely to the philosophy of postmodern text critics such as Derrida.

Stahlberg and others have more recently questioned this reading of midrash, asking if such literary critics have in fact recast the genre in a way that is not true to its intention or its form. While the aim of deconstruction is to seek out the ways a text undermines itself, to show that binary oppositions cannot be relied upon to convey truth, the rabbis have the opposite aim. All believe that God lies behind the text, and so seek to reveal the ways that inconsistencies might be resolved. The text's unity is to be preserved or restored even at the expense of its literal sense. Underlying all their midrashic free play is the common assumption that all depths of meaning in the text cohere in God. Midrash is appropriate only for scripture, not as an approach towards any text, because it is a theological enterprise reflecting a particular understanding about the relationship between God, Israel and the Bible. This is reading with a didactic purpose, a closer relationship with the God of the text, usually in response to a crisis that has created a gap between the text and the situation of the readers. For Stahlberg, literary criticism's appropriation of midrash as a model of postmodern interpretation is built on a misunderstanding of the basis on which midrash stands. Midrash may still be an important and illuminating genre to consider from a postmodern, or any other, perspective, but its unifying theological purpose should not be ignored.

Certainly indeterminacy is not part of a midrashist's concerns, as there is for him a divine guarantor of meaning: but deconstruction is also constrained by the text it is reading to some extent. Both seem to revel in the ceaseless deferment of meaning in the flux of textuality. The similarities between a deconstructive reading and a midrashic reading are perhaps closest where midrash is at its most playful and discursive, and deconstruction is most closely anchored to one primary text, offering a closely argued reading of it. Both highlight that earlier discourses as conscious or unconscious citations are to be found in all texts; that texts may argue against themselves; and that cultural codes both constrain and allow new texts to be produced within that culture. There is an ideology – sometimes better described as a theology – behind the reading and interpreting of texts, and the production of new ones.

And so more relevant for Stahlberg, and for us, than asserting the postmodern credentials of rabbinic midrash, is perhaps the insight offered by that midrash into the way the Bible may be retold in different times

---

7 Handelman, *Slayers of Moses*, p. 47.

and places. Stahlberg calls this 'co-opting the vocabulary of midrash'.[8] Midrash on this view highlights the world of the reader and the interpretation rather than the world behind the text, with its focus on its original intention. It makes the text of the Bible fresh and relevant for new readers, without overwhelming it. And it is presented with the expectation that it too will be retold, as it does not have the final word. These concerns of midrash are effective reminders or models of the way other texts, perhaps the literary texts we are interested in, may be read as retelling the Bible.

On an even more technical level, Stahlberg's interest is in close definitions of the approach of later texts to the Bible, and so she finds in Rabbi Hillel's seven rules of halakhic midrash plenty to discuss. These seven rules include inference from major to minor: if one thing applies to a harder case – such as respect for the body of an executed criminal (Deuteronomy 21.22–3) – it should also apply to a less difficult situation (such as in the case of an ordinary, innocent person); inference from one phrase to another similar phrase: a word, phrase or narrative may be interpreted in the same way each time it occurs, or is alluded to, causing stories to ripple through one another; and deduction from context: the wider context of an original verse may be grafted onto the retelling of that one verse (a procedure very similar to Hollander's and Hays's cave of resonance that we discussed in Chapter 4). For Stahlberg, these rules, when explored, reveal the variety of ways that it is possible for interpreters of scripture to build on and return to the original text. Although midrash has a distinctly Jewish perspective, it also offers a more general way to understand the textual bridging of the distance between the Bible and later readers, and may provide a new way to discuss secular texts and their relationship to scripture.

Midrash and literature

Certainly 'midrash' has been a term applied, in Jewish literary circles, to describe personal retellings of biblical stories in fictional texts,[9] and in wider circles also to describe the influence of the Bible on modern literature.[10] For our purposes, perhaps this is the most useful way to relate midrash, the Bible and literature, as indeed we have already seen in

---

8 Handelman, *Slayers of Moses*, pp. 136ff.

9 See, for example, David C. Jacobson, 1987, *Modern Midrash: The Retelling of Traditional Jewish Narratives by Twentieth Century Hebrew Writers*, Albany: State University of New York Press.

10 See, for example, David Curzon, 1994, 'A Hidden Genre: Twentieth-century Midrashic Poetry', *Tikkun* 9, pp. 70–1, 95. Curzon includes poets such as W. B. Yeats, Rainer Maria Rilke and Jorge Luis Borges, as being engaged, whether consciously or not, in the making of midrash.

the work of Stephen Marx on Shakespeare. This understanding of midrash is perhaps, in Stahlberg's view, limited and at some remove from classical rabbinic midrash in all its complexity, especially if the close application of rules of interpretation are not the focus of interest. However, it would be important on this reading not just to recognize the free playfulness of a midrashic use of the Bible in fiction, but also that this is reading and interpretation with a purpose, which may indeed be theological. The two poets we will consider below, Gerard Manley Hopkins and Emily Dickinson, certainly had strongly held theological beliefs, and while it is unclear whether either of them wished or expected their work to be read by a wide circle of others, their retelling of the story of Jacob wrestling with God certainly has theological purpose and significance. It is this combination of freedom and conviction that makes midrash, in their case, an appropriate and meaningful way to describe their work.

Emily Dickinson

Emily Dickinson was born in 1830 in the small rural New England town of Amherst. Her family was well off and influential in the town, involved in the setting up of Amherst Academy and College, the former of which Dickinson attended before being sent to Mount Holyoke Female Seminary. The household was a religious one and their house, 'The Homestead', was a hub of church and political life in the town. From the late 1840s and into the 1850s, Dickinson took an active part in this society, although she chose not to join the church. Gradually she withdrew from the outside world, and after 1860 she only left the house twice, for treatment on her eyes.

Dickinson was well versed in the literature of the day, and received news of the world through her many correspondents and the select visitors she allowed to see her. Her most productive period was between 1858 and 1861, when she wrote more than 1,000 poems, but only a dozen or so of these were published in her lifetime, and many of those anonymously. Despite encouragement from friends to publish more, Dickinson actively avoided all publicity beyond a close circle of friends and critics, and hoped for fame only after her death. There has been much debate about the nature of her relationships with both men and women, but much remains uncertain. From the letters that survive it appears she was a passionate woman who chose to renounce marriage, although the reasons for this are unclear. Intense and private, from whose inner life sprang poems covering a wide range of religious, political, psychological and philosophical subjects, Dickinson died at home in 1886.

It is a commonplace to say that Dickinson's religious faith, like her poetry, is hard to fathom. Her context has been considered from many angles – social, political and ecclesiastical – and her surviving letters and the plethora of poems found after her death have all been quarried for information. She evades categorization, however, seeming to say many different, even contradictory, things in prose and in verse throughout her life. A child of her Darwinian age, she asserts the God's right 'hand is amputated now/And God cannot be found', a sense of his providential care is lost, and this is to be regretted because 'The abdication of Belief/Makes the behaviour small'.[11] Nevertheless she is drawn to Jesus the 'Tender Pioneer', and sees in his suffering a mirror of her own and the world's: 'I like a look of Agony, /Because I know it's true' (Poem 339, p. 152). Overall, the evidence suggests that while she stopped attending church in her early thirties, and could make derogatory remarks about her devout family, such as 'They are all religious – except me – and address an Eclipse, every morning – whom they call their "Father"',[12] she retained strong spiritual inner convictions, although not always orthodox by the standards of her time. Furthermore, while a poem such as 'Those – dying then' (Poem 1581, p. 1882), quoted above, presents a bleak view of God's absence, we as readers should be wary of assigning such views to Dickinson herself, rather than simply to the speaker of the poem.

A characteristic of her poetic style is the presentation of different views from many perspectives, without necessarily coming to a conclusion. If we return again to 'Those – dying then', we see this clearly. A contrast is set up between the past, when those who died knew where they were going, and now, when God 'cannot be found'. His place of honour for the faithful dead, his 'right hand', has been 'amputated', although no clue is given as to the identity of the one who wielded the scalpel. Nor is it obvious if the speaker approves of or condemns that brutal act – the poem could be read at this point as an attack on those such as the followers of Darwin who had cast doubt on the validity of God's role in creation as detailed in Genesis. In the next stanza, this loss of faith is a cause for regret: it takes away any universal moral framework, making human behaviour 'small'. Whether this means human behaviour is immoral, or moral behaviour is overshadowed by the immoral, or simply there is a change of perspective, is not stated. The poem closes with the suggestion that even a religion based on illusory appearances, like a will o' the wisp ('*ignis fatuus*'), would be better than having no light or guidance at all. The dash with which the poem closes suggests that the speaker lacks

---

11 Poem 1581, Emily Dickinson, 1998, *The Poems of Emily Dickinson: Reading Edition*, R. W. Franklin (ed.), Cambridge, MA: Belknap Press, p. 1882. All poems quoted are from R. W. Franklin's edition of *The Poems of Emily Dickinson*, 1998, using the numbering system he follows.

12 From a letter to her literary friend Thomas Wentworth Higginson on 25 April 1862, quoted in Roger Lundin, 2004, *Emily Dickinson and the Art of Belief,* 2nd edition, Grand Rapids, MI: Eerdmans, pp. 126–7.

certainty about whether she is right, or what the future holds. This is in contrast to the certainty of those 'dying then'. While this poem is made up of contradictory statements about present and past belief, the speaker's views on any of them are not asserted. And in the end, with the use of the dash, the reader is left with no sense of closure.

While 'Those – dying then' has a very controlled and steady tone, other poems are less measured, and suggest more of a conflict around theological ideas. Towards the end of her life, in spring 1886, Dickinson wrote to her friend Higginson, in an affectionate leave-taking of himself and his family, that 'Audacity of Bliss, said Jacob to the Angel "I will not let thee go except I bless thee" – Pugilist and Poet, Jacob was correct' (quoted in Johnson's edition of *The Poems of Emily Dickinson*, p. 45). This image, from Genesis 32, of Jacob wrestling with an angel, is a powerful one and appears in several of her poems, bringing together these two ideas of creativity and of aggressive interaction with God. And through a discussion of the most obvious of these re-readings of this biblical story, we will assess the connection between midrash as it has been appropriated by literary criticism, and the sorts of retelling that Dickinson offers.

The biblical text to which Dickinson's poem, 'A Little East of Jordan' (Poem 145, p. 72), is intertextually related is itself a difficult one. It is certainly allusive rather than clear, and lacks specificity, for example, about which 'he' is being referred to as the story unfolds (see vv. 26–7). The identity of the figure who wrestles with Jacob in the dark is a mystery: referred to as a 'man' at the start, who refuses to give his name (why does Jacob demand to know it in the first place?), but in the interaction, Jacob comes to believe it is God he has fought (v. 30). Many interpreters, including rabbinic midrashists, have offered further suggestions about the man's identity, from an angel (the midrashic choice), to a river or evil spirit, the spirit of Esau, who Jacob is nervously preparing to encounter years after his trickery, to Christ himself in traditional Christian typogy. Indeed, this typological reading was a common one in the eighteenth and nineteenth centuries, when this story was frequently used to exemplify the struggle leading to conversion. The message taken from the text is then focused on verse 26 – 'I will not let thee go, except thou bless me'. See, for example, Charles Wesley's 'Wrestling Jacob' from 1742.[13]

In vain thou strugglest to get free;
I never will unloose my hold!
Art thou the Man that died for me?
The secret of thy love unfold:
Wrestling, I will not let thee go,
Till I thy name and nature know. (v. 3)

---

13 Quoted in David Jasper and Stephen Prickett, 1999, *The Bible and Literature: A Reader*, Oxford: Blackwell, p. 138.

The oddity of verses 27–8, in which the pinned-down figure asks Jacob his name, and then goes on to rename him 'Israel', saying he has 'prevailed' over Elohim ('gods') and men, when this is left unresolved in the narrative, seems to interrupt the flow of the story. So too, on this view, does the second half of verse 30, in which the identification of the man as 'god' seems incongruous. Both of these have been suggested by modern scholars as later additions to an originally much shorter and even more mysterious text,[14] along with verse 32 and its explanation of a food law, of course, which has given rabbinic, halakhic midrash much to discuss.[15]

This strange story begs many questions, of narrative cohesion, theological significance (what sort of God initiates such an encounter – and places himself at the mercy of a man – if he does here?) and plain narrative sense. Classical, rabbinic midrash might be expected to focus on the implications of the story for the keeping of food laws. However, midrash as a way to understand a biblical text in a creative literary context, with the purpose of gleaning new meanings for a contemporary readership, might be expected to be a rich and fruitful approach to this biblical text and its re-tellings. And so we return to Dickinson and her poem, 'A little East of Jordan' (Poem 142, p. 72).

Dickinson and Jacob

The poem, as it is found in collections of Dickinson's poems such as R. W. Franklin's, shares with 'Those – dying then' a regular, hymn-like rhythm, right up until the shocking final line. Jacob is not named until the second verse: in the first, he is given the title of 'A Gymnast', while the mysterious man is identified unequivocally as 'an Angel'. The identity issue is not of interest here, and it is a demand for a blessing that is the focus in verse 3, although the angel is addressed, more by the narrator than by Jacob, as 'Stranger!' in this verse. Jacob's role in the drama is extended and highlighted in the poem. As 'Gymnast' he is a strong, supple even modern figure, very much in control of events, 'waxing strong' in comparison to the Angel who is forced to 'beg [. . .] permission . . . to return'. That he wishes to return in order 'To Breakfast' gives his character a peculiarly earthbound, mundane aspect. From his demonstration of physical strength at the opening of the poem, it is Jacob's mental agility that is noted in the third verse. He is 'cunning' in his refusal to allow the angel to escape until a blessing is given. However, when light comes beyond the hills he will rename 'Peniel', a pun, the reader is aware from the Genesis

---

14 Claus Westermann, 1988, *Genesis*, Edinburgh: T & T Clark, pp. 228–31.

15 See, for example, the midrashic discussion of this text clearly translated and compiled by Norman Solomon in *The Talmud: A Selection*, 2009, London: Penguin, pp. 612–16.

version, on the word for 'face', Jacob the Gymnast is left 'bewildered'. The light somehow brings the revelation that, in a jarring break with the expected rhythm, 'he had worsted God'. Again, using contrasts, Dickinson uses a soft, pastoral image ('the silver fleeces') in the same verse as the hard, shocking moment of revelation. Jacob's injury to his hip at the hands of the man in Genesis 32.31 is not mentioned and there is no interest in this verse's power to explain any sort of current behaviour as there is in verse 31. Nor is Jacob's physical supremacy in any doubt. Jacob's physical and mental strength are maintained up until the final two lines. Even here, while there is surprise and perhaps shock, the use of the word 'worsted' places Jacob in an apparently powerful position. God is beaten, placed in a lower position than the victorious Jacob. Perhaps a pun on the noun 'worsted', meaning yarn or material, is also included here: God is twisted and pulled, by the wrestling, into a new form with new uses at the creative hands of humanity.

The dynamics of Dickinson's poem are very different from those of Genesis 32. Some of the ambiguities of that passage are resolved, and the outcome of the encounter is one that places Jacob in a much stronger position: 'bewildered', but once the darkness has gone, strong, whole and in a new relationship with God. There is little hint in this poem's retelling of the biblical story of any reference to Jacob's troubled relationship with Esau. However, in the second line, there is perhaps a slight hint that the angel may have some connection with Jesus – which would place this poem in a similar context to that of Wesley mentioned above. The setting is near the Jordan, the site of Jesus' baptism by John; and the story, the poet tells us, has been preserved because 'Evangelists' have 'record[ed]' it. The use of the word 'Evangelists' introduces us to an aspect of Dickinson's poetry that places her in a similar situation to that of the midrashists. In some cases, Dickinson appears to have written, and to have retained, more than one version of a poem, including this one, without leaving any editorial direction. Here, the version published by Martha Dickinson Bianchi, Dickinson's niece, in 1914,[16] has 'As *Genesis* records': a much less significant and resonant phrase, with no allusion to the Gospel witness at all. If the 'Evangelists' have a hand in preserving this story, it becomes a metaphor for the struggle to accept conversion, which the poet ultimately wins. Otherwise, if 'Genesis records', this is a much more straightforward retelling of the Genesis text.

---

16 Johnson suggests that the version in the 1914 edition came from a copy sent to Dickinson's sister-in-law, Sue, now lost, while the version now found in most editions came from one of the packets of poems found at home after Dickinson's death. See Thomas H. Johnson (ed.), 1955, *The Poems of Emily Dickinson, Including Variant Readings Critically Compared with all Known Manuscripts*, vol. 1, Cambridge, MA: Belknap Press, p. 45.

The suggestion that this alternative, 'Genesis', version is more straight-forward is strengthened considerably by its use of 'Wrestler' rather than 'Gymnast' for Jacob, and the description of him at the end as an 'astonished Wrestler' rather than a 'bewildered Gymnast'. 'Wrestler' merely follows the Genesis account, adding little, while 'Gymnast' gives a completely new understanding of the figure of Jacob. While other variations between the two versions are less significant, and they both stand as re-tellings of the one story, their readings of that story have quite different theological and literary implications.

A further aspect of Dickinson's work which gives it a midrashic feel is her frequent offering of alternatives within the one poem. This could be a list of possible words or even phrases, with no guidance offered about which to choose. One example of this is found in this poem. In the third verse, following the words of Jacob demanding a blessing, there is the option of identifying the angel as either 'Stranger' or 'Signor'. The meaning of each is quite different, implying either equality but uncertainty on the part of Jacob, or a sense of acknowledgement that he has encountered a being superior to himself. In most editions, it is 'Stranger' that is given, as this perhaps follows the flow of the rest of the poem. But clearly both or either, from the perspective of the poet, are available and appropriate. The reader (or editor) is given the task of choosing between them, or deciding not to choose.

This practice of offering alternatives in the text itself is of great interest to postmodern readings of Dickinson's poetry, and brings it close to the realm of midrash as a way of responding creatively and purposefully to the Bible. Sharon Cameron, in her book aptly titled *Choosing Not Choosing*, writes, 'it is assumed . . . that choice is required, even as the requirement is repeatedly, if subversively, transgressed'.[17] As she comments, it is not the case that Dickinson seems to be suggesting, as other poets such as Walt Whitman and W. B. Yeats do when they offer alternatives joined with 'or', that both alternatives are intended. In the poem we are discussing, the Angel cannot meaningfully be both 'Stranger' and 'Signor'. Lundin relates this ambiguity to the polyphony described by the Russian philosopher and literary critic Mikhail Bakhtin as being behind the great literary texts of modern times. For him, the reader and the multiple voices in the text, one of which may represent the author's point of view, engage in dialogue, but there is no domination by any one voice, and the final meaning of the work is never ultimately determined. This unfinalizable dialogue resonates with the hermeneutics of midrash as we have discussed it: although midrash is perhaps closer to Dickinson's poetry than Bakhtinian polyphony as it retains a theological significance beyond itself. As she wrote in a letter to Otis Phillips Lord in 1882, 'on

---

17 Sharon Cameron, 1992, *Choosing Not Choosing: Dickinson's Fascicles*, Chicago: University of Chicago Press, p. 24.

subjects of which we know nothing, or should I say *Beings* – . . . we both believe and disbelieve a hundred times an Hour, which keeps Believing nimble'.[18] Nimbleness of belief, perhaps the nimbleness of Jacob the gymnast, which ranges across the spectrum from conviction to no belief, still takes the struggle and the enterprise seriously. The internal strife generated by this struggle is real and in writing about it in the way she does, its reality is asserted and affirmed as spiritually significant. Something lies behind it, and in this Dickinson shares the concerns of rabbinic midrash, and this midrash gives us an angle from which to view her poetry.

With its very different tone, a later poetic retelling of the Jacob story offers a more anguished reading of the biblical text:

> The Battle fought between the Soul
> And No Man – is the One
> Of all the Battles prevalent –
> By far the Greater One –

> (Poem 629, p. 282)

This is a 'Bodiless Campaign' without direct reference to Jacob the Gymnast or the Angel, a battle in which all are engaged in their souls. Invisible, history does not 'record it': but the poem itself testifies to it in an oblique way that leaves its outcome uncertain:

> As Legions of a Night
> The Sunrise scatters – These endure –
> Enact – and terminate –

There are enough clues here to relate this poem to the Genesis story, but the significance of the story is transposed into a context of existential struggle. The identity of the adversary is in much more doubt, as it is in Genesis, but the struggle is real although its resolution is left unsaid. What it is which 'endure[s] . . . enact[s] . . . and terminate[s]' – the first two positively suggestive of God and his word, the final word more doom-laden – is unclear. There is certainly dialogue here between biblical text, reader and a variety of voices, but if the poem is read as midrash on the Jacob story, the free play of the dialogue is constrained by a theological purpose centred on the reality of the struggle to engage with something beyond the self.

While Dickinson could write, in rather downbeat terms, that

> The Bible is an antique volume
> Written by faded men,
> At the suggestion of Holy Spectres

> (Poem 1577, p. 581)

---

18 Roger Lundin, 2004, *Emily Dickinson and the Art of Belief*, 2nd edition, Grand Rapids, MI: Eerdmans, p. 140.

it also provided her with much inspiration and fascination, as that poem goes on to suggest. Midrash has been offered as an interpretative lens through which to understand her retellings of biblical stories as endlessly creative expressions of theological significance. We turn now to consider the work of a poet from a similar time but a completely different religious context. Does midrash offer such a useful perspective when applied to the poetry of Gerard Manley Hopkins?

Hopkins and Jacob

Gerard Manley Hopkins

Gerard Manley Hopkins was born into a prosperous middle-class family in Stratford, Essex, in 1844. A gifted scholar, at Oxford University he came under the influence of many of the powerful forces in the Anglican Church, including E. B. Pusey and Benjamin Jowett. However, in 1866 he was received by John Henry Newman into the Roman Catholic Church, a move that horrified his family. Two years later he entered the Novitiate of the Society of Jesus and began his nine years' training to become a Jesuit priest. At this stage, he burnt all he had written, and resolved not to write any more until or unless his superiors requested that he do so.

The discovery of the writings of Duns Scotus, with their stress on the individuality of things, knowable through their interaction with the senses of the beholder, resonated with his developing understanding of the individual energy of each thing encountered. As part of his training Hopkins moved to various locations and teaching positions in Britain and Ireland, although his mental and physical health was at times poor. While in Wales in 1875, he was asked by his superior to write about the tragic loss of a ship taking Catholic exiles from Germany, and 'The Wreck of the Deutschland' was the result. Further sonnets and other poems followed, although very little was accepted for publication, even in the Jesuits' own literature. After stints as priest in London, Oxford, Glasgow and Liverpool, and teacher of Greek at Stoneyhurst College in Blackburn, Hopkins became Chair of Classics at University College, Dublin in 1884. The teaching regime was exhausting, his political views were tested in Ireland, and he missed his family and friends in England. The 'Terrible Sonnets' of this period suggest intense spiritual and creative struggle. He died of typhoid fever in 1889 in Ireland.

In his seminal article on the interpretation of the Bible in Jewish midrashic and in literary contexts, Geoffrey H. Hartman takes as his subtitle the thirteenth line of Gerard Manley Hopkins' sonnet, 'Carrion Comfort'.[19] In 'The Struggle for the Text', Hartman, with Hopkins, asks 'O which

---

19 Gerard Manley Hopkins, 1967, *The Poems of Gerard Manley Hopkins*, 4th edn, W. H. Gardner and N. H. Mackenzie (eds), London: Oxford University Press, p. 99.

one? Is it each one?'.[20] The question in the poem comes from the speaker, agonizing over the motives that drew him to 'kiss the rod'. At the moment of conversion, he 'lapped strength, stole joy, would laugh, cheer'. But now he questions whether he was cheering the 'hero whose heaven-handling flung [him]', or 'foot trod [him]' himself. Here is Dickinson's battle with 'the Soul and No Man' in ghastly detail. Later in the same article, Hartman quotes from the midrash found in *Genesis Rabbah*, quoting R. Berekiah:

> There is none like God (Deuteronomy 32.26); yet who is like God? Jeshurun, which means Israel the Patriarch. Just as it is written of God, And the Lord alone shall be exalted (Isaiah 2.11), so of Jacob too; And Jacob was left alone (Genesis 32.25).[21]

The proof text under discussion is 'There is none like unto God, O Jeshurun'. In the midrash, the word 'alone' takes on two senses. Of all men, Jacob alone is sufficiently noble to be compared to God himself; but also, the aloneness of Jacob in his struggle with the man reminds us of the loneliness of God. 'Jacob wrestles with God as God wrestles with Himself'. In Hopkins' tortured retelling of the story from Genesis, midrash and poetry, and our readings of these texts, may reflect on one another in a way that brings new theological significance to them all.[22]

But first we should return to Hopkins' poem for a closer reading. The poem opens with a series of statements: 'Not, I'll not, carrion comfort, Despair, not feast on thee;' but even these violent, bloody assertions give way to a litany of questions all addressed to God:

> But ah, but O thou terrible, why wouldst thou rude on me
> Thy wring-world right foot rock? Lay a lionlimb against me? Scan
> With darksome devouring eyes my bruisèd bones?

While there is little to connect this first part of the sonnet with the Genesis 32 story, its clear echo in the closing lines ('I wretch lay wrestling with

---

20 Geoffrey H. Hartman, 1986, 'The Struggle for the Text', in Geoffrey H. Hartman and Sanford Budick (eds), *Midrash and Literature*, New Haven and London: Yale University Press, p. 3.

21 Hartman, 'The Struggle for the Text', p. 7.

22 For a more nuanced discussion of the relationship between midrash and Hopkins' poetry, see Rachel Salmon, 'Reading Hopkins: A Dialogue Between Two Traditions', in Joaquin Kuhn and Joseph J. Feeney, SJ (eds), 2002, *Hopkins Variations: Standing round a Waterfall*, Philadelphia: Saint Joseph's University Press, pp. 237–45. She comments that there is a similarity in the primacy of language in both Hopkins and midrash, which 'expresses itself in his semantic and syntactic eccentricity which gives rise to multiple, sometimes even contradictory, readings that do not appear to privilege univocality' (p. 244).

[my God!] my God') allows a second-time reader the potential to find in these earlier lines a new retelling of the story. Certainly the punishing nature of the Genesis encounter is here, in stark and brutal detail and perhaps with a Christian overlay. The obscure verb 'Rude' suggests the imprint of the cross; the 'right foot rock' suggests the might of the Church of Peter, Jesus' rock on which he will build his Church. The 'lionlimb' so delicately 'laid against [him]' suggests the power of a triumphant Christ in the language of the majestic beasts of Revelation. It is Jacob's injured weakness that is stressed here, in his struggle with a Christian God, rather than his hold of his attacker, against which the stranger is unable, temporarily, to 'prevail' (Genesis 32.25). However, in the speaker's determination to question his assailant, while 'frantic to avoid [him] and flee', there is something of the persistence of Jacob to wrestle a blessing out of the darkness.

And yet the poem will not allow such an easy conclusion or outcome suggested by the blessing that Jacob receives out of his struggle. The questions are left unanswered, and while Jacob is given a new voice, God and the assailant are silent here. The speaker's conversion is open to doubt ('since (seems) I kissed the rod'); 'O which one? Is it each one?' is left open as a possibility as the impetus for the turning to God. In the final line, the 'night' of Jacob's struggle is turned into 'that year', and the 'now done darkness' may refer to darkness that is finished and over, or has achieved its aim, or is simply exhausted for the moment, and waiting for its moment to return as day turns to night. The significance of the struggle is suggested by the bracketed and exclaimed 'my God', but the sense of fearful apprehension is also present, suggesting that little blessing has come out of the experience. In the violence of this scene, which is a present moment ('Not, I'll not, carrion comfort, Despair'. . .) continually provoked by the memory of a previous struggle, there is no sense of progress or moving on as a result of it. Like the open-endedness of Dickinson's 'and terminate–', this is an ongoing experience of God that offers little grounds for hope.

A reader familiar with the New Testament might want to read the story of Jesus in Gethsemane as a midrashic commentary on both the story of Jacob and this poem, particularly in the form of the story in Luke as it is found in the King James Version (Luke 22.41–6).[23] Jesus asks for the 'cup' to be removed from him, if it is God's will, and in his 'agony', 'his sweat was as it were great drops of blood falling down to the ground'. The scene is at night, and he is alone as his disciples are sleeping, although there is mention of an angel who 'ministers' to him. The struggle is a spiritual, mental one rather similar to that of the poem, but

---

23 Later versions of the passage remove verses 43–4 in which the angel, the agony and the blood-like sweat are mentioned, as they do not appear in the most reliable manuscripts of this Gospel.

the mention of Jesus' turmoil in the dark is suggestive of the Jacob text. The ministering angel is then either a redeeming feature of the original story or a rather menacing presence, if the figure in Genesis is also understood to be an angel. However, clearly this Christianizing of the wrestling story may be read as a fulfilment or closing down of the ambiguities of the Genesis text, as Jesus is firmly portrayed as overcoming his fears and accepting the will of God – and this is a charge often made of the use of the Hebrew Bible in the New Testament.[24] By drawing on both the Genesis and the Gospel stories, freely and allusively, Hopkins suggests that both Testaments retain their power to generate new, literary meanings, and perhaps even demand it. As Hartman reminds us, a defining feature of scripture is its 'frictionality', its 'capacity to leave traces, which incite and even demand interpretation of what it has incorporated'.[25] Whether the New Testament, in large or small measure, is a midrash on elements of the Hebrew Bible, or whether the New Testament and Christianity itself marked the end of the playful freedom of midrash for its readers and followers, is not an issue for this book. The ongoing retelling of scripture in the literature of later centuries, when read as midrash encourages us to read, certainly remains open and imaginative while potentially having something purposefully theological to impart.

When literary studies are reminded of the 'richness and subtlety of those strange rabbinic conversations which have been disdained for so long in favour of more objective and systematized modes of reading',[26] new possibilities are opened up. Invoking midrash as an interpretative perspective involves acknowledging the subjective beliefs of readers and the creators of texts, as well as being open to hearing many voices in the one text and accepting there may be no definitive answers. The story of Jacob wrestling with the man is both a metaphor for midrash's relationship with the written text, and a story that is ripe for midrashic readings throughout the centuries. The work of Emily Dickinson and Gerard Manley Hopkins has suggested that theological reflection on this text is not confined to doctrinal discussion, and that poetry may, in the tradition of midrash, read and be read as having something creative to say about theological truths.

---

24 For Susan Handelman, in her *Slayers of Moses*, 1982, New Testament allegorical interpretation, the taking of Old Testament narratives as figures or types of truer realities now revealed in Christ, closes down the endless possibilities of midrash. The Jesus of the New Testament, and of subsequent biblical exegesis, was taken to stabilize meaning and provide an ultimate answer to issues of interpretation. No longer was the process of interpretation taken to be a communication with God himself.

25 Hartman, 'The Struggle with the Text', p. 130.

26 Hartman, 'The Struggle with the Text', pp. 8–9.

Questions

1. What characteristics do rabbinic midrash and modern literary criticism share? In what ways are they different?
2. Are there any literary texts familiar to you that may be read as midrashim on specific biblical texts? What does this perspective add to our understanding of literature?

Further reading

Sharon Cameron, 1992, *Choosing Not Choosing: Dickinson's Fascicles*, Chicago: University of Chicago Press.

Emily Dickinson, 1998, *The Poems of Emily Dickinson: Reading Edition*, R. W. Franklin (ed.), Cambridge, MA: Belknap Press.

Paul S. Fiddes, 'G. M. Hopkins', in Rebecca Lemon, Emma Mason, Jonathan Roberts and Christopher Rowland (eds), 2009, *The Blackwell Companion to the Bible in English Literature*, Chichester: Wiley-Blackwell, pp. 563–76.

David Jasper and Stephen Prickett, 1999, *The Bible and Literature: A Reader*, Oxford: Blackwell.

Thomas H. Johnson (ed.), 1955, *The Poems of Emily Dickinson, Including Variant Readings Critically Compared with all Known Manuscripts*, vol. 1, Cambridge, MA: Belknap Press.

Susan A. Handelman, 1982, *The Slayers of Moses: The Emergence of Rabbinic Interpretation in Modern Literary Theory*, Albany: State University of New York Press.

Geoffrey H. Hartman, 1986, 'The Struggle for the Text', in Geoffrey H. Hartman and Sanford Budick (eds), *Midrash and Literature*, New Haven and London: Yale University Press, pp. 3–18.

Gerard Manley Hopkins, 1967, *The Poems of Gerard Manley Hopkins*, 4th edn, W. H. Gardner and N. H. Mackenzie (eds), London: Oxford University Press.

Roger Lundin, 2004, *Emily Dickinson and the Art of Belief*, 2nd edition, Grand Rapids, MI: Eerdmans.

Jacob Neusner, 1987, *What is Midrash?*, Philadelphia: Fortress Press.

Jacob Neusner, 2001, *The Halakhah and the Aggadah: Theological Perspectives*, Lanham, MS: University Press of America.

Rachel Salmon, 2002, 'Reading Hopkins: A Dialogue Between Two Traditions', in Joaquin Kuhn and Joseph J. Feeney, SJ (eds), *Hopkins Variations: Standing round a Waterfall*, Philadelphia: Saint Joseph's University Press, pp. 237–45.

Lesleigh Cushing Stahlberg, 2008, *Sustaining Fictions: Intertextuality, Midrash, Translation, and the Literary Afterlife of the Bible*, New York: T & T Clark.

Claus Westermann, 1988, *Genesis*, Edinburgh: T & T Clark.

9

Recurring Themes: Apocalypse

Creation and apocalypse form the bookends to the sweep of the Bible story. Both have permeated literature, endlessly fascinated with the beginnings and endings of things. In this chapter, the Apocalypse or Revelation of John, the final book of the Bible, will be introduced in all its complexity and violence. Its literary relationship with Genesis will be considered, and then two poems from writers we met in Chapter 3, W. B. Yeats and Edwin Muir, will be read for the ways apocalyptic imagery works in modern literary texts.

> The Revelation of Jesus Christ, which God gave unto him, to shew unto his servants things which must shortly come to pass; and he sent and signified it by his angel unto his servant John: Who bare record of the word of God, and of the testimony of Jesus Christ, and of all things that he saw. (Revelation 1.1–2)

With this confident assertion, the book known as the Revelation of John opens. The word often associated with this book, and the movement of which it is part, 'apocalypse', comes from the Greek word for 'revelation', from the first verse here. Receiving and passing on information about the future given in the form of words, visions and dreams, is at the heart of apocalyptic literature. The genre emphasizes, even creates, a sense of being part of a privileged group with inside knowledge about what is to come, and how to avoid the destruction that seems inevitably to be involved in the last days. There is comfort and encouragement for this group 'in the know', but warning of judgement and tribulation to come for those who either refuse to accept the revelation, or whose wickedness has already consigned them to eternal punishment or annihilation. Mercy and grace are not given much of a role in these texts, and the choice presented to their readers is usually stark. Little wonder that texts such as Revelation have both fascinated and repelled readers, often polarizing them into widely diverging camps. Even for those who do not accept the literal picture of the future that such texts present, however, apocalyptic imagery may be a powerful way to express fearfulness about the way the world is heading.

The Book of Daniel

The Revelation of John, of course, did not appear unique and freshly minted. It stood in a line of Jewish literary tradition that went back at least to the Book of Daniel. This very popular book of just 12 chapters clearly illustrates the background of persecution that marks apocalyptic writing. The book is set during the time of the Babylonian exile. From the seventh chapter, the Jewish folk hero Daniel is presented, in the first person, as someone who experiences dreams and visions, and who needs angelic envoys to interpret them. Four apocalypses are presented in Chapters 7–12: two are visions interpreted by a heavenly visitor; one is Daniel's meditation on scripture, which is responded to by an angel; the fourth is the result of a trance in which he receives the teaching of an angel about events in the past, the future and the final days of the world, which are imminent.

The majority of modern commentators argue that the Book of Daniel refers to events within the history of Israel from the Babylonian captivity (sixth century BCE) to the time of the conquest of the Greek Antiochus IV Epiphanes (second century BCE), the latest in a long line of Babylonian, Persian and Greek invaders and persecutors of the Jewish people. The focus in the Book of Daniel, for most commentators, lies at the end of this period, when persecution at the hands of Antiochus was particularly fierce. In 167 BCE, Antiochus had set up an altar to Zeus in the Jerusalem temple, and was forcing the Jews to participate in pagan practices on pain of death. The suggestion is that the Book of Daniel, written just after this date, offers a solution to the horrors the Jewish people were experiencing: these troubles, the book argues, are the climax of all the travail the Jews will ever have to face, for God will intervene with his heavenly host and destroy Antiochus and his army. No human resolution is now possible, only God is able to bring an end to the situation by inaugurating the Last Days. The book offers comfort by assuring its readers that once God claims his victory, faithful Jews living and dead will be brought to judgement and given eternal reward for having withstood such persecution.

An important distinction between prophetic writing such as we find in other places in the Hebrew Bible, for example in Jeremiah and Isaiah, and the apocalyptic writing of the Book of Daniel, is that there is no call to repentance and no expectation that a resolution to the current state of affairs will come from the world of humanity. Instead, the emphasis in Daniel is on the unstoppable will of God, which, it is promised, is determined to bring the current intolerable situation of the readers of the book to a dramatic and final end, in their favour. This sudden and decisive intervention of God in a world deemed beyond human repair is a distinguishing feature of apocalyptic writing, and will be seen clearly in Revelation. Meanwhile, while the fall of Antiochus IV Epiphanes did not herald the end of the world as it was foretold in Daniel, the book nevertheless gained huge and swift popularity, and was imitated widely in the succeeding centuries. Its combination of cosmic conflict between the ultimately victorious God and a shockingly powerful adversary, and assessment of history within a stereotypical time frame, setting the present age against the age to come, spoke to generations of Jews suffering persecution of one kind or another. The writers of such texts found the literary construct of the seer, the vision, the one who interprets and the interpretation itself, to be a suitably allusive and appealing method to deliver comfort and encouragement. The fantastic, horrific and strange imagery employed to describe the fate of the enemy, but demanding the interpretation of a divinely appointed intermediary, had both imaginative power and enough room for ambiguity to allow such texts to continue to speak to readers long after the crisis they originally addressed was past. While the interpretation, itself quite open, may no longer fit, or even be understood, the vision remained.

In Daniel 7.1–8, 15–18 we find many of the characteristics of apocalyptic writing: a vision given in a dream of four strange and violent creatures, with both familiar and unfamiliar features, set on a cosmic plane, needing the interpretative insight of an other-worldly figure. Readers through the ages have sought to identify the four kings whom the four beasts represent. The specific meaning of the ten horns has also been scrutinized, as standard symbols of power and kingship (see Psalms 75.4; 89.24; 132.17), while the mention of a little horn in the following verse is traditionally identified with Antiochus IV Epiphanes.

Where did the Book of Revelation come from?

The Book of Revelation does not follow one of the standard conventions of apocalyptic texts, namely the pseudepigraphic use of a heroic figure from the past, such as Enoch, Isaiah or Ezra (or Paul or Peter, whose names some later apocalyptic writers chose to adopt). Assuming John and the author of the book are the same person, Revelation appears to have been written by someone who was living at the same time as the book was produced and the suffering it describes was being endured. It is always possible that John the Christian prophet had such an exalted reputation, although now obscure to us, that his name was used by another writer in the same way that the author of the Book of Daniel used his name. However, there is an immediacy about the work, and no pretence at the end that it comes from a time before the present age of suffering, but was not understood then (as we find in Daniel 12.9), which suggests that this convention was not followed here. Otherwise, the Book of Revelation falls squarely within the tradition of apocalyptic literature, and is most usefully and meaningfully read as such.

Most commentators agree that Revelation arose at a time of great persecution and anguish for the early Church, just as Daniel was written and found favour when the Jewish people were experiencing deep distress at the hands of a foreign oppressor. Such a time came for the Christian Church in the closing decade of the first century CE, when the might of the Roman Empire was demanding co-operation in emperor worship from its subjects, and exacting a heavy penalty from those who refused, as many Christians did. Violent, public persecution became a possibility for many and a reality for some. Against the Empire, it would have been natural for those in the Church to look to the intervention of God as their only hope, as the only force capable of defeating such an all-powerful and fearful system pitted against them. They waited and longed for a time when eternal rewards and punishments were handed out, and their position, apparently so lacking in power, would be vindicated finally and forever.

Apocalyptic writing in Judaism had begun to lose its influence after the fall of Jerusalem in 70 CE to the Romans. This destruction of Jerusalem and all it represented was the Roman response to a Jewish rebellion begun in 66 CE, which had aimed to force a divine reaction along apocalyptic lines. Some of those who had rejected such a high-risk and, ultimately, futile course of action, had established a new centre of Jewish learning and observance in Jamnia, west of Jerusalem. Here it appears that a decision was made that Jewish scripture would only comprise literature composed before the time of the prophet Ezra (late fifth century BCE), thus rejecting the apocalyptic texts that had been so popular in recent years – although the Book of Daniel, perhaps because of its deep popularity and its claim to have been written during the Babylonian exile, survived. In place of apocalyptic hope, those in control of Judaism as it was defined at Jamnia concentrated on finding contemporary meaning in the ancient laws of their tradition. And so the Mishnah, Talmud and other midrashic traditions were born, as was discussed in Chapter 8.

Meanwhile, apocalyptic as a literary movement continued to offer meaning to those Christian communities under pressure from Roman imperialistic religion, or fearing such pressure. Such an uneven confrontation and such a direct and brutal threat to what was understood as the community of God's faithful seemed hopelessly insurmountable without direct and final intervention by God himself, in Christian terms in the shape of the return of his Son. The first coming of God's anointed had been limited, showing the way of salvation to those who put their trust in him, although his resurrection from the dead demonstrated and inaugurated the power over the forces of evil with which he would return to claim a final victory. While apocalyptic texts were being rejected and suppressed by the Jews, Christians were searching through them for new messages and recycling them in their own writing. Daniel clearly echoes through Revelation, and citations of 1 Enoch are to be found in Jude

14–15. Mark 13 is often called the 'Little Apocalypse' as it is infused with images of Jesus' dramatic and decisive return to claim a final victory. Paul too has apocalyptic passages, as in 1 Thessalonians 4.13–18. Later in the early Church, pseudonymous writings of Christian figures such as Peter, Paul and Mary appeared, all offering apocalyptic visions and consolation for current trials. The richness of apocalyptic images and ideas continues to be woven in sacred and secular texts in modern times, and their after-life will be considered later in this chapter. However, it is to the Book of Revelation that we must now return.

Revelation is not a book to be read from start to finish with any hope of finding a narrative thread or developing argument. Many commentators have attempted to find a structure in the book that explains its complexity and shifting images. None has gained academic or popular consensus. After the introductory sentence, which we read above, establishing the credentials of the seer and, we assume, the writer John, who has been handed the revelation first given to Jesus by God himself, there is an abrupt shift of genre. Rather than plunging into the expected world of grotesque vision, the reader is offered seven letters of advice to named churches in Asia Minor, rather in the style of Paul himself, prefaced by an announcement that John had received what follows while in exile due to his faith. The apocalyptic tone resumes in chapter 4, in which John describes a vision of being taken to the throne of God in heaven. Familiar apocalyptic furniture appears in the following chapters: scrolls and seals, to be opened by an exalted lamblike creature. As each seal is revealed, a series of disasters is shown to befall the earth. On the opening of the seventh seal, seven angels blowing trumpets appear, and a new series of disasters begins, with a message from seven thunders given between the sixth and seventh thunders, which are not to be passed on. Jerusalem is shown to be the centre of great destruction and terror. But on the seventh trumpet, the heavenly realm erupts with songs of praise to God.

By Revelation 12, there is a shift of scene and a new set of characters: a woman about to give birth and a devouring dragon. God rescues the child, the dragon enters into cosmic battle and is defeated, but begins a reign of terror on the earth, separating humanity into two groups, those who bear his mark and are able to carry on as before, and those who do not. Another sevenfold series is introduced, this time involving bowls that are poured out, creating plagues on the world. This leads to a battle at Armageddon involving all the kings of the earth. In Revelation 17 to 18, another female figure appears, the Whore of Babylon, 'drunk with the blood of the saints' (17.5), ultimately destroyed by one of the beasts mentioned earlier in the text. Christ appears on a white horse to enter into battle with the dragon and his followers. The dragon is defeated and chained for 1000 years, during which time Christian martyrs are raised from the dead and live in a state of happiness with Christ on earth. But at the end of the 1000 years, war between the dragon and his followers and God erupts once again until divine fire is ultimately victorious. Judgement follows, and for those who are saved, the heavenly Jerusalem appears, with a promise of everlasting communion with God. The book itself closes with an angelic warning to John not to keep what he has been shown a secret, and a warning to readers not to change anything that has been written.

The heavenly setting of the vision, the ideal vantage point to view the dramatic intervention of God in the desperate and godless world of humanity; the repeated attacks on the godly by a powerful and cruel oppressor; the promise of a new age and the final defeat of the enemy: all of these features make sense to a reader familiar with apocalyptic writing. The narrative thread may be impossible to follow, and is not important to this genre of literature. While the identity of the various characters may have been obvious to some of the text's original readers, they are hard to assign at this remove. The strange power of the imagery has continued to attract and speak to readers in hard-pressed situations, as it was designed to do, but the attempt to find literal connections between contemporary history and the events described in Revelation is not within the scope of this book. From a literary perspective it is probably more important and fruitful to offer reflections on the ways in which apocalyptic images have continued to echo in literature as part of the vocabulary of fear and hope for the future.

Creation and apocalypse

Let us first take a step backwards, however, and connect these apocalyptic images that close the Bible with the story of creation with which it opens. Such a step allows us to focus on a small section of the Book of Revelation, the closing two chapters in which the newly created Jerusalem appears and the presence of the tree of life signals a close relationship between Genesis and Revelation in this section at least.

In Genesis 3, Adam and Eve are expelled from the Garden of Eden in case, in his new state of knowledge, Adam 'put[s] forth his hand and take[s] also of the tree of life, and eat[s], and live[s] forever' (v. 22). The verse is cryptic and no further explanation is offered as to why this is to be considered something to be avoided at all costs. Perhaps for this reason, the tree of life is not a common image in the rest of the Old Testament. The Garden of Eden itself plays a significant role in Ezekiel 28, 30 and 40–8. In the earlier chapters, the tree of life is not mentioned, although in the description of the new temple in Ezekiel 47 we read of a life-giving river and 'all kinds of trees' growing on its banks, their fruit appearing monthly for food, and their leaves for healing (47.12). While there is a straightforward allusion in Revelation to the single tree in Genesis 3.22 in John's promise to the Church at Ephesus that they will 'eat from the tree of life that is in the paradise of God' (Revelation 2.7), it is this much more complex verse in Ezekiel that is surely alluded to in Revelation 22.1–2. Here, on either side of the 'water of life' sits the tree of life 'which bare twelve manner of fruits, and yielded her fruit every month: and the leaves of the tree were for the healing of the nations'.

The puzzle in the Revelation text is to explain how one tree of life can sit on both sides of the river. It is not as simple as suggesting, as G. K. Beale does in his Commentary on Revelation,[1] that the singular is to be understood in a collective sense, the multiplication of trees as part of the overflowing and exaggerated nature of the new paradise in comparison to the old. Elsewhere, references to the tree of life in God's eschatological garden in Revelation are firmly in the singular (2.7; 22.14, 18–19), and it is only here, in the context of monthly fruit and healing leaves, that the tree has apparently multiplied. As Steve Moyise argues,[2] John seems to have two traditions to draw on, one from Genesis and one from Ezekiel: in his text, the awkward and uncertain image of the tree of life is resurrected from obscurity in the Hebrew Bible, and given a prominent and fertile place in the geography and theology of the new Eden that his new Jerusalem represents.

Further elements of the creation stories to be found in Revelation suggest that this final book of the Bible envisages a time when God will act as he did at the beginning of the world, and create something new and transformed. In Revelation 12.9, the dragon who attacks the woman about to give birth is identified as 'that old serpent ... which deceiveth of the whole world': his ultimate fate is to be 'thrown into the lake of fire and brimstone' (20.10), to be tormented eternally. In 21.4, death is described as being 'no more'; in 22.3, it is promised that nothing accursed will be allowed in the new Jerusalem. Taken together, these statements suggest that the punishments of the fall are being understood as facing reversal in the age to come; while the removal of the sea (21.1) and of night (22.5) also hints that the creation story of Genesis is due for a winding backwards. This new creation will be very different from the original.

While the intertextual imagery of creation in Revelation is not extensive, it is woven throughout the text, from both Genesis stories, and in such a way that there is encouraging and inspiring continuity and hope for the future offered. However, this is re-creation only for those on the right side, it is not universally available and there is none of the sense of its potential as the beginning of a new story that we find in both Genesis

---

1 G. K. Beale, 1999, *The Book of Revelation*, NIGTC; Grand Rapids, MI: Paternoster, p. 1106.

2 Steve Moyise, 2012, 'Models for Intertextual Interpretation of Revelation', in Richard B. Hays and Stefan Alkier (eds), *Revelation and the Politics of Apocalyptic Interpretation*, Waco, TX: Baylor University Press, pp. 39–41.

accounts. The new Jerusalem as the new Eden is fixed and closed, an ending rather than a beginning.

Some commentators have found this fixity uncomfortable, and have found destabilizing elements in the text of Revelation that undermine the vision as it is apparently presented.[3] One such image is the lake of fire in Revelation 20.15 and 21.8. Here, right in the centre of the new creation, continues to exist a threatening and devouring place: it may be outside the gates of the city (22.15), but it is very much part of its wider landscape. Moreover, a feminist reading of this text would raise the troubling issue of the image of the city as the Bride, being entered not only by her husband, the Lamb (21.9), but also by those whose names are written in the Lamb's book (21.27). There is something about the massed nature of this entering of the personified city that to many modern readers has a sordid ring to it. The Bride stands in contrast to the other women in the text, in particular the Whore of Babylon (Revelation 17), who is described in such fascinated and gory detail. Both, however, are ultimately at the mercy of the masculine figures who control their fate. This overpoweringly masculine and deeply violent portrayal of God is discussed from a postmodern perspective by Stephen Moore, who, in his book *God's Gym: Divine Male Bodies of the Bible*, questions whether this God is worthy of worship.[4] Modern readers are perhaps more alert to such difficulties in the text than readers from earlier ages, and it may be that literature that draws on apocalyptic images both encourages and reflects such unease. Let us turn now to the poets we met in Chapter 3 to explore their response to this apocalyptic new age.

Apocalypse in Yeats and Muir

Both W. B. Yeats's poem 'The Second Coming'[5] and Edwin Muir's 'The Horses'[6] were written at times of social uncertainty and fear for the future. Like the Book of Daniel and the Revelation of John, they offer a response to a period of turmoil in which the only hope left seems to be intervention on a cosmic scale. Humanity has failed and its fate lies in the hands of forces beyond its control. While in 'The Horses' that fate has a positive outcome, in 'The Second Coming' the nature of the cosmic

---

3 See for example Tina Pippin, 1994, 'Peering into the Abyss: A Postmodern Reading of the Biblical Bottomless Pit', in E. S. Malbon and E. V. McKnight (eds), *The New Literary Criticism and the New Testament*, Sheffield: Sheffield Academic Press, pp. 251–67.

4 Stephen D. Moore, 1996, *God's Gym: Divine Male Bodies of the Bible*, New York and London: Routledge.

5 W. B. Yeats, 1981, *The Collected Poems of W. B. Yeats*, 2nd edn, London: Macmillan, p. 210.

6 Edwin Muir, 1984, *Collected Poems*, London: Faber & Faber, p. 246.

intervention is much less joyfully anticipated. It is into the latter poem in particular that some of the troubling aspects of Revelation seep, Yeats being apparently attuned to the horror and volatility of the vision offered there and reflecting it as he reflected on the menacing uncertainties of his age.

'The Second Coming' was written at the beginning of 1919, and published at the end of 1920. The horror of the First World War must be considered as a backdrop to the poem, but there were other more specific and unsettling events that are reflected there. The poem speaks of international disorder, even anarchy, and early extant versions of it refer implicitly to the Treaty of Brest-Litovsk in 1918, which made possible the handover of control of semi-autonomous Baltic States and the Ukraine from Germany. In the month in which the poem was completed, the Spartacist Uprising was quelled with great violence in Germany and civil war raged in Russia. Although it was later to be associated with the upheaval of the Irish War of Independence, because of its late publication date, the poem was in fact written just in advance of that tumultuous series of events, and is more concerned with reactionary fears about revolution sweeping across Europe. The more personal context in which it arose for Yeats himself was the imminent birth of his first child, and the influence of the occult, in which he and his wife were immersed. For him, everything seemed to point to a soon-to-be-realized time of chaos that would bring in a new world order. However, while the 'rocking cradle' and 'Bethlehem' in the poem evoke the Christ-story, there is no expectation of a triumphant return of a saviour. The rocking cradle vexes its sleeping seers to 'nightmare' and it is a 'rough beast' who 'slouches' towards its birth at Bethlehem.

In terms of its relationship to the apocalyptic of Revelation, 'The Second Coming' shares much in both structure and imagery. The poem's opening lines offer an assessment of the current situation. Much has been written about the image of the 'gyre', part of Yeats's personal understanding of history worked out in collaboration with occultists and magicians. Of more interest here is the choice of the word 'loosed' to describe the effect of 'mere anarchy' on the world, and also the 'blood-dimmed tide'. In Revelation, the sea becomes 'as the blood of a dead man' in response to the pouring out of the second angel's bowl (15.3), and Satan is loosed from his 1000-year long imprisonment in the pit (20.3, 7) to wage war on the world and God one last time. Taking these cues from Revelation, the poem is set in the tumultuous world just prior to the final battle between God and his age-old adversary. Like the address to the Churches in the opening chapters of Revelation, the first section of the poem warns that 'lack of conviction' is an inadequate response to the 'passionate intensity' of their foes.

In the second section, a revelation of the Second Coming comes unbidden to the speaker, acting in the apocalyptic tradition of the seer such as

John. The vision comes not from the throne of God, but from the 'Spiritus Mundi', grounding it literally in the 'waste of desert sand' rather than in the rich opulence of the heavenly court of John's visions. The fantastic creature that is the object of the vision, and that will presumably intervene in the affairs of the world, is defined obliquely, a 'shape with lion body and head of a man', with a focus on its 'slow thighs', signalling its power and inexorability but not its exalted status. Compare the symbols of power focused on in Revelation: eyes like flaming fire; multiple crowns; a sharp sword coming from his mouth and the name of the king of kings inscribed upon his robe and thigh (Revelation 19.11–16). The companions of the 'shape' are the 'shadows of the indignant desert birds', an echo, surely, of the call in Revelation of the angel in response to the appearance of the magnificent rider on the white horse, to all the 'fowls that fly in the midst of heaven' to gather for the 'supper of the great God' (Revelation 19.17). Here perhaps we find an intersection between the horrified fascination of the seer in the poem and the visionary John's account, for the supper the birds are called to participate in in the biblical text is 'the flesh of kings, and the flesh of captains, and the flesh of mighty men, and the flesh of horses, and of them that sit on them, and the flesh of all men, both free and bond, both small and great' (Revelation 19.18). Yeats has been criticized for twisting Revelation into an anti-Christian message, but here it may be argued that he is drawing out of the apocalypse a horror that is already present, and even treated with some relish.

Darkness falls again on the speaker's vision, but he feels able to offer his own interpretation of what he has experienced ('now I know') in terms of the effect of the incarnation on 20 centuries of history. His closing question about the identity of the 'rough beast' inexorably moving towards its destiny lacks the acclamatory feel of the ending of Revelation, although there is an anxiety even in these verses expressed in the warning not to amend the words of the text as it stands (22.18–19), and a longing in the plea to Jesus to come as he has promised (22.20). Both texts end with a sense of lack of fulfilment and waiting, and both have spoken to the imaginations of the hard-pressed. It is often commented that 'The Second Coming' is the most anthologized of Yeats's poems, although it is not considered among his most critically acclaimed work. However, by appealing to the vivid images of Revelation, and shaping them within a terse, pointed and self-contained poem, Yeats has highlighted their power and horrific intensity for a new generation of readers.

Like 'The Second Coming', Edwin Muir's 'The Horses' is one of the poet's most anthologized poems. It comes from the same late collection, One Foot in Eden, as 'Adam's Dream', and reflects the intense fear of nuclear war that the Cold War between the superpowers of the USSR and the USA threatened, which was widely felt in the 1950s and beyond. The setting of the poem is in a period after apocalyptic disaster. In structure it has similar features to both Revelation and Yeats's poem: first it describes something of the effect of the disaster and the response of the surviving community; then in a visionary section it portrays hope for a new beginning in the arrival of a herd of horses and the possibility of a new relationship with those who remain. This first descriptive section deliberately echoes the creation story in Genesis 1, but in reverse. It was a 'seven days war' that 'put the earth to sleep', and the 'second', 'third' and 'sixth' days are marked with increasing horror and dread. The disaster is described as a gradual descent into silence, alluding to the fading of the divine and creating Word: the survivors make their 'covenant with silence', the stillness makes them 'afraid', and the failure of the radios on the second day means they offer 'no answer'. God is absent, but the description of the disaster in terms of its effect on technology suggests the cause of the destruction is humanity. The plane plunging into the sea and the warship with its 'dead bodies piled on deck', the tractors 'like dank sea-monsters couched and waiting', are all turned away from and taken as evidence that the modern world has failed. If the radio should speak again, the survivors assert that they 'would not listen . . . would not let it bring /That bad old world that swallowed its children quick/ At one great gulp.' Instead, they find meaning in the past, 'Far past . . . [their] . . . fathers' land'. Their existence may not be the bliss of the New Jerusalem, but like that mythical place it reflects the past as much as the future.

But the poem turns at this point into a much more hopeful statement of the potential of humanity to respond to the past and to an 'old command' that brings a new sense of meaning. The arrival of the horses is described not visually, as 'Adam's Dream' describes its vision of the potential of human endeavour, but aurally: the 'distant tapping' becomes a 'deepening drumming' and then a 'hollow thunder'. Their appearance is dramatic, powerful and cleansing, 'like a wild wave charging', a sharp contrast to the inert and decaying tractors. Many have written of Muir's love and respect for horses, stemming from his childhood on farms in Orkney where survival depended on the power of horses. Here the vision also taps into ancient memories of the mythic majesty of 'fabulous steeds'. The 'wilderness of the broken world' into which the young horses have arrived is contrasted with 'their own Eden': they bring their own sense of the innocence of a world before the Fall. They also bring 'archaic companionship' in place of the mechanized and alienating technology that has failed so dramatically. The relationship of 'free servitude' by which they work for the survivors changes the people from damaged and fearful individuals to those who know what it means to have 'pierce[d] . . . hearts'.

This is a very different image of the horse from the one offered in Revelation, although both texts are in awe of their power. The sixth angel's trumpet unleashes a great cavalry of fire-breathing horses with heads like lions and tails like serpents (9.13–19). Their role is to kill a third of humanity, wounding them with their tails and poisoning them with their sulphuric breath. Although the riders of the horses are mentioned, it is the 'power' of the horses (v. 19) that brings about destruction. Later in the vision, in Revelation 19, heaven opens and a white horse appears, bearing the 'King of kings and Lord of lords' (v. 16): here it is the rider whose sword 'smites the nations' (v. 15) and slays the followers of the beast, rather than the horse itself. 'The Horses', with its apocalyptic starting point, clearly echoes the cyclical pattern of creation made new that is found in Revelation. However, just as creation is reversed by humanity's descent into mechanization and loss of relationship with anything deeper, so the message of Revelation is transformed in the poem. The image of the horse that offers 'free servitude' rather than violent conquest reverses the apocalyptic vision of Revelation, and re-aligns the image of true salvation with a sense of relationship, mutuality and sacrifice. The Christlike redemption the horses offer and symbolize is an alternative vision to that of Revelation. It continues to offer hope to those in fear of the future, and to demand a change of perspective from those who receive the vision and experience its power. It speaks to those who find the violence of Revelation troubling with an alternative hope, in the mythic language of vision.

In all of the texts we have considered in this chapter, shared and powerful images have been used to speak to contexts of fear and powerlessness. Hope for change, and a sense that humanity is inadequate to bring about such change, runs through them all. Just as creation is understood in Genesis to be the work of God alone, so the working out or unworking of creation, in the worlds of these texts, demands intervention on a cosmic scale. In all of them, humanity is shown to be at the mercy of outside forces. Change is viewed as inevitable, whether it is to be feared, hoped for or simply endured. Apocalyptic, like creation to which it is closely related, it has been argued here, remains a resonant theme within the Bible itself and through later literature.

Questions

1. Consider any literary texts that have apocalyptic themes: does the reading of the book of Revelation offered here shed any light on these texts?
2. In your view, does apocalyptic as a literary genre arise more often in times of crisis, and if so, can you give any examples?

Further reading

G. K. Beale, 1999, *The Book of Revelation*, NIGTC; Grand Rapids, MI: Paternoster.
Ian Boxall, 2002, *Revelation: Vision and Insight: An Introduction to the Apocalypse*, London: SPCK.
John J. Collins, 1993, *Daniel* (Hermeneia), Minneapolis: Fortress Press.

John J. Collins, 1998, *The Apocalyptic Imagination: An Introduction to Jewish Apocalyptic Literature*, 2nd edition, Grand Rapids, MI: Eerdmans.

Donald E. Gowan, 2001, *Daniel*, Abingdon Old Testament Commentaries, Nashville: Abingdon Press.

Scott M. Lewis, 2004, *What are They Saying about New Testament Apocalyptic?*, New York: Paulist Press.

Stephen D. Moore, 1996, *God's Gym: Divine Male Bodies of the Bible*, New York and London: Routledge.

Steve Moyise, 2012, 'Models for Intertextual Interpretation of Revelation', in Richard B. Hays and Stefan Alkier (eds), *Revelation and the Politics of Apocalyptic Interpretation*, Waco, TX: Baylor University Press, pp. 31–43.

Edwin Muir, 1984, *Collected Poems*, London: Faber & Faber.

Tina Pippin, 1994, 'Peering into the Abyss: A Postmodern Reading of the Biblical Bottomless Pit', in E. S. Malbon and E. V. McKnight (eds), *The New Literary Criticism and the New Testament*, Sheffield: Sheffield Academic Press, pp. 251–67.

Joseph Trafton, 2005, *Reading Revelation: A Literary and Theological Commentary*, rev. edn, Macon, GA: Smyth & Helwys.

W. B. Yeats, 1981, *The Collected Poems of W. B. Yeats*, 2nd edn, London: Macmillan.

Conclusion

In the preceding chapters, we have read a wide range of texts from a variety of perspectives. We have considered themes that have run through biblical texts and literary texts. A sense of the history of attempts to read the Bible as literature, and of the Bible in literature, has been offered. We have read biblical and literary texts beside each other, trying to apply theories of intertextuality, narratology, reader-response criticism, feminist interpretation and midrash to both. Some of these approaches, and some of these readings, might be deemed more successful than others in terms of the insights they have offered. Perhaps each reader of these readings will make different assessments of them, and find a varying set of approaches more amenable than others. They have been discussed here with little in the way of critical comment, beyond their historical development and an indication of their fate in the broader fields of biblical and literary studies. In recent years, however, the very application of such approaches in both biblical and literary studies has been questioned by the same critics who were earlier keen to explore their potential. The arrival of 'post-theory' on the scene of textual studies will be considered here, as it challenges all of the neat categories of readings we have covered thus far.

In Chapter 2, we raised the substantial objections of critics such as T. S. Eliot and C. S. Lewis from the 1950s against the very idea of the Bible being read as if it were literature. For these critics, and others like them, the Bible was another category of texts altogether. Its status as a sacred text, as scripture, had guaranteed its powerfulness in the literature of the succeeding centuries. For Lewis, the biblical text itself resisted any attempt to be read for its literary worth alone. And certainly, as was noted in Chapter 2, interest in the Bible as literature is stronger in the world of biblical studies than in the literary world, where it might have been expected to be read with relish, although there are exceptions to this, as will be discussed further below in terms of a wider understanding of literary criticism. Moreover, in biblical studies, historical-critical study remains a powerful force, and is often taken as being in opposition to more literary readings. The biblical text as 'window' onto its recoverable world model continues to be a dominant view in biblical studies, the idea of the text having literary value in itself remaining for many an insignificant aspect of its importance. The role of the reader, especially the modern reader, in the creation of meaning in the text, for literary critics a commonplace, is still a step too far for many traditional biblical critics.

However, as we have seen throughout this book, the strict boundaries created around literary, sacred and historical texts, and between readings that take a literary, historical or theological perspective, are now much less fixed in all fields than they used to be. There is at least the potential to draw on insights from many perspectives in any one reading of any text, whether literary or biblical, without prejudicing any of them. We have noted that the historical context of a text, for some literary critics, has gained importance, both in the opening up of a reading of the text, and in the illumination offered by that reading. In this new world of possibilities, biblical studies may find it has much to learn but also much to offer. But we should be aware of a further development in the broad field of literary studies, which is challenging the traditional understandings of theory, canon, history and text, and which is beginning to make its mark in biblical studies too. Stephen Moore, who has done more than most to introduce the world of biblical studies to the theories of literary criticism and their implications, offers a discussion of this new development in the closing chapters of his book, *The Bible in Theory*. While his work is challenging in places, and often methodologically dense, his insights are grounded in both a thorough knowledge of the world of the Bible, in particular the New Testament, and in an understanding of critical theory and its implications. Here I will focus on one of his essays, which explores the new world in which the theories that have sustained a relationship between biblical and literary critics for the past few decades are gone 'beyond'.

Reading the Bible 'after' theory

The title of Moore's article sums up its thesis: 'A Modest Manifesto for New Testament Literary Criticism: How to Interface with a Literary Studies Field that is Postliterary, Post-theoretical, and Postmethodological'. He opens with an assertion related to the assimilation of certain strands of literary criticism into mainstream biblical studies, as we have noted in previous chapters: narrative criticism for Moore 'seems in retrospect to have been a singularly painless extension of redaction criticism',[1] both approaches intent on uncovering the original intentions of the Evangelist through the unravelling of the design he placed in the text with infinite care. Similarly, reader-response criticism as it has been taken up

---

1 Stephen D. Moore, 2007, 'A Modest Manifesto for New Testament Literary Criticism: How to Interface with a Literary Studies Field that is Postliterary, Post-theoretical, and Postmethodological', in Stephen D. Moore, 2010, *The Bible in Theory*, Atlanta: Society of Biblical Literature, p. 358.

in biblical studies, in effect a close cousin, as we have already argued, of narrative criticism, remains concerned at heart with the implied reader as constructed by the author. Only deconstruction as a literary theory from the poststructuralist branch of the discipline has resisted assimilation into traditional, author-recovery-centred biblical criticism. And it is not hard to understand why: by reading a text against itself and its author's intention, deconstruction challenges the privilege of the inherited historical reading, but also the unpicking of theological themes and perspectives that makes up another strand of biblical studies. All of this is subject to deconstruction's close interrogation. While the New Testament has been of interest to deconstructors such as Derrida,[2] poststructural criticism in its most powerful guise from the 1980s and 1990s, when it was a guiding force in literary studies, particularly in America, has not taken firm hold in biblical studies. Meanwhile, the apparent decline of such criticism in academia, with a return to a focus on literary texts and authors rather than on theories and those who have promoted them, for Moore is a backward step for those working on the Bible with an interest in literary studies. Whereas theory had offered such scholars a language to be shared with readers of literature, and a fresh way to approach a very small, very well-covered canon, a return to the text and its context in literary studies does not promise much in the way of new inspiration.

Poststructuralism, which has not been covered in this book in any detail, partly because of its marginal status in biblical studies, has however provoked and often collaborates with a more political approach to texts, of which the feminist readings we offered in Chapter 7 are an example. For Moore, these approaches, which also include postcolonial, queer and cultural studies, are now the dominant discourse in contemporary literary studies. Liberationist forms of this movement, in particular feminist exegesis and hermeneutics, have been established in biblical studies, although not directly via literary channels, and certainly not generally in their more poststructuralist incarnations. Moore offers queer and masculinity studies, as well as postcolonialism, as further political approaches that have had some influence on the edges of biblical studies. Each of these brings together poststructuralist and to some extent historicist studies to reveal ways in which categories such as gender or colonialism are constructs and performances that have influenced other cultures. These constructs are shown to be both contingent and powerful. In biblical studies, there has been a continuing tendency to adapt and de-theorize such trends to fit particular biblical concerns (Moore cites the current popularity of what he calls 'Empire studies' in biblical studies: a strand

---

2 Moore cites, for example, Derrida's 'Post-Scriptum: Aporias, Ways and Voices', translated by John P. Leavey Jr., in Harold Coward and Toby Foshay (eds), 1992, *Derrida and Negative Theology*, Albany: State University of New York Press, pp. 283–323.

of study that rarely engages with postcolonial critical writing, although it claims a relationship to it). This brand of post-colonialism 'lite' is, for Moore, quite understandable, as

> literary studies is a field that embraces difficulty of one sort – the sort monumentalized in disciplinary landmarks such as Jacques Derrida's *Of Grammatology* or Homi Bhaba's *The Location of Culture* – whereas biblical studies is a field that embraces difficulty of another sort – the sort enshrined in the Documentary Hypothesis or the Synoptic Problem.[3]

That difficult discontinuity is a hard bridge for any one scholar to cross with confidence and aplomb.

A fourth branch of these more political approaches, cultural studies, might be transferred to a study of the Bible as a cultural icon – a move that has been attempted in fields such as film studies (seen in academic interest both in 'Jesus' films, such as *The Passion of the Christ*, and in the role of the Bible in 'secular' films); and its influence may be seen in the rising tide of the explicit foregrounding of a critic's location in sociocultural terms, particularly from scholars from minority backgrounds. But this remains peripheral to mainstream biblical studies, and has had little to do with literary criticism as it has been commonly understood up until now, and not least in this book.

All of these current developments in literary studies in its broadest sense – queer, masculinity, postcolonial and cultural studies – share a lack of a stable, transferable methodology underpinning them. It was such a methodology that enabled biblical studies to appropriate literary critical approaches, such as reader-response, or even deconstruction, and to apply them to their reading of the Bible. Moore argues that the rising influence of the more recent, political or cultural studies across many academic disciplines, most particularly in America, has led to very little in the way of repeatable strategies of reading. Perhaps these share something in common with feminist literary and biblical approaches, which do not share one methodology, but rather all exhibit a 'critical sensibility, an encompassing angle of vision that, in a more fundamental fashion than a methodological framework, brings previously unperceived or disavowed data into focus'.[4]

For Moore, the move away from method in literary studies has implications for biblical studies too. As he notes, the common practice of biblical scholars who share an interest in literary issues (indeed of biblical scholars in general, although not all have been as self-conscious about it as literary critical ones) has been to present the method they have chosen to follow, and then apply it by rote to the passage selected. The aim has

---

3 Moore, 'Modest Manifesto', p. 365.
4 Moore, 'Modest Manifesto', pp. 369–70.

been to maintain an objective, academic stance in relation to the text, in contrast to the aim of the homiletic approach to the text. 'Methodology, in short, is what maintains the partition between sermon and scholarship.'[5] The result has been less than inspiring in terms of academic output, and for Moore, the challenge presented by post-theory in literary studies is now how to go beyond the methodological approach in biblical studies, without ending up with interpretations that are sermons.

Moore suggests that there is currently a field of biblical studies that attempts to do this, and names it 'contextual hermeneutics', or biblical 'cultural studies', as mentioned above. The aim of approaches within this field is to 'bring an ancient text into meaningful and explicit dialogue with a contemporary context': an aim they share with the sermon.[6] The professional and personal are thus brought into dialogue; and the inherited discipline of biblical studies is seriously challenged by such a move. One way forward for biblical literary criticism in the current posttheoretical world would be to bring together the sort of cultural studies found in wider academia with the cultural studies already germinating in biblical studies. For Moore, this would involve a rather disconcerting deprivileging of the biblical text itself, to consider the wider influence of that text in the contemporary world, wherever it was to be found. When he asks, 'Isn't it time we exited the methodone clinic once and for all?',[7] he is suggesting something profoundly unsettling to all that most of us from the world of biblical studies know and are in some cases addicted to. However, the vista in this postmethodological space is potentially liberating and certainly more creative than much that has been offered in the past.

Moore's interest lies in the side of the equation we have defined from the start as 'the Bible as literature'. But there is a sense in which the enterprise known as the 'Bible in literature' implicitly takes this approach, although admittedly rarely with the self-conscious positioning of the reader for which he argues. Perhaps courses and books that consider the Bible in literature are more pre-critical than post-critical in the terms he sets out. The debate created by theories of intertextuality and midrashic interpretation may point in the direction of the possibility of readings that are post-theoretical, radically reader-centred, although the end results of such readings rarely live up to the potential. The question for any reader of the Bible, or indeed of the Bible in literature, for the two tasks are related in this regard, is the age-old one of where meaning lies. Or even, is there meaningful meaning to be found in any of the classic places in which biblical studies, borrowing from literary studies' classifications, have sought it: the intention of the author; the understanding of the original audience;

5 Moore, 'Modest Manifesto', p. 370.
6 Moore, 'Modest Manifesto', p. 371.
7 Moore, 'Modest Manifesto', p. 372.

the text; the reader; the reader in an interpretative community. Moore, it seems to me, is suggesting that instead of meaning we should be looking for meaningful readings. These will be positioned in cultural terms, explicit about their 'encompassing angle of vision', and will engage the object of interpretation, whether it is the biblical text itself or another context in which the Bible may be one of several intertexts, from this perspective. The endeavour may well involve insights from the historical or sociological context in which any of these texts originated; evidence about the reception history of the texts, where it is available; a close reading and interrogation of the text itself; and an acknowledgement, even a celebration, of the role of the specific reader and his or her academic, cultural or personal community. The resulting reading is likely to have the passionate force of a sermon, and to be resistant to the critique of objectivity. It will not be commentary as the discipline of biblical studies has traditionally known it; and it will not be literary criticism as that has been traditionally understood either. Perhaps a new name for such readings will have to be found, beyond the broad title of 'cultural studies'. In this concluding chapter, a tentative reading in these terms is presented as a possible way forward for the discipline that is encompassed, somewhat uncomfortably, under the phrase 'the Bible and literature'.

The Prodigal Son in post-theoretical perspective

We have considered the parable of the Prodigal Son in Chapter 5, when we read it from the perspective of narrative criticism, and compared it to Charlotte Brontë's *Jane Eyre*. Characterization and point of view were offered as ways to understand these texts more fully, and although this was not explicitly stated, there was an assumption in that chapter that these elements were the products of a combination of the author's intention and something inherent in the texts themselves. In a footnote, the interpretation of Mary Ann Beavis was mentioned, as an example of a reading that lifts the focus from the parable's recovered historical context to the concerns of a reader with a specific experience of family life. Here we will explore this reading in more detail, and supplement it with a reading of a poem by Christina Rossetti, which is itself a retelling of a part of the parable.

In '"Making up Stories": A Feminist Reading of the Parable of the Prodigal Son (Luke 15.11b–32)', Mary Ann Beavis reads the parable from the perspective of a runaway from an abusive situation in childhood. The term 'feminist' in the title is misleading, as in fact the main section of this reading sits equally well within a broader critical field, the sort of field Moore has described as 'contextual hermeneutics'. Moreover, although Beavis uses the language of narrative criticism, by invoking an implied

CONCLUSION

reader, I suggest this playing with the role of the reader in the creation of meaning is a far cry from the intended meaning usually assumed in that terminology. From the outset, Beavis asserts that

> the interpretation that follows does not purport to uncover the 'true' or 'original' meaning of the parable, the meaning intended by Jesus, or the meaning intended by Luke. Rather, informed by the skills of a professional biblical scholar, it attempts to read the parable from the perspective of an implied reader with the life experience of [a] . . . runaway [child].[8]

The modern perspective informs the reading, rather than any attempt to reconstruct an 'original' meaning, although the available context in which the story originated is also brought into dialogue with this particular meaning-making experience. Using insights from the socio-historical work of R. L. Rohrbaugh, Beavis stresses the dysfunctional nature of the prodigal son's family. His request for his share of his inheritance is tantamount to a public declaration that he wished his father were already dead. This public dishonouring of the father would have brought shame on the whole family, in a society in which family reputation was of fundamental importance. In religious terms, the younger son breaks the commandment to honour his parents (Exodus 20.12), but the older son is little better by apparently agreeing to the breaking up of the family inheritance, centred on the land. The father himself, on this view, is portrayed as a fool, by undermining his authority and honour in the family and in the wider community in this way. For Beavis, the entry-point into this parable comes in the unanswered questions such behaviour raises, which few commentators have addressed: 'why the sons disdain their father so much that they would publicly humiliate him and his entire household, and why the father accepts such appalling conduct'.[9] Most later readers have assumed that the problem lies in the sons, who are deemed either spoiled and insensitive, or mean-spirited, and the father is regarded as simply over-indulgent. However, for Beavis, the actions of these characters suggest a serious dysfunctionality between them, and she suggests that the underlying cause could be read as the sexual molestation of the younger son, and possibly the older son also, by the father. As she notes, 'child sexual abuse inevitably arouses strong feelings of hatred and anger, which can finally be expressed only when the victim reaches an age when she/he can challenge the perpetrator'.[10]

---

8 Mary Ann Beavis, '"Making Up Stories"': A Feminist Reading of the Parable of the Prodigal Son (Luke 15.11b–32)', in M. A. Beavis (ed.), 2002, *The Lost Coin: Parables of Women, Work and Wisdom*, London: Sheffield Academic Press, p. 103.

9 Beavis, '"Making Up Stories"', p. 105.

10 Beavis, '"Making Up Stories"', pp. 106–7.

The younger son's actions, on this view, would be an effective way to express his deeply felt emotions against his father, so that he was publicly shamed but the offence remained unspecified.

From the perspective of a reader who was the survivor of such incestuous abuse, Beavis suggests that there would be no surprise that most readers of the parable have assumed the guilt of the son, while siding with the father. She points to evidence that indicates that victims of sexual child abuse have often been ignored or disbelieved by those in authority. Equally, she notes that teenage victims of incest often run away from the home in order to escape the abuse – again, to such a victim, the younger son's actions are understandable rather than incredible. And his vulnerability to further sexual exploitation (hinted at in the older brother's accusation that the prodigal had 'been with prostitutes' (Luke 15.30; and in the sexual connotations of the verb used to describe the way he 'attaches himself' to his patron in the far country (15.15)) would not be a surprise to those who had been in his situation. The one he looked to for help ironically abuses him further by requiring him to take on a task that was degrading to both Jews and Gentiles – the care of the swine.

The phrase in the parable that has often been read as indicating repentance, the prodigal's moment of 'coming to himself' (15.17), which leads to his rehearsal of his moment of return and his request to be accepted back as a servant, may also have a very different meaning for a victim of abuse. This 'splitting' of himself may be read as a coping strategy: it enables him to return to a place where he might be fed and survive, while remaining separate from his father the abuser. The moment of return might also be read as having deeply ominous and threatening overtones. In a family where patriarchal power is maintained by the sort of sexual abuse Beavis is positing, the father's remarkably enthusiastic response is a public sign that the patriarch is back in control. The son's plan to ask for the 'safety' of a servant's role in the household is overwhelmed and interrupted by the father's eagerness to have him back in the position of honoured son. The reaction of the father may be read as a loving, even maternal response, but its embraces and kisses may also have sexualized overtones. The son's return signals his resumption of the role of the child in the family hierarchy, and all the dangers this might entail for him.

The reaction of the older brother, in this reading, is also understandable: it is the jealous response of one child to the perceived 'favourite' status afforded to the sibling who is the object of abuse. Addressed not as an adult, but as the father's 'child' (15.31a), the older son remains heir to what is left of the estate, and must now take responsibility for his poverty-stricken younger brother, while remaining under his father's domination. As Beavis comments:

> the *status quo* is preserved, the family's 'status' in the community is restored in the eyes of the celebrating villagers (vv.24–25); the

'dysfunctional' family is back under the control of the father . . . From the perspective of an incest survivor, the parable offers scant hope for healing of the abusive patterns that prompted the younger son to leave in the first place.[11]

While Beavis asserts that the parable may be read as a positive story of reconciliation and forgiveness, as it has been traditionally, especially where abuse has not taken place, she cautions against the universal use of this story to encourage the abused to forgive the perpetrator of the abuse against them. Any suggestion that their reading of the story is 'wrong', that the father figure in the parable is god-like in his acceptance, not like their own father; and the son is really a sinner and not a victim, is potentially deeply damaging. Most significantly, the aim of the article is to affirm the insight that 'the ability to decide on what is the true word of God resides in . . . human . . . experience'.[12] The power of these stories, even their theological significance as scripture, is not denied. But the meaning must be allowed to come from the situation and experience of those who read them. As Beavis shows in the 'exemplary story' she offers at the end of her article, loosely based on the autobiographical novel of a survivor of incest, the parable of the Prodigal Son may thus inspire a new story, which demonstrates that 'the angels of Godde rejoice more over one innocent person who survives than over the repentance of the sinners who have abused them!'.

Ranging widely from a close reading of the text, through contextual studies of the law and society at the time the parable was written, to the testimony of modern survivors of abuse, Beavis's interpretation, while claiming a feminist stance, sits well within Moore's post-theoretical world. Is it a literary reading, in the terms we have assumed in this book? I would suggest that it is, as it is deeply concerned with the reception of the text as text; and it shares features of the reception of the Bible with the reception of the Bible in literature. Both are personal and contingent, while contextually driven.

Christina Rossetti

Christina Rossetti was born in London in 1830, the daughter of an English mother and an exiled Italian nationalist and scholar of Dante. Often overlooked and in the shadow of her more famous and flamboyant brother, the Pre-Raphaelite painter and poet, Dante Gabriel, Rossetti wrote large numbers of poems and devotional works. Drawn first to the evangelical wing of the Church of England, she, like her mother and sister, was later

---

11 Beavis, '"Making Up Stories"', p. 119.
12 Beavis, '"Making Up Stories"', p. 122.

influenced by the Tractarian Movement of the 1840s. The sacramental-ism of Tractarianism, allied with a belief in the hiddenness of God in creation, informed much of her poetry. The sensual symbolism of the Pre-Raphaelite movement was also a guiding force, although she was to reject the later agnosticism of many who followed that path. Her most famous poem, 'Goblin Market', was published in 1862, and demonstrates this voluptuous enjoyment of the senses, while promoting a moral mes-sage about self-restraint. She did not marry, although her poetry speaks powerfully of love and loss, and she was engaged in the home for much of her life caring for her elderly relatives, ultimately leading a secluded life until her death in 1894.

As a final point of comparison, I offer one such literary intertextual ex-ample, and my experience of reading it. Christina Rossetti's poem, 'A Prodigal Son', appeared in *A Pageant and Other Poems* in 1881.[13] It offers four tightly constructed stanzas which are an expansion of Luke 15.17–19, the moment when the prodigal son 'comes to himself' and decides to 'arise and go' back to his father's house, planning his words carefully. The first stanza focuses on the image of the lamp the son re-members turning back and seeing as he left his father's house: he wonders if it was kindled to light him 'home some day'. The second focuses on the current experience of the son and its harsh realities: 'Hungry here with the crunching swine'. His home exists 'in a dream' in which he sees and hears his father's sheep in carefree protection – the lambs 'browse and leap'. The third stanza continues the sensuality of the rest, with its mention of abundant bread, 'purple wine-fat froths with foam' and 'oil and spices' which 'make sweet the air'. The contrast is expressed in the line 'While I perish hungry and bare'. The poem closes with the realiza-tion that the servants have the blessings that are denied the son, and they are centred around being able to see the father's face. The final couplet expresses his intention:

'Fallen from sonship, beggared of grace,
Grant me, Father, a servant's place.'

The poem may be read as an expression of both Pre-Raphaelite sensual symbolism, and Tractarian sacramentalism. Contemporary reviewers of Rossetti's work had long commented on her use of rich material symbolism – Richard Le Gallienne in 1866 referred to her practice of 'dwelling elaborately on details'.[14] But more than this, for Rossetti there is a sacramental element to the sensual, physical world: in a Ruskinian

---

13 Christina Rossetti, 1986, *The Complete Poems of Christina Rossetti*, vol. 2, R. W. Crump (ed.), Baton Rouge: Louisiana State University Press, p. 109.

14 Richard Le Gallienne, *Review of Poems. Academy* 39, 7 February 1891, pp. 131.

sense the physical world is the language of God, demanding the decoding of humanity. In *Seek and Find*, subtitled '*A Double Series of Short Studies of the Benedicite*', published in 1879, Rossetti had written: 'All the world over, visible things typify things invisible' and 'objects of sight may and should quicken us to apprehend objects of faith, things temporal suggesting things eternal'.[15] This sensuous spirituality of course sits very well within the Pre-Raphaelite tradition, seeing sensory phenomena as figures of transcendent truth – and in the early religious paintings of Pre-Raphaelites such as her brother Dante Gabriel, of course, no detail is without its symbolic significance.

Attention to the significance of the detailed symbolism in the poem 'A Prodigal Son' yields new insights. I suggest the references are more to the Johannine 'I am' figure than to the Lukan Jesus, who speaks the parable in its original setting, but perhaps this scarcely matters to one such as Rossetti who had such a high view of the divine inspiration of all scripture. The lamp of the first verse invokes Jesus as the light of the world, shining in the darkness, the light that the darkness, in Johannine terms, cannot extinguish. The flock owned in such a pastoral idyll of the second verse places Jesus the Good Shepherd in central view, who knows his sheep by name, protects them, lays down his life for them. The bread and wine of the third verse suggest Jesus as the bread of life, but also the presence of Jesus in the Eucharistic elements. The oil and spices 'making sweet the air' speak of both the anointing worship of Mary before the Last Supper, filling the house with the fragrance of the perfume and pre-paring Jesus for burial (another Johannine story), and the unused spices brought by the women to the empty tomb. In the final verse, the reference to seeing the father's face might echo the transfiguration, the moment of revelation so filled with further echoes of Moses meeting God on Mount Sinai. The numinous face of God, embodied here in Jesus, provokes wor-ship – just as the servants in the poem are 'rich and blessed'.

What is significant about this sensualized sacramentalization of the parable is its Christocentric focus. The father is the named figure around whom the hopes and longings of the son are focused, in accordance with the narrative framework of the parable. However, this metaphor is pushed hard into a Christological mould: this is Jesus as the father, with all the sustaining attributes he has claimed for himself in his Jo-hannine incarnation – as light, shepherd, bread, object of worship. Of course, these attributes also go back to God as father, and have plenty of echoes in the Hebrew Bible. But their concentration here in the con-structed dream or memory of the son, and their ordering that very closely follows the narrative of John's Gospel, and specifically chapters 6–12

---

15 Christina Rossetti, 1879, *Seek and Find: A Double Series of Short Studies of the Benedicite*, London: SPCK, pp. 244, 180, quoted in Antony H. Harrison, 1988, *Christina Rossetti in Context*, Brighton: Harvester Press, p. 31.

that Gospel, suggest that their focus is on the figure of Christ. Overall, the reader is left with a sense of completeness and fulfilment in the story, centred on the over-arching work of Christ the redeemer. The powerful memory of the whole story of the parable of the Prodigal Son – or at least up until the arrival of the elder son, which does not figure at all here – gives the poem a hopeful and resolved sense, although the moment of reconciliation is not described.

However, the parable of the Prodigal Son also forms the cave of resonance for a very different Rossetti poem in this regard, which appears directly before this one in the collection *A Pageant and Other Poems*. The contiguous placement of the first undermines the resolution of the second.

'I Will Arise' is the title of the poem,[16] a direct quotation from the words of the son as he decides to return in the parable (Luke 15.18), and found also in the closing verse of 'A Prodigal Son'.[17] Here, however, the statement is a painful expression of hope in spite of experience rather than a statement of intent. The experience is of 'breathless haste, of long-drawn straining effort across the waste'. The knowledge of 'thy love of me' seems not to be able to overcome the 'chill', 'cold' and 'nigh to death' sense that the speaker cannot shift. The poem takes the form of a prayer, and the determination to repent is clear if in the implied future:

> I will arise, repenting and in pain;
> I will arise, and smite upon my breast
> And turn to thee again.

There is an acknowledgement that the prayers are 'feeble', which makes the assertion that closes the poem, 'O Lord, I will arise', perhaps unconvincing as a statement of intent, although the depth of despair is very real. The sensual delight of 'A Prodigal Son' is missing from this poem, replaced by cold, chilled wasteland. Whether the Lord who is addressed is God the father or the son seems unimportant, although it is technically an incarnational, anthropomorphic image that is summed up in the plea to be carried 'a little way'. If the intertextual relationship with the parable of the Prodigal Son is explicit on many levels in the first poem we considered, in this one it is tangential, and perhaps not even obvious without the contiguity of the two – although the one image of life and heat among the chill, at the very heart of the 'I Will Arise' poem, 'a craving flame of selfless love of me which burns in thee,' perhaps alludes to the long-standing and ever-seeking love of the father in the parable.

---

16 Rossetti, *Complete Poems*, p. 107.

17 We have already noted the use of the phrase in Chapter 1, in the first line of W. B. Yeats's nostalgic poem, 'The Lake Isle of Innisfree'. Here the place of memory is a refuge from the urban busyness of adult life.

Taken together, the two poems offer a much more complete reading of the parable and its strengths and weaknesses than each does on its own. The world of the senses is integrated with the world of intense feeling. The strange and allusive phrase in the parable that describes the moment of revelation of the son, 'coming to himself', is illuminated and made personal in the faltering determination of the 'I Will Arise' poem. The sensual world of the subject, the contrast between hunger and satisfaction, physical and spiritual, is given full expression in 'A Prodigal Son', placing the parable in a wide sacramental and scriptural context. Perhaps both worlds could not be accommodated in one poem. But in the two, sensuous spirituality and intense pathos are explored through one pivotal scriptural text, and the effect is powerful, just as the glimpse of Rossetti's faith offered is profound and surprising.

The above was my presentation to my 'Bible and Literature' Honours class at Edinburgh University recently. It was a reading based on some knowledge of and sympathy for the life of Christina Rossetti, and her religious background, combined with a familiarity with the parable, its hermeneutical gaps and difficulties and the history of its reception. The response of the students, particularly to the 'A Prodigal Son' poem, was quite different, however. For many of them, the poem's form was too simple and controlled, more like a nursery rhyme than an expression of the psychological angst they found in the parable in the son's moment of decision to return. The concentration on hunger seemed to point more to physical rather than spiritual emptiness, while the pastoral imagery of the second verse seemed trite rather than sincere. For one, the closing couplet was too artful to have arisen out of repentance or desperation, and the suggestion that the younger son might ask to have the place of a servant was manipulative and not a sign of humility, with its vocative appeal to his 'father' – although another member of the group, from an evangelical Christian background, thought that a servant ministry might be considered an approach to aspire to, following the example of Christ himself.

The strongest criticism, however, came from those who found the absence of the older son's voice left the poem deeply lacking in a sense of fairness. For some readers, many who professed to be older children themselves, the poem, and the parable's critique of the older son's complaints, made them angry and dismissive of these texts. The issue of justice was more acute than the dysfunctional nature of the family unit that Beavis identified, especially for the one student who had not read the parable before. The younger son assumes that the reaction to his return will not be rejection, signalled obliquely by the first verse and its reference to the lamp the father lit on the night of his leaving – 'Did he think to light me home some day?' While the parable's resolution of the younger son's story is also unheard here, it overshadows the moment described with affirmation that the expectation will be realized, and the hunger expressed will be more than satisfied. The silenced older brother's presence, however, was perceived as a major inadequacy in the poem; although he is effectively silenced by the father in the parable also, the fact that he is given a voice to present his complaints at all was felt to be important. In the parable, there was felt to be a completeness of possibilities of response to the moment of reconciliation; in the poem, the perspective offered was considered to be incomplete and unconvincing, although some in the class expressed, with a wry acceptance, that younger siblings were sometimes treated in this indulgent way. But there was general resistance to the poem as a reading of the parable.

The spiritual angst expressed in the other poem, 'I Will Arise', did little to offset this feeling of unease. Certainly the central affirmation of the 'craving flame/Of selfless love of me which burns in Thee'; and the 'sore distress' of the speaker were deemed more sincere than the moment of 'repentance' described in 'A Prodigal Son'. The form of the poem, while regular and fixed, was less simple than the other poem, the rhymes were less perfect and the alternating of long and short lines made these readers pause and reflect. However, the obliqueness of this poem's relationship to the family setting of the parable made its connection with my group of readers tenuous and lacking significance. The child – parent relationship, so important to the parable and most later readings of it, is subsumed in a rather destructively portrayed lover-to-lover relationship. The speaker's love has grown 'chill', 'cold and nigh to death', while the love of the one addressed remains a 'craving flame'. The speaker's experience is of 'long-drawn straining effort across the waste', but she/he, although 're-penting and in pain', asserts that she/he 'will arise . . . And turn to Thee again', despite the disappointments and 'distress' of the past, when the relationship was presumably stronger. The relationships of power read awkwardly to a modern ear – 'Lead me a little way, and carry me/ A little way . . . And deign replies/ To feeble prayers': the speaker is reduced to begging the one addressed for a response, which will involve a giving up of her/his will. This is a relationship that the speaker is forcing him/her-self to re-establish, out of guilt arising from the overwhelming love apparently still burning in the other. Whether she/he carries out this act of return is left unstated, although again the strong echo of the parable leads the reader to assume that she/he will.

Although Beavis's reading of the parable was not discussed in the class, the students' reading of the poem offered in fact chimes well with it. Something inappropriate, destructive and sexual may be read at the heart of Rossetti's 'I Will Arise', which 'A Prodigal Son' seems to attempt to silence and control. Reading Beavis's interpretation alongside 'I Will Arise' reinforces its disturbing consequences, although the poem itself, on its own and without reference to 'A Prodigal Son' either, drifts away in modern readings from its connection to the parable. Read together, or alongside one another, these texts, one biblical, two poetic and one from a specific interpretative perspective, interact and interrogate the meaning of each of them.

In the post-theoretical world described by Stephen Moore, this bringing together of texts and readings from different contexts and periods is a commonplace. All are held together in the experience and context of the reader or the community of readers who attempt the task of interpretation. Bible and literature, text and reader, all have a role to play in the restless search for significance and meaning. It is a world in which Bible and literature need to remain in dialogue with each other, for their concerns are shared and their futures may be intertwined in the interdisciplinary world we now inhabit.

Questions

1. Reread the parable of the Prodigal Son in light of Mary Ann Beavis's reading of it. Is your perspective changed, or have new possibilities of interpretation opened up?
2. Are there other texts that have struck you differently from other people, because of your particular experiences, including, perhaps, your reading of other texts?

Further reading

Mary Ann Beavis, '"Making Up Stories": A Feminist Reading of the Parable of the Prodigal Son (Luke 15.11b–32)', in M. A. Beavis (ed.), 2002, *The Lost Coin: Parables of Women, Work and Wisdom*, London: Sheffield Academic Press, pp. 17–33.

John J. Collins, 2005, *The Bible after Babel: Historical Criticism in a Postmodern Age*, Grand Rapids, MI: Eerdmans.

Terry Eagleton, 2003, *After Theory*, New York: Basic Books.

Antony H. Harrison, 1988, *Christina Rossetti in Context*, Brighton: Harvester Press.

Stephen D. Moore, 2007, 'A Modest Manifesto for New Testament Literary Criticism: How to Interface with a Literary Studies Field that is Postliterary, Post-theoretical, and Postmethodological', in Stephen D. Moore, 2010, *The Bible in Theory*, Atlanta: Society of Biblical Literature, pp. 355–72.

R. L. Rohrbaugh, 'A Dysfunctional Family and Its Neighbours', in V. G. Shillington (ed.), 1997, *Jesus and His Parables: Interpreting the Parables of Jesus Today*, Edinburgh: T & T Clark, pp. 141–64.

Christina Rossetti, 1986, *The Complete Poems of Christina Rossetti*, vol. 2, R. W. Crump (ed.), Baton Rouge: Louisiana State University Press.

Index of Names and Subjects

THE BIBLE AND LITERATURE